Collins | English for Exams

PRACTICE TESTS FOR THE TOEFL iBT® TEST

T0312455

Published by Collins
An imprint of HarperCollins Publishers
Westerhill Road
Bishopbriggs
Glasgow
G64 2QT

HarperCollins Publishers
Macken House
39/40 Mayor Street Upper
Dublin 1
D01 C9W8
Ireland

Third Edition 2024

10 9 8 7 6 5 4 3 2 1

© HarperCollins Publishers 2012, 2023, 2024

ISBN 978-0-00-869525-5

Collins® is a registered trademark of HarperCollins Publishers
Limited

ETS, MYBEST, TOEFL and TOEFL iBT are registered
trademarks of ETS. This publication is not affiliated with or
endorsed by ETS.

www.collins.co.uk/elt

A catalogue record for this book is available from the British
Library

Series Editor: Celia Wigley
Author of additional content for second and third editions:
Louis Harrison
Editor for second edition: Eleanor Barber
Audio: New York Audio Productions
Typesetting: Sharon McTeir Creative Publishing Services and
Jouve, India
For the Publisher: Maree Airlie, Gillian Bowman,
Kerry Ferguson, Lisa Todd

Printed and bound in the UK by Ashford Colour Press Ltd

Entered words that we have reason to believe constitute
trademarks have been designated as such. However, neither
the presence nor absence of such designation should be
regarded as affecting the legal status of any trademark.

The contents of this publication are believed correct at the
time of printing. Nevertheless, the Publisher can accept no
responsibility for errors or omissions, changes in the detail
given or for any expense or loss thereby caused.

HarperCollins does not warrant that any website mentioned
in this title will be provided uninterrupted, that any website
will be error-free, that defects will be corrected, or that the
website or the server that makes it available are free of
viruses or bugs. For full terms and conditions please refer to
the site terms provided on the website.

A catalogue record for this book is available from the British
Library.

If If you would like to comment on any aspect of this book,
please contact us at the given address or online.
E-mail: collins.elt@harpercollins.co.uk

Acknowledgements
We would like to thank those authors and publishers who
kindly gave permission for copyright material to be used
in the Collins Corpus. We would also like to thank Times
Newspapers Ltd for providing valuable data.

Photo credits: Photos on pages 18, 24, 30, 68, 118,
130, 170, 180, 182, 185, 205 © Toby Madden/
HarperCollinsPublishers. All other images from
Shutterstock.com.

Contents

Introduction   iv

TOEFL iBT Practice Test 1:   1
  Reading Section   3
  Listening Section   17
  Speaking Section   29
  Writing Section   37

TOEFL iBT Practice Test 2:   51
  Reading Section   53
  Listening Section   67
  Speaking Section   79
  Writing Section   87

TOEFL iBT Practice Test 3:   101
  Reading Section   103
  Listening Section   117
  Speaking Section   129
  Writing Section   137

TOEFL iBT Practice Test 4:   151
  Reading Section   153
  Listening Section   167
  Speaking Section   179
  Writing Section   187

Guide to the TOEFL iBT® Test   201

Mini-Dictionary   249

Audio Script   269

Answer Key   295

Sample Answers   301

Introduction

Welcome to *Practice Tests for the TOEFL iBT® Test*. This comprehensive resource for TOEFL iBT® preparation provides you with practice, support, and knowledge about the test to help you succeed in the TOEFL iBT® Test.

The TOEFL iBT® test is offered in three ways:

- Test at a test center
- Test at home
- Test on paper

This book prepares you for all three options:

- the TOEFL iBT test on computer at a test center
- the Home Edition, and
- the TOEFL iBT Paper Edition.

This book has been fully updated to match the changes to the TOEFL iBT test that took effect on July 26 2023.

For more information on the differences between the versions of the test, please see the Guide to the TOEFL iBT® Test on page 201.

About this book

Practice Tests for the TOEFL iBT® Test contains **four full-length practice tests for the TOEFL iBT test**. Each test includes all four sections (Reading, Listening, Speaking, Writing) to allow you to experience the full exam as part of your study and preparation. These tests include realistic test questions, showing you the types of question you can expect to find on the test. Knowing what to expect is an important part of preparing for the test.

In addition to the practice tests, the book includes the **answer key** to the practice tests, the **audio script**, and **sample answers** for the Writing and Speaking questions. These tools will help you practice and check your answers as you prepare for the TOEFL iBT test.

The book also contains a **mini-dictionary** of high-level words used in the practice tests, with definitions and examples to help you build your vocabulary. All definitions are from Collins COBUILD dictionaries.

Audio — All files for the Listening, Speaking, and Writing sections of the practice tests are available online. You can download the audio at **www.collins.co.uk/eltresources**.

Guide to the TOEFL iBT® Test — This comprehensive guide presents you with strategies for success and essential test information. By using this guide you will feel completely confident about how the TOEFL iBT test works, and know what to expect on the day of the test.

Specifically the guide contains:

• **Tips** for success — Best practice strategies and useful advice on how to prepare for the test and make the best use of the resources in the book.

• A TOEFL iBT test **overview** — Use this as a quick reference to the TOEFL iBT test whenever you need to remind yourself of specifics about test question types and what to expect on test day.

• **Quick guides** — Four quick guides present key information about question types for each test section in easy-to-read charts, making it simple for you to quickly understand what it is important to know in order to answer the questions correctly.

• Detailed, **step-by-step guides** to each part of the test that include explanations of question types, what correct answers must include, and how responses are scored.

• **Challenges and solutions sections** — These sections offer strategy and skill reviews to help you learn how to overcome the most common challenges on each part of the test.

How to use this book

Studying the resources in *Practice Tests for the TOEFL iBT® Test* gives you the unique advantage of taking four complete TOEFL iBT practice tests as you prepare for this important test. Because the test is divided into distinct skill sections, you will quickly discover where you need to focus your time in order to maximize your score as you work through the practice tests.

Once you have identified areas in which you need to improve, refer to the appropriate Challenges and Solutions section of the Guide to the TOEFL iBT® Test for strategies and solutions.

After you complete each practice test, check the answer key to see where you chose incorrect answers and in which areas you need to improve. Study the correct answers in order to understand why they are correct.

Be sure to make the best use of all the resources in this book in order to be prepared and feel confident on test day. Good luck!

TOEFL iBT Practice Test 1

TOEFL iBT Practice Test 1

Reading Section

This section tests your ability to understand academic passages in English. The section is divided into separately timed parts.

Questions are worth 1 point except for the last question for each passage, which is worth more than 1 point. The directions for the last question explain how many points you can receive.

TOEFL iBT test on the computer

There are two reading passages in this section. You should plan to spend **18 minutes** reading each passage and answering the questions about it. You should take no more than **35 minutes** to complete the entire section.

Reading Section Timing Guide TOEFL iBT test on the computer		
Passage	**Number of Questions**	**Time to Complete Test**
Passage 1	10	35 minutes
Passage 2	10	

The above information does not apply to the TOEFL iBT Paper Edition.

TOEFL iBT Paper Edition

There are three reading passages in this section in the TOEFL iBT Paper Edition. You should plan to spend **20 minutes** reading each passage answering the questions about it. You should take no more than **60 minutes** to complete the entire section.

Reading Section Timing Guide TOEFL iBT Paper Edition		
Passage	**Number of Questions**	**Time to Complete Test**
Passage 1	10	
Passage 2	10	60 minutes
Passage 3	10	

READING 1

Directions: Read the passage.

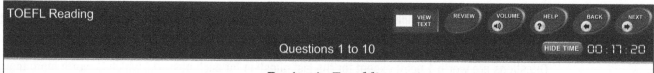

Benjamin Franklin

1. Benjamin Franklin, born in 1706 and died in 1790, was a truly versatile person. As a statesman, he, and several notable others, contributed to the formation of the United States as a nation. He was the only person to sign all four key documents of American history: the Declaration of Independence, the Treaty of Alliance with France, the Treaty of Peace with Great Britain, and the Constitution of the United States. He served as a diplomat, often praised as the most successful one America has ever sent abroad. What is not as well known, however, are Franklin's many contributions to science, education, and culture.

2. Longing to be his own master at 17, Franklin ran away from Boston to Philadelphia, then the largest city in the American colonies. The story of his arrival is part of American folklore. Numerous tales describe the young runaway apprentice bravely marching down Market Street with only one Dutch dollar in hand, carrying a loaf of bread. After seven years of working for various printers, he began publishing *The Pennsylvania Gazette*, soon turning it into one of the most successful papers in the colonies. He explained that successful people work harder than their competitors. He is also credited with publishing the first newspaper cartoon as well as the first story with an accompanying map. Franklin achieved even greater publishing success than the newspaper with his *Poor Richard's Almanac*. Each issue included Franklin's clever and witty sayings, many of which preach the value of hard work and thriftiness. These sayings remain part of American speech. Famous ones include: "Early to bed and early to rise, makes a man healthy, wealthy, and wise." "A penny saved is a penny earned." "Lost time is never found again." "Guests, like fish, begin to smell after three days." "Three can keep a secret if two of them are dead."

3. Although he never sought public office, he was doggedly interested in public affairs. Observing the poor state of the colonial postal service, he agreed to become Philadelphia's postmaster in 1737. The British government, observing his competency, appointed him deputy postmaster of all the colonies in 1753, and he initiated many needed reforms. Constantly aiming to make Philadelphia a better city, he helped establish the first American colony library, lending books free of charge. He also organized a fire department in response to the numerous fires overwhelming the city. He reformed the city police. He began a program to pave, clean, and light the streets. He raised money to build a city hospital for disadvantaged people, the first city hospital in the colonies. With others, he helped found a school for higher education that became the renowned University of Pennsylvania.

4. Franklin's contributions as a scientist and an inventor are perhaps his most noteworthy. He was one of the first people in the world to experiment with electricity. Flying a homemade kite during a thunderstorm, Franklin conducted his most famous electrical experiment in Philadelphia in 1752. A bolt of lightning struck a pointed wire that was attached to the kite and traveled down the kite string to a key fastened at the end, resulting in a spark. Then he tamed lightning by inventing a lightning rod. As a result, he proved that lightning is electricity. He urged his fellow citizens to use this instrument as a "means of securing the habitations and other buildings from mischief from thunder and lightning." His own home, equipped with the rod, was saved when lightning struck. He knocked himself unconscious at least once and suffered electrical shocks while proving his hypothesis and developing his rod.

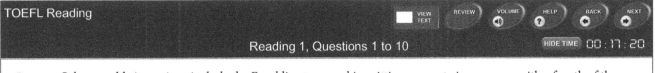

5.   Other notable inventions include the Franklin stove, making sitting rooms twice as warm with a fourth of the fuel they had been using. People around the world appreciate his inventions, bifocal eyeglasses in particular. They enable both reading and distance lenses to be set in one frame. He encouraged the enactment of daylight saving time so that people would use less candlelight. He also showed colonists how to improve acid soil by using lime. He neither patented his inventions nor made profits from them, claiming his inventions were for all. He appreciated the inventiveness of others and often stated he wished he could return to Earth in a hundred years to see what progress humanity had made.

Directions: Answer the questions.

1. The word "key" in paragraph 1 could best be replaced by

   Ⓐ successful

   Ⓑ mandatory

   Ⓒ fundamental

   Ⓓ opening

2. The author mentions "The story of his arrival is part of American folklore." in paragraph 2 in order to

   Ⓐ support Franklin's mythological heritage

   Ⓑ suggest that the actual events are unknown

   Ⓒ highlight Franklin's music connections

   Ⓓ document the connection to Philadelphia

3. The word "apprentice" in paragraph 2 could best be replaced by

   Ⓐ adventurer

   Ⓑ criminal

   Ⓒ ingénue

   Ⓓ trainee

4. Look at the four squares [■] that show where the following sentence could be added to paragraph 2.

One need only examine Franklin and his accomplishments to support this belief.

Where would the sentence best fit?

² Longing to be his own master at 17, Franklin ran away from Boston to Philadelphia, then the largest city in the American colonies. [4A] ■ The story of his arrival is part of American folklore. Numerous tales describe the young runaway apprentice bravely marching down Market Street with only one Dutch dollar in hand, carrying a loaf of bread. After seven years of working for various printers, he began publishing *The Pennsylvania Gazette*, soon turning it into one of the most successful papers in the colonies. He explained that successful people work harder than their competitors. [4B] ■ He is also credited with publishing the first newspaper cartoon as well as the first story with an accompanying map. Franklin achieved even greater publishing success than the newspaper with his *Poor Richard's Almanac*. Each issue included Franklin's clever and witty sayings, many of which preach the value of hard work and thriftiness. [4C] ■ These sayings remain part of American speech. Famous ones include: "Early to bed and early to rise, makes a man healthy, wealthy, and wise." "A penny saved is a penny earned." "Lost time is never found again." "Guests, like fish, begin to smell after three days." "Three can keep a secret if two of them are dead." [4D] ■

(A) [4A]

(B) [4B]

(C) [4C]

(D) [4D]

5. Which of the following best restates the saying in paragraph 2 "Three can keep a secret if two of them are dead."?

(A) People have difficulties keeping secrets.

(B) If you want to keep a secret, tell only three people.

(C) It's better to have three friends than two.

(D) Don't tell a secret to a dying person.

6. The word "doggedly" in paragraph 3 could best be replaced by

(A) minimally

(B) animatedly

(C) determinedly

(D) domestically

7. Which of the sentences below most clearly expresses important information in the highlighted sentence in paragraph 3? *Incorrect* choices change the meaning or leave out important information.

Ⓐ Franklin encouraged Great Britain to appoint him deputy postmaster.

Ⓑ In 1753 Great Britain initiated a postal service in the colonies.

Ⓒ The British government reformed the postal service in the colonies.

Ⓓ Franklin improved and overhauled the postal service in the colonies.

8. It is implied in the passage that

Ⓐ Philadelphians installed Franklin's lightning rod

Ⓑ Franklin spent most of his life traveling abroad

Ⓒ Franklin's death was caused by his work with thunder and lightning

Ⓓ due to its location, Philadelphia is a lightning-prone city

9. The word "they" in paragraph 5 refers to

Ⓐ bifocals

Ⓑ inventions

Ⓒ people

Ⓓ sitting rooms

10. **Directions:** Read the introductory sentence for a summary of the passage below. Complete the summary by choosing the THREE answer choices that include the key ideas in the passage. Some answer choices are incorrect because they include ideas that are not presented in the passage or are not significant in the passage. **This question is worth 2 points** (2 points for 3 correct answers, 1 point for 2 correct answers, and 0 points for 1 or 0 correct answers).

The passage discusses the most important contributions Benjamin Franklin made to early American life.

-
-
-

Choose 3 answers.

① Franklin's *Poor Richard's Almanac* is widely read today.

② Franklin's proof that lightning is electricity had far-reaching implications.

③ Franklin was among the American nation builders.

④ Franklin worked as a police officer, a librarian, and a firefighter.

⑤ Franklin never sought public office.

⑥ Franklin's many inventions improved the quality of life for many.

READING 2

Directions: Read the passage.

Training the Brain

1. People who can accomplish unbelievable mnemonic feats, such as memorizing thousands of random digits in under an hour, claim they have normal brains and that they do not have photographic memories: a gift that some people are born with that enables them to remember anything and everything. Some of these memory superstars compete annually in Olympic-like World Memory Championships. What these athletes do utilize are techniques that anyone can incorporate into everyday life to train one's memory. In addition to using techniques, these competitors undergo serious training and practice.

2. The World Memory Championships begin with the competitors sitting at a table with two shuffled decks of cards. Each person will have exactly five minutes to memorize the order of both decks. These mental athletes, or MAs for short, can memorize the first and last names of dozens of strangers in only a few minutes or any poem handed them. Ed Cooke, a 24-year-old MA from England, explains that MAs see themselves as "participants in an amateur research program" trying to rescue the long-lost art of memory training. In the not-so-distant past, Cooke contends, culture depended on individual memories. Almost all of Cooke's mnemonic techniques were invented in ancient Greece. These techniques existed not to recall useless information, such as playing cards, but to carve into the brain foundational texts and ideas.

3. A study in the journal *Nature* examined eight of the people who finished near the top of the World Memory Championships. The scientists examined whether these contestants' brains were fundamentally different from everyone else's or whether these people were simply making better use of memorizing abilities that we all possess. The researchers put the MAs and control subjects into brain scanners and had them memorize numbers, photographs of people, and snowflakes. What they found surprised everyone. The brains of the MAs and those of the control subjects were anatomically indistinguishable. On every test of mental ability, the MAs scored in the normal range. One surprising difference between the MAs and the control group surfaced; when the researchers examined what part of the brain was being utilized during a memory activity, they found the MAs relied more heavily on regions in the brain involved in spatial memory.

4. MAs offer a simple explanation. Anything can be imprinted upon our memories and kept in good order, simply by constructing a building in the imagination and filling it with images of what needs to be recalled. Dating back to the fifth century, this building is called a Memory Palace. Even as late as the fourteenth century, when there were perhaps only a dozen copies of any text, scholars needed to remember what was read or told to them. Reading to remember requires a very different technique than speed reading. If something is going to be made memorable, it has to be repeated. Until relatively recently, people read only a few books intensively over and over again, usually out loud and in groups. Today we read extensively, usually only once and without sustained focus.

5. What distinguishes the great mnemonist is the ability to create lavish images on the spur of the moment, to paint a picture in one's mind so unlike any other it cannot be forgotten, and to do it quickly. Using memory palaces—of course not actual buildings—contestants create memorized images. For example, take a deck of cards and recombine the pictures to form unforgettable scenes such as routes through a town or signs of the zodiac. One competitor used his own body parts to help him memorize the entire 57,000-word Oxford English–Chinese dictionary.

6. Any novice who wishes to train the mind needs first to stockpile palaces. By visiting the homes of old friends, taking walks through various museums, or compiling a collection of famous artists, one can build new, fantastical structures in the imagination. Then carve each building up into cubbyholes for memories. One mnemonist associates every card in a deck with a different celebrity performing a strange act. Another puts every card into a different exhibit at her favorite museum. In a short amount of time, one will notice improvement with remembering license plate numbers or shopping lists. In order to keep the skill sharp, MAs deliberately empty their palaces after competitions, so they can reuse them again and again and recommend that novices do the same.

Directions: Answer the questions.

11. The word "undergo" in paragraph 1 could best be replaced by

   Ⓐ participate in

   Ⓑ contemplate

   Ⓒ transport

   Ⓓ travel to

12. According to paragraph 2

   Ⓐ mental athletes are all from England

   Ⓑ mental athletes are strangers to the competition

   Ⓒ ancient Greeks used memory techniques

   Ⓓ ancient Greeks memorized first and last names of strangers

13. According to paragraph 3, it is NOT true that mental athletes

   Ⓐ have brains that are fundamentally different from everyone else's

   Ⓑ score in the normal range of mental ability tests

   Ⓒ depend more on areas of the brain that control spatial memory

   Ⓓ have brains that surprised everyone

Go on to the next page ➜

14. Look at the four squares [■] that show where the following sentence could be added to paragraph 4.

They were able to recall large amounts of information by storing information in such a structure.

Where would the sentence best fit?

⁴ MAs offer a simple explanation. [14A] ■ Anything can be imprinted upon our memories and kept in good order, simply by constructing a building in the imagination and filling it with images of what needs to be recalled. Dating back to the fifth century, this building is called a Memory Palace. [14B] ■ Even as late as the fourteenth century, when there were perhaps only a dozen copies of any text, scholars needed to remember what was read or told to them. [14C] ■ Reading to remember requires a very different technique than speed reading. If something is going to be made memorable, it has to be repeated. Until relatively recently, people read only a few books intensively over and over again, usually out loud and in groups. [14D] ■ Today we read extensively, usually only once and without sustained focus.

(A) [14A]

(B) [14B]

(C) [14C]

(D) [14D]

15. Why does the author mention "speed reading" in paragraph 4?

(A) To discuss a fourth century technique

(B) To illustrate why people read a few books intensively

(C) To explain the copies of texts fourteenth century scholars needed to recall

(D) To contrast the type of reading done nowadays with that of earlier times

16. The phrase "spur of the moment" in paragraph 5 is closest in meaning to

(A) timetable

(B) clock

(C) fly

(D) brain

17. It can be inferred from paragraph 5 that

(A) there are 57,000 body parts

(B) there is a variety of unforgettable scenes

(C) memory palaces can be quickly forgotten

(D) decks of cards build actual buildings

18. Which of the sentences below most clearly expresses important information in the highlighted sentence in paragraph 6? *Incorrect* choices change the meaning or leave out important information.

    Ⓐ Those new to memory training need to create multiple memory palaces.

    Ⓑ Stockpiling memory palaces enables those new to memory competitions to win.

    Ⓒ Training the mind happens when one is new to competitions.

    Ⓓ When one stockpiles in battle, one enters a memory palace.

19. The word "cubbyholes" in paragraph 6 is closest in meaning to

    Ⓐ black holes

    Ⓑ zodiac signs

    Ⓒ confined spaces

    Ⓓ playing cards

20. **Directions:** Read the introductory sentence for a summary of the passage below. Complete the summary by choosing the THREE answer choices that include the key ideas in the passage. Some answer choices are incorrect because they include ideas that are not presented in the passage or are not significant in the passage. **This question is worth** 2 points (2 points for 3 correct answers, 1 point for 2 correct answers, and 0 points for 1 or 0 correct answers).

The passage discusses how mental athletes are able to memorize astounding amounts of data.

-
-
-

Choose 3 answers.

    ① Memory athletes create lavish images that they delete after competitions.

    ② Memory athletes need to remember what is read to them.

    ③ Memory athletes use memory palaces to help them recall memorized images.

    ④ Unlike memory athletes, most people today read without attempting to remember details.

    ⑤ Ed Cooke is 24 years old.

    ⑥ Techniques memory athletes employ can be used by average people.

STOP. This is the end of the Reading section for test-takers taking the TOEFL iBT test on the computer.

If you are preparing to take the Paper Edition of the test, continue to READING 3.

READING 3

Read the passage.

The Endangered Turtle

In 2012, a 655-pound leatherback sea turtle was released by the New England Aquarium after aquarium staff rescued the stranded and injured turtle off a mud flat in Cape Cod. The aquarium turtle was actually considered underweight, for these turtles typically weigh around 1,000 pounds. Forty percent of the turtle's front left flipper was gone due to a recent trauma. Leatherbacks, who use their large front flippers to pull their bodies through the water, often lose part of them to sharks or other large predatory fish and can still survive while at sea. These endangered sea turtles are rarely found alive after stranding. A tracking device was inserted under its shell so that it could be closely monitored.

The leatherback is the largest living turtle in the world. It is also the longest-living marine species ever to populate the world's oceans. Leatherbacks roam tropical and subtropical waters of the Pacific, Atlantic, and Indian Oceans. Finding this turtle as far north as Massachusetts is a rarity. They survived catastrophic asteroid impacts and outlived the dinosaurs; however, scientists question whether these animals will survive into the next decade. If these turtles that lived for 150 million years are allowed to vanish, scientists fear it will foreshadow the extinction of a host of other marine species. In 1980 the population was estimated to be about 115,000 adult females. In recent years, however, the number of nesting leatherbacks has been declining at an alarming rate, in excess of 95 percent. Historically, these turtles were captured not for their meat but rather for their eggs, considered a delicacy even today in many parts of the world.

However, with fewer leatherback turtles in existence today, the number of eggs to poach has also waned. What then are major causes in the decrease? Scientists blame fishing nets, beach erosion, entanglement in other ship equipment, and sea trash. In 1987 shrimp fleets alone captured 640 leatherbacks in their nets. The turtles have been decimated by a fishing technique known as longlining, in which vessels lay out 40-to-60-mile-long lines of vertically hanging baited hooks. The turtles get caught up and tangled in these hooks. In response, the United States made the use of Turtle Excluded Devices (TEDs) mandatory for all fishing fleets, but scientists fear that this restriction will not be enough to save the leatherbacks from extinction. In addition to fishing nets, the turtles become entangled fairly often in anchors, buoys, other ropes, and cables. Another problem is their preferred nesting sites. The leatherbacks favor open-access beaches, possibly to avoid damage to their soft flippers. Unfortunately, such open beaches with little shoreline protection are vulnerable to beach erosion, triggered by seasonal changes in wind and wave direction. A presumably secure beach can undergo such severe and dramatic erosion that eggs laid on it are lost. The turtles have also been severely impacted by trash in the seas. Leatherbacks have mistaken floating plastic bags, plastic and Styrofoam objects, and balloons for their natural food, jellyfish. Ingesting this debris can obstruct their digestive organs, leading to the ingestion of toxins that reduce the absorption of nutrients from real food. Ten of 33 dead leatherbacks washed ashore between 1979 and 1988 had ingested plastic bags or other plastic material.

Saving the leatherbacks will take cooperation from nations around the world, for more than 90 percent of longline fishing takes place in international waters. Most nations, however, have taken steps to protect leatherback sea turtle nesting beaches in the last decade. Scientists are asking that all beaches where leatherback sea turtles are known to nest and lay eggs be protected and all egg harvesting be banned.

Refer to the passages below and answer the questions that follow.

The Endangered Turtle

[1] A 655-pound leatherback sea turtle was released by the New England Aquarium after aquarium staff rescued the stranded and injured turtle two months ago off a mud flat in Cape Cod. The aquarium turtle is actually considered underweight, for these turtles typically weigh around 1,000 pounds. Forty percent of the turtle's front left flipper was gone due to a recent trauma. Leatherbacks, who use their large front flippers to pull their bodies through the water, often lose part of them to sharks or other large predatory fish and can still survive while at sea. These endangered sea turtles are rarely found alive after stranding. A tracking device was inserted under its shell so that it could be closely monitored.

Directions: Answer the questions.

21. Why is it mentioned in paragraph 1 that the aquarium sea turtle is 655 pounds?

    (A) To foreshadow its subsequent release back into the ocean

    (B) To illustrate its being endangered

    (C) To explain why its flipper is gone

    (D) To contrast its weight with other sea turtles

22. The word "predatory" in paragraph 1 could best be replaced by

    (A) hunting

    (B) historic

    (C) irritable

    (D) crafty

23. It can be inferred from paragraph 1 that the turtle has been inserted with a tracking device in order to

    (A) follow its future movements

    (B) watch it come ashore

    (C) monitor its front left flipper

    (D) measure its weight gain

Go on to the next page ➜

² The leatherback is the largest living turtle in the world. It is also the longest-living marine species ever to populate the world's oceans. Leatherbacks roam tropical and subtropical waters of the Pacific, Atlantic, and Indian Oceans. Finding this turtle as far north as Massachusetts is a rarity. They survived catastrophic asteroid impacts and outlived the dinosaurs; however, scientists question whether these animals will survive into the next decade. If these turtles that lived for 150 million years are allowed to vanish, scientists fear it will foreshadow the extinction of a host of other marine species. In 1982 the population was estimated to be about 115,000 adult females. In recent years, however, the number of nesting leatherbacks has been declining at an alarming rate, in excess of 95 percent. Historically, these turtles were captured not for their meat but rather for their eggs, considered a delicacy even today in many parts of the world.

24. The author mentions "They survived catastrophic asteroid impacts and outlived the dinosaurs; however, scientists question whether these animals will survive into the next decade" in paragraph 2 in order to

(A) compare sea turtles with their dinosaur ancestors

(B) emphasize the demise of the long-living sea turtles

(C) question whether the impact of asteroids led to sea turtle extinction

(D) calculate how many sea turtles will survive the decade

³ However, with fewer leatherback turtles in existence today, the number of eggs to poach has also waned. What then are major causes in the decrease? Scientists blame fishing nets, beach erosion, entanglement in other ship equipment, and sea trash. In 1987 shrimp fleets alone captured 640 leatherbacks in their nets. The turtles have been decimated by a fishing technique known as longlining, in which vessels lay out 40-to-60-mile-long lines of vertically hanging baited hooks. [25A] ■ The turtles get caught up and tangled in these hooks. In response, the United States made the use of Turtle Excluded Devices (TEDs) mandatory for all fishing fleets, but scientists fear that this restriction will not be enough to save the leatherbacks from extinction. [25B] ■ In addition to fishing nets, the turtles become entangled fairly often in anchors, buoys, other ropes, and cables. Another problem is their preferred nesting sites. The leatherbacks favor open-access beaches, possibly to avoid damage to their soft flippers. Unfortunately, such open beaches with little shoreline protection are vulnerable to beach erosion, triggered by seasonal changes in wind and wave direction. A presumably secure beach can undergo such severe and dramatic erosion that eggs laid on it are lost. [25C] ■ The turtles have also been severely impacted by trash in the seas. Leatherbacks have mistaken floating plastic bags, plastic and Styrofoam objects, and balloons for their natural food, jellyfish. Ingesting this debris can obstruct their digestive organs, leading to the ingestion of toxins that reduce the absorption of nutrients from real food. [25D] ■ Ten of 33 dead leatherbacks washed ashore between 1979 and 1988 had ingested plastic bags or other plastic material.

25. Look at the four squares [■] in the passage on the previous page that show where the following sentence could be added to paragraph 3.

Without egg production, sea turtle extinction is inevitable.

Where would the sentence best fit?

(A) [25A]

(B) [25B]

(C) [25C]

(D) [25D]

26. According to paragraph 3, all of the following contribute to the decrease today of sea turtles EXCEPT

(A) sea trash

(B) anchor entanglement

(C) egg poaching

(D) beach erosion

27. The word "decimated" in paragraph 3 could best be replaced by

(A) destroyed

(B) injured

(C) captured

(D) tended

28. What is stated in paragraph 3 about why sea turtles prefer open-access beaches?

(A) The sites prohibit fishing nets.

(B) The sites offer exposure to wind and wave direction.

(C) The sites provide the natural food of the turtles: jellyfish.

(D) The sites may offer protection for their appendages.

[4] Saving the leatherbacks will take cooperation from nations around the world, for more than 90 percent of longline fishing takes place in international waters. Most nations, however, have taken steps to protect leatherback sea turtle nesting beaches in the last decade. Scientists are asking that all beaches where leatherback sea turtles are known to nest and lay eggs be protected and all egg harvesting be banned.

29. According to paragraph 4, why will international cooperation to save the sea turtle be essential?

(A) Scientists from many nations regulate Turtle Excluded Devices.

(B) US regulations alone are insufficient.

(C) Sea turtle eggs are an international delicacy.

(D) Sea turtle egg harvesting has been banned around the world.

30. **Directions:** Read the introductory sentence for a summary of the passage below. Complete the summary by choosing the THREE answer choices that include the key ideas in the passage. Some answer choices are incorrect because they include ideas that are not presented in the passage or are not significant in the passage. This question is worth 2 points (2 points for 3 correct answers, 1 point for 2 correct answers, and 0 points for 1 or 0 correct answers).

Sea turtles are facing extinction.

Choose 3 answers.

① US regulations alone are insufficient to protect endangered sea turtles.

② Fishing fleets use plastic bags and Styrofoam to attract sea turtles into their nets.

③ Scientists from many nations use TEDs to regulate fishing fleets.

④ Sea turtle meat is considered a delicacy in many parts of the world.

⑤ Scientists fear that sea turtle extinction may signal that of other sea mammals.

⑥ Sea turtles become entangled in fishing lines, contributing to their demise.

STOP. This is the end of the Reading section for the Paper Edition.

Listening Section

This section tests your ability to understand conversations and lectures in English. You can listen to each conversation and lecture only **one** time.

After each conversation or lecture, you will answer some questions. The questions usually ask about the main idea and supporting details or about a speaker's attitude or purpose. Answer the questions based on what the speakers say or imply.

You can take notes while you listen. The notes may help you answer the questions. You will NOT receive a score for your notes.

You will see the **audio icon** 🎧 in some questions. This means that you will hear a part of the question that does not appear on the test page.

Questions are worth 1 point. If a question is worth more than 1 point, specific directions will tell you how many points you can receive.

You will have approximately **36 minutes** to listen to the conversations and lectures and to answer the questions. You should answer each question even if your answer is only a guess. For this practice test, a useful guideline is to spend no more than 35 seconds to answer a question.

The Listening section is relevant for test-takers taking the computer-based version and the Paper Edition of the TOEFL iBT Test.

QUESTIONS

Questions 1–5

🎧 Listen to Track 1.

NOTES:

Directions: Answer the questions.

1. Why does the student go to the university office?

   (A) To find his advisor so he can register

   (B) To pay the parking ticket

   (C) To sign up for the monthly tuition payment plan

   (D) To have the financial hold removed

2. Which of these are true about the student's experience?

   Choose 2 answers.

   (A) He cleared up the issue of the hold.

   (B) He was told he had an academic hold.

   (C) He is used to having his name mispronounced.

   (D) He can't find his advisor.

🎧 3. Play Track 2 to listen again to part of the passage. Then answer the question.

   Why does the student say this?

   (A) The student knows his last name is unusual.

   (B) The bursar doesn't know who he is.

   (C) The student can recall his ID number.

   (D) The bursar can't pronounce his name correctly.

4. What must a student do in order to register for classes?

   (A) Have his tuition bills disbursed monthly

   (B) Not have any holds on his account

   (C) Speak with the bursar

   (D) Make sure to pay the ninety dollars

5. What will the student most likely do next?

   (A) Go back to the library

   (B) Discuss the payment option with his parents

   (C) Look for his advisor

   (D) Update his account with the university

Go on to the next page ➜

Questions 6–11

🎧 Listen to Track 3.

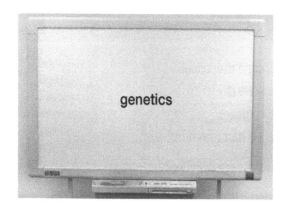

NOTES:

Directions: Answer the questions.

6. What does the professor mainly discuss in the lecture?

   (A) The explanation of why his wife has red hair

   (B) Mendel's personality traits and their impact

   (C) Mendel's theories and their applicability

   (D) Predicting the shape of garden pea plants

7. Which of the following are reasons the professor mentions for taking the course?

   Choose 2 answers.

   (A) To fulfill the science elective

   (B) To compare high school genetics coursework

   (C) To major in one of the natural sciences

   (D) To complete the final premed requirement

🎧 8. Play Track 4 to listen again to part of the passage. Then answer the question.

   What does the professor mean when he says this?

   (A) That the students need to be paying attention to the lecture

   (B) That the students' memories may be damaged

   (C) That the students may have forgotten what he's about to discuss

   (D) That the students have too many things to remember

9. What are variants called?

   (A) Gametes

   (B) Genes

   (C) Offspring

   (D) Alleles

10. What does the professor say about red hair?

   (A) That if both parents are carriers for red hair but do not have red hair, their children will have red hair

   (B) That if one parent has red hair, the child will be red-headed

   (C) That redheads might die off in the near future

   (D) That it takes two carriers to have a red-headed child

11. What will probably be discussed in the next class?

   (A) The number of children the professor has

   (B) The hair color of the professor's wife

   (C) Gregor Mendel's hair color theories

   (D) Garden pea plants and their offspring

Go on to the next page ➜

Questions 12–17

🎧 Listen to Track 5.

philosophy

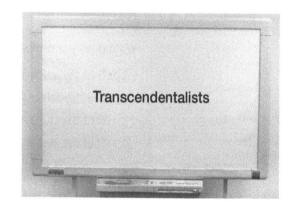

Transcendentalists

NOTES:

Directions: Answer the questions.

12. Why does the professor want the class to visit Brook Farm?

    (A) To see the remaining cellar holes

    (B) To educate area children about the Transcendentalists

    (C) To learn about the Transcendentalists

    (D) To assist with a new Brook Farm project

13. What is true about the original Brook Farm?

    (A) It never had more than 15 members.

    (B) Nathaniel Hawthorne subsidized the community.

    (C) The members wanted to work the land.

    (D) The members rebuilt the site after the fire.

14. What is true about Transcendentalism?

    Choose 2 answers.

    (A) The spiritual world is the most important.

    (B) It includes literature as well as social issues.

    (C) It excludes social interaction.

    (D) It limits the number of community members.

15. Why was the professor contacted to promote the new Brook Farm?

    (A) Because he is a Transcendentalist

    (B) Because he has had farming experience

    (C) Because he is a Transcendentalist academic

    (D) Because he has student teachers in his class

🎧 16. Play Track 6 to listen again to part of the passage. Then answer the question.

    Why does the professor say this?

    (A) Teacher trainees can help with the neighboring children.

    (B) Teaching certificate students can get credit working there.

    (C) The new Brook Farm is looking for teachers.

    (D) His students will work in the area schools.

17. Which of the following is NOT mentioned as an after-dinner activity of the original Brook Farm members?

    (A) parties

    (B) outdoor physical activity

    (C) playing cards

    (D) singing

Go on to the next page ➔

Questions 18–22

🎧 Listen to Track 7.

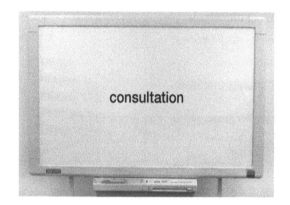

NOTES:

Directions: Answer the questions.

18. **Why does the student go to see the professor?**

    Ⓐ To practice his speech

    Ⓑ To choose between two topics

    Ⓒ To find an original idea

    Ⓓ To complete a quick survey

19. **Which of these are true about the student's experience with the professor? This question is worth 2 points** (2 points for 3 correct answers, 1 point for 2 correct answers, and 0 points for 1 or 0 correct answers).

    Choose 3 answers.

    Ⓐ The professor suggests the student switch topics.

    Ⓑ The student needs to return during office hours.

    Ⓒ The student is still undecided on a speech topic.

    Ⓓ The student is reminded to include expert testimony.

    Ⓔ The student will present a week from Thursday.

20. **What does the professor suggest the student do?**

    Ⓐ Ask how many classmates vote

    Ⓑ Find a less academic topic

    Ⓒ Conduct an in-class survey

    Ⓓ Take a later shuttle to class

🎧 21. **Play Track 8 to listen again to part of the discussion. Then answer the question. Why does the student say this?**

    Ⓐ He is concerned that she may not get back to campus on the weekend.

    Ⓑ He thinks the professor may not be familiar with the shuttle system.

    Ⓒ He would like her to give him a ride back to campus on weekends.

    Ⓓ He needs her to know that students go downtown on the weekend.

22. **What will the student probably do next?**

    Ⓐ Have the class sign a petition

    Ⓑ Order new bars of shampoo with logos

    Ⓒ Decide which topic to choose

    Ⓓ Practice his persuasive speech

Questions 23–28

🎧 Listen to Track 9.

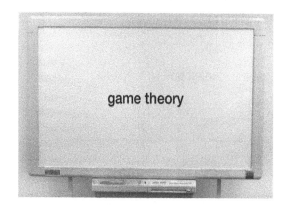

NOTES:

Directions: Answer the questions.

23. How is the information in the lecture organized?

    (A) The causes of human behavior are clarified

    (B) Various types of games are contrasted

    (C) A topic is explained through an extended example

    (D) The process is compared with another one

24. What is NOT mentioned as a type of situation that can be applied to game theory?

    (A) a card game

    (B) sports

    (C) a military decision

    (D) games of luck

25. What is stated in the lecture about game theory?

    Choose 2 answers.

    (A) All game theory games are reduced to board games.

    (B) It is more complicated than it appears to be.

    (C) It uses math to examine strategy.

    (D) The players need to be people.

26. Are these statements true about the prisoner's dilemma? **This question is worth 2 points** (2 points for 4 correct answers, 1 point for 3 correct answers, and 0 points for 2, 1, or 0 correct answers).

    For each sentence check the *YES* or *NO* column.

	YES	NO
If A betrays, and B is silent, B goes to jail for 6 months.		
If A betrays, and B is silent, A does not go to jail.		
If A and B betray each other, neither goes to jail.		

Go on to the next page →

🎧 27. Play Track 10 to listen again to part of the passage. Then answer the question.

What does the professor mean when she says this?

    Ⓐ Since each country does not know what the other one will do, it should protect itself.

    Ⓑ Both countries always need to make weapons.

    Ⓒ Countries are like people, and sometimes they are altruistic.

    Ⓓ Countries need to study game theory before making weapons.

28. **Why does the professor mention what is called a repeated game?**

    Ⓐ To make clear that it is always the better strategy

    Ⓑ To explain why it is always better to betray the other player

    Ⓒ To indicate that in some circumstances players care about each other

    Ⓓ To show that participants will play the game a second time

STOP. This is the end of the Listening section.

Speaking Section

This section is the same for the computer-based TOEFL iBT test and the Paper Edition.

This section tests your ability to speak about different topics. You will answer four questions.

Question 1 asks you to make and defend a personal choice between two contrasting behaviors or courses of action.

Question 2 will include a reading and a listening passage. First, you will read a short passage which presents a campus-related issue. Then you will hear comments on the issue in the reading passage. Next you will summarize the speaker's opinion within the context of the reading passage

Question 3 will also include a reading and a listening passage. First, you will read a short passage that broadly defines a term, process or idea from an academic subject. Then you will hear an excerpt from a lecture which provides examples and specific information to illustrate the term, process or idea from the reading passage. Next you will answer a question which asks you to combine and convey important information from the reading passage and the lecture excerpt.

Question 4 will include part of a lecture that explains a term or concept and gives concrete examples to illustrate that term or concept. The question asks you to summarize the lecture and demonstrate an understanding of the relationship between the examples and the overall topic.

While you read and listen, you can take notes that should help you answer the questions.

Listen carefully to the directions for each question. The preparation time begins right after you hear the question. You will be told when to begin to prepare and when to begin speaking.

The Speaking section is relevant for test-takers taking the computer-based version and the Paper Edition of the TOEFL iBT Test.

QUESTIONS

Track 11

1. You will be asked your opinion about a familiar topic. Listen to the question, and then prepare your response. You will have 15 seconds to prepare a response and 45 seconds to speak. You can take notes on the main points of a response.

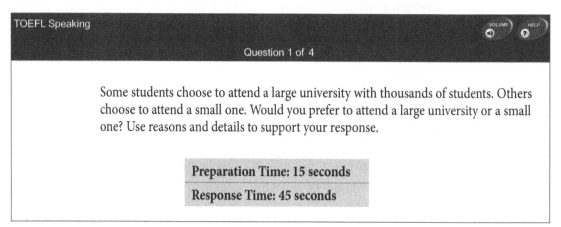

TOEFL Speaking

VOLUME   HELP

Question 1 of 4

Some students choose to attend a large university with thousands of students. Others choose to attend a small one. Would you prefer to attend a large university or a small one? Use reasons and details to support your response.

Preparation Time: 15 seconds

Response Time: 45 seconds

NOTES:

2. You will read a short passage and then listen to a conversation about the same topic. You will then answer a question about about them. You will have 45 seconds to read the passage. You can take notes on the main points of the reading passage.

Reading Time: 45 seconds

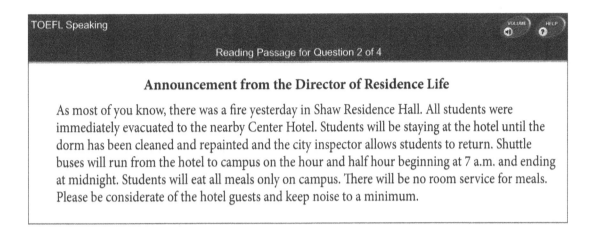

Listen to two students discuss the announcement. You can take notes on the main points of the conversation.

NOTES:

Now answer the following question:

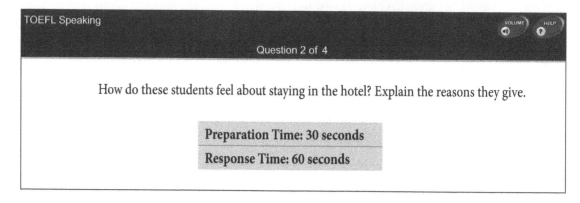

3. You will read a short passage and then listen to a conversation about the same topic. You will then answer a question about about them. You will have 45 seconds to read the passage. You can take notes on the main points of the reading passage.

Reading Time: 45 seconds

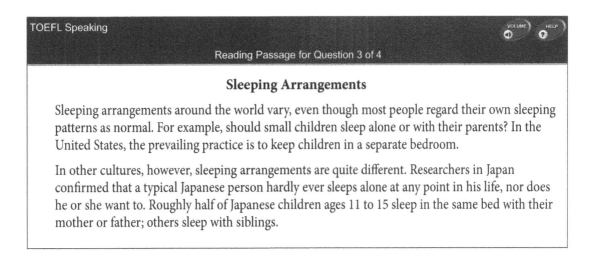

Sleeping Arrangements

Sleeping arrangements around the world vary, even though most people regard their own sleeping patterns as normal. For example, should small children sleep alone or with their parents? In the United States, the prevailing practice is to keep children in a separate bedroom.

In other cultures, however, sleeping arrangements are quite different. Researchers in Japan confirmed that a typical Japanese person hardly ever sleeps alone at any point in his life, nor does he or she want to. Roughly half of Japanese children ages 11 to 15 sleep in the same bed with their mother or father; others sleep with siblings.

Listen to the passage. You can take notes on the main points of the listening passage.

NOTES:

Go on to the next page →

Now answer the following question:

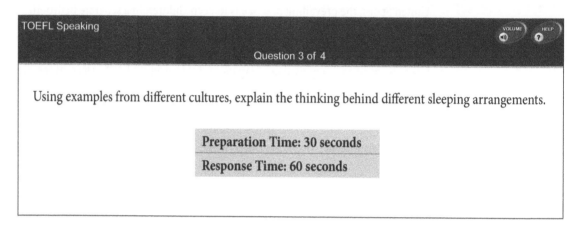

TOEFL Speaking

VOLUME   HELP

Question 3 of 4

Using examples from different cultures, explain the thinking behind different sleeping arrangements.

Preparation Time: 30 seconds

Response Time: 60 seconds

Track 14

4. You will listen to part of a lecture. You can take notes on the main points of the listening passage.

Now answer the following question:

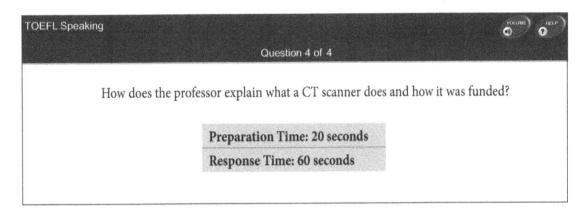

STOP. This is the end of the Speaking section.

Writing Section

This section tests your ability to use writing in an academic setting. There will be two writing tasks.

In the first writing task, the integrated writing task, you will read a passage and listen to a lecture where the speaker discusses the same topic from a different perspective. You will then write a summary. You may take notes on the reading and listening passages.

TOEFL iBT test on the computer

The second task on the computer-based TOEFL iBT test is the academic discussion task. In this task, you will write a response to the professor's question using the information in the texts and your own ideas.

TOEFL iBT Paper Edition

The second task on the Paper Edition of the TOEFL iBT test is the independent writing task. In this task, you will answer a question using your own background knowledge.

Integrated Writing Directions

For this task, you will read a passage about an academic topic, and then you will hear a lecture about the same topic. You may take notes on both.

Then you will read a question about the connection between the reading passage and the lecture. In your written response try to use information from both the passage and the lecture. You will **not** be asked for your own opinion. You can refer to the reading passage while you are writing.

You should plan on **3 minutes** to read the passage. Then listen to the lecture and give yourself **20 minutes** to plan and write your response. A successful response will be about 150 to 225 words. Your response will be judged on the quality of the writing and the correctness of the content.

QUESTION 1

Read the passage. On a piece of paper, take notes on the main points of the reading passage.

Reading Time: 3 minutes

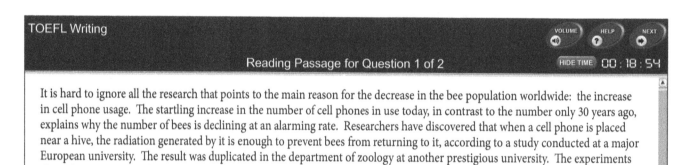

TOEFL Writing

Reading Passage for Question 1 of 2

VOLUME HELP NEXT

HIDE TIME 00 : 18 : 54

It is hard to ignore all the research that points to the main reason for the decrease in the bee population worldwide: the increase in cell phone usage. The startling increase in the number of cell phones in use today, in contrast to the number only 30 years ago, explains why the number of bees is declining at an alarming rate. Researchers have discovered that when a cell phone is placed near a hive, the radiation generated by it is enough to prevent bees from returning to it, according to a study conducted at a major European university. The result was duplicated in the department of zoology at another prestigious university. The experiments show that microwaves from cell phones appear to interfere with worker bee navigational skills. When cell phones were placed near beehives, the hives collapsed completely in five to ten days. The worker bees simply failed to return home. Adding to the mystery, wildlife, which would normally raid the abandoned hives, would not go near the collapsed colonies.

The navigational skill of the worker bees is dependent on the Earth's magnetic properties. The electro-magnetic waves emitted by the cell phones and relay towers interfere with the Earth's magnetism, resulting in the loss of the navigational capacity of the bee. Then the bee simply fails to return to the hive. The radiation causes damage to the nervous system, and it becomes unable to fly. Although the rapid bee population decline began as a mystery, the cell phone magnetism proliferation explains the reduction.

🎧 Play Track 15 to listen to the passage.

Now answer the following question:

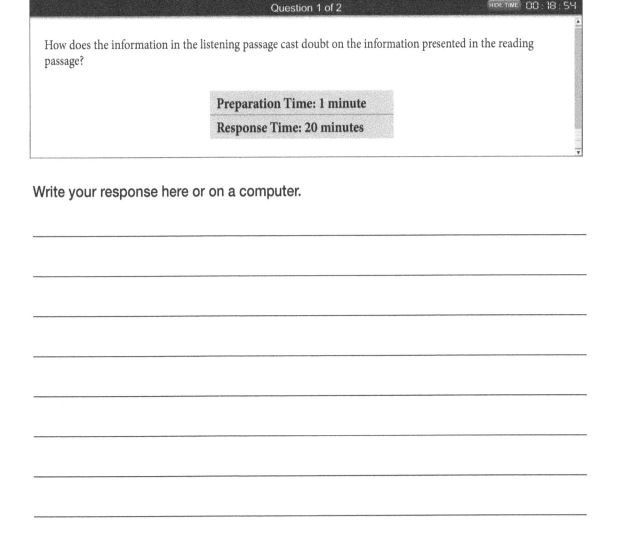

TOEFL Writing

Question 1 of 2

HIDE TIME 00 : 18 : 54

How does the information in the listening passage cast doubt on the information presented in the reading passage?

Preparation Time: 1 minute

Response Time: 20 minutes

Write your response here or on a computer.

Writing for an Academic Discussion

For this task, you will read an online discussion. A professor has posted a question about a topic, and some classmates have responded with their ideas.

Write a response that contributes to the discussion. You will have **10 minutes** to write your response. It is important to use your own words in the response. Including memorized reasons or examples will result in a lower score.

QUESTION 2 for the computer-based TOEFL iBT Test

Your professor is teaching a class on psychology. Write a post responding to the professor's question.

In your response you should:

- express and support your opinion.
- make a contribution to the discussion in your own words.

An effective response will contain at least 100 words.

Professor Thorn

'Talent' is a word we often hear today – we have talented people and talent shows and even talent coaches. But although talent is highly prized in our society, it is a hard concept to define. So I'd like you to think about this question: What is talent, are all of us talented or are some people born with talent but not others? Some say that people are born with talent, other psychologists say it is the rate at which you improve in comparison with other people. What do you think?

Hiroko

I wish that I was talented. I've taken singing lessons for three years now but I'm terrible at singing. I definitely think that talent is inherited, think about families who pass talents on from generation to generation.

Ryan

In my country, we believe that everyone can be good at something, no matter the starting point. With training and effort anyone can take their bit of talent to the next level and compete with other people. Talent is just effort and determination.

Go on to the next page ➜

FOR THE PAPER EDITION ONLY

Independent Writing Directions

For this task, you will write an essay that explains, supports, and states your opinion about an issue. You will have **30 minutes** to plan, write, and edit your essay. You can take notes on the main points of a response.

A successful response will be at least 300 words. Try to show that you can develop your ideas, organize your essay, and use language correctly to express your ideas. The essay will be judged on the quality of your writing.

QUESTION 2 for the Paper Edition

Write your response here.

_____

_____

_____

_____

_____

_____

_____

_____

Go on to the next page →

Go on to the next page ➜

_____

_____

_____

_____

_____

_____

_____

_____

_____

_____

_____

_____

_____

_____

_____

_____

_____

_____

_____

_____

STOP. This is the end of the Writing section.

TOEFL iBT Practice Test 2

TOEFL iBT Practice Test 2

Reading Section

This section tests your ability to understand academic passages in English. The section is divided into separately timed parts.

Questions are worth 1 point except for the last question for each passage which is worth more than 1 point. The directions for the last question explain how many points you can receive.

TOEFL iBT test on the computer

There are two reading passages in this section. You should plan to spend **18 minutes** reading each passage and answering the questions about it. You should take no more than **35 minutes** to complete the entire section.

Reading Section Timing Guide TOEFL iBT test on the computer		
Passage	Number of Questions	Time to Complete Test
Passage 1	10	35 minutes
Passage 2	10	

The above information does not apply to the TOEFL iBT Paper Edition.

TOEFL iBT Paper Edition

There are three reading passages in this section in the TOEFL iBT Paper Edition. You should plan to spend **20 minutes** reading each passage answering the questions about it. You should take no more than **60 minutes** to complete the entire section.

Reading Section Timing Guide TOEFL iBT Paper Edition		
Passage	Number of Questions	Time to Complete Test
Passage 1	10	
Passage 2	10	60 minutes
Passage 3	10	

READING 1

Directions: Read the passage.

The French Encyclopedia

1. Neither Denis Diderot nor Jean d'Alembert were scientists. Living in the mid-1700s in France, Diderot was disowned by his father for wanting to become a writer and not entering one of the learned professions. Fortunately for history, Diderot followed his passion, for he and d'Alembert, ranked among the sharpest intellects of the day, fostered an environment in which earth-shattering discoveries could be made. They, and an army of experts and writers, published a set of encyclopedias about science, art, and trades in pre-revolutionary France.

2. Their encyclopedia began as a simple venture: a translation of a successful English work. Initially the two were writers, but once they advanced to be editors, they expanded the scope of the project to include all knowledge, not just literature. During the translation process Diderot's creative mind and astute vision transformed the original publication. Instead of a mere translation, the two collected the works of all the active writers as well as ideas and knowledge that were transforming the cultivated French population.

3. The first volume was published in 1751. This encyclopedia was unlike any other publication. The ideas expressed within its pages were unorthodox and quite progressive for the time. Diderot declared within the work his belief that there was a need for such an encyclopedia, and that it should include not only disciplines studied by the academies but every branch of knowledge. This was a revolutionary idea. In fact, the encyclopedia was one of the first works published during the Enlightenment. The Enlightenment was an eighteenth-century philosophical movement stressing the importance of reason and the critical reappraisal of existing ideas and social institutions.

4. The encyclopedia comprised knowledge from scholars in the academies as well as knowledge of trades and business. The objective was to collect all knowledge of the time and present the information in a condensed form for all people to use. The encyclopedia covered different points of view, processes, and methods for its subjects. Reading these would be a means of betterment. This knowledge of various subjects would benefit individuals and society collectively.

5. Their encyclopedias contained numerous errors. Diderot and d'Alembert lived and worked in a time when printed material was anything but permanent. Rather than adhering to the original text, publishers themselves often changed the content depending on where the books were published and for what audience. Diderot felt disdain for some of the finished volumes. However, their primary belief, emphasizing observation over faith in traditional beliefs, remained intact. For example, they debunked a popularly held belief at the time that baby boys first utter the sound "A" while baby girls emit the sound "E." They devoted as much space to the manufacture of stockings as to the human soul. Needless to say, their books regularly came under fire, and Diderot had to spend some time in jail. The encyclopedias were plagued by controversy from the beginning. Just one year after the first volume was published the courts halted the project. But Diderot persevered, and the project resumed. Worn down by the constant controversy surrounding the encyclopedia, d'Alembert left the effort after the French government banned the work in the late 1750s.

6. As the books gained in popularity, the government could no longer endure their influence and power. The encyclopedias threatened the governing social classes of the French aristocracy because it took for granted freedom of thought and the value of science and industry. The encyclopedias asserted that the main concern of the nation's government should be the nation's common people. The publication told the average man that he could know what only kings, emperors, and their lieutenants were supposed to know. It suggested that anyone should have access to rational truth. Although formally suppressed by the government, the decree did not stop the work, but it then was forced to continue in secret. Almost 400 years since the encyclopedia's first publication, many credit d'Alembert and Diderot's work with fostering freedom of the press, the right for every man to vote, and the advance of science.

Directions: Answer the questions.

1. Which of the sentences below most clearly expresses important information in the highlighted sentence in paragraph 1? *Incorrect* choices change the meaning or leave out important information.

   (A) Diderot had to support himself as a writer.
   (B) Diderot initially studied one of the learned professions.
   (C) When Diderot lived, becoming a writer was atypical.
   (D) In the mid-1700s in France one could not survive as a writer.

2. The word "earth-shattering" in paragraph 1 is closest in meaning to

   (A) detrimental
   (B) categorical
   (C) consequential
   (D) disastrous

3. The word "venture" in paragraph 2 is closest in meaning to

   (A) trip
   (B) undertaking
   (C) expenditure
   (D) prank

4. The word "unorthodox" in paragraph 3 is closest in meaning to

   (A) unconventional
   (B) anti-religious
   (C) illogical
   (D) untruthful

Go on to the next page →

5. Which of the following statements about the Enlightenment is supported by paragraph 4?

   Ⓐ The encyclopedia contained scholarly works.

   Ⓑ Ordinary people worked in trades.

   Ⓒ Information included alternative positions.

   Ⓓ Knowledge of the time was condensed.

6. Why did d'Alembert stop working on the encyclopedia?

   Ⓐ Because he was forced to go to jail

   Ⓑ Because the project was suspended by the courts

   Ⓒ Because the unrelenting difficulties became tiresome

   Ⓓ Because he was dismayed by the numerous printing errors

7. Look at the four squares ■ that show where the following sentence could be added to paragraph 5.

When a factually incorrect belief is accepted as the truth, it is difficult to challenge it.

Where would the sentence best fit?

⁵ Their encyclopedias contained numerous errors. Diderot and d'Alembert lived and worked in a time when printed material was anything but permanent. Rather than adhering to the original text, publishers themselves often changed the content depending on where the books were published and for what audience. Diderot felt disdain for some of the finished volumes. However, their primary belief, emphasizing observation over faith in traditional beliefs, remained intact. [7A] ■ For example, they debunked a popularly held belief at the time that baby boys first utter the sound "A" while baby girls emit the sound "E." [7B] ■ They devoted as much space to the manufacture of stockings as to the human soul. Needless to say, their books regularly came under fire, and Diderot had to spend some time in jail. [7C] ■ The encyclopedias were plagued by controversy from the beginning. [7D] ■ Just one year after the first volume was published the courts halted the project. But Diderot persevered, and the project resumed. Worn down by the constant controversy surrounding the encyclopedia, d'Alembert left the effort after the French government banned the work in the late 1750s.

   Ⓐ [7A]

   Ⓑ [7B]

   Ⓒ [7C]

   Ⓓ [7D]

8. The phrase "plagued by" in paragraph 5 is closest in meaning to

   Ⓐ troubled by

   Ⓑ ridiculed by

   Ⓒ offset by

   Ⓓ infested with

9. It is implied in the passage that

   (A) Diderot and d'Alembert did not get along

   (B) the government believed the books would empower the common people

   (C) Diderot became a wealthy man from the sale of the encyclopedias

   (D) Diderot and d'Alembert's background in science and trades helped immensely

10. **Directions:** Read the introductory sentence for a summary of the passage below. Complete the summary by choosing the THREE answer choices that include the key ideas in the passage. Some answer choices are incorrect because they include ideas that are not presented in the passage or are not significant in the passage. **This question is worth 2 points** (2 points for 3 correct answers, 1 point for 2 correct answers, and 0 points for 1 or 0 correct answers).

    The passage discusses the most important contributions The French Encyclopedia made to French life.

    ┌───┐
    │ •   │
    │   │
    │ •   │
    │   │
    │ •   │
    └───┘

    Choose 3 answers.

    (1) Due to the publication of the books, printing errors decreased.

    (2) The books declared the government should concern itself with ordinary people.

    (3) Kings and emperors gave access to what they knew.

    (4) Ordinary people gained access to rational truth.

    (5) The books condensed what was known about the world for all to use.

    (6) People were free to study what they chose, not what was expected.

READING 2

Directions: Read the passage.

Questions 11 to 20

The Land-Grant College System

1. The history of land-grant colleges of agriculture in the United States is closely tied to the rise in higher-education opportunities for children of working families. The land-grant system began in 1862 with a piece of legislation known as the Morrill Act. This act funded educational institutions by granting federally controlled land to all states for them to develop or sell to raise funds to establish and endow "land-grant" colleges. The mission of these institutions as set forth in the 1862 Act is to focus on the teaching of practical agriculture, military tactics, science and engineering, though without excluding classical studies, as a response to the industrial revolution and changing social mobility. This mission was in contrast to the historic practice of higher education to focus on an abstract liberal arts curriculum. The legislative mandate for these land-grant colleges helped extend higher education to broad segments of the US population so that members of the working classes could obtain a liberal, practical education.

2. Public universities existed already in some states, such as the University of Michigan founded in 1814; however, higher education was still widely unavailable to many agricultural and industrial workers. The Morrill Act was intended to provide a broad segment of the population with a practical education that had direct relevance to their daily lives. Most states responded to the Morrill Act by legislating new agricultural and mechanical arts colleges rather than by endowing already existing state institutions. The act gave rise to a network of often poorly financed colleges known as the 1862s. The Second Morrill Act, which provided for annual appropriations to each state to support its land-grant colleges, was passed in Congress in 1890.

3. The first land-grant bill was introduced in Congress by Vermont Representative Justin Morrill—hence the name of the Act—in 1857. After much struggle, the bill passed in 1859, only to be vetoed by President James Buchanan. In 1861, Morrill resubmitted the bill that increased to 30,000 acres the grant for each senator and representative and added a requirement that institutions teach military tactics. The need for trained military officers to fight in the Civil War, along with the absence of Southern legislators who had opposed the earlier bill, helped the Act sail through Congress in just six months. President Abraham Lincoln signed it into law on July 2, 1862. Iowa was the first state legislature to accept the provisions, designating the State Agricultural College, known today as Iowa State University, as the land-grant college in 1864. The oldest school to hold land-grant status is Rutgers University, founded in 1766 and designated the land-grant college of New Jersey in 1864.

4. Over the decades, as the US economy grew and changed, so did the nature of demands for education and scientific pursuit. As more and more US citizens began to attend college, most colleges of agriculture were transformed into full-fledged universities. In some states, like California, Maryland, Minnesota, and Wisconsin, land-grant universities have become the foremost public institutions of higher education and scientific research. In others, such as North Carolina, Michigan, and Oregon, higher education and research functions are shared with other prominent institutions. Ultimately, most land-grant colleges became large public universities that offer a full spectrum of educational opportunities. Only a very few land-grant colleges are private schools, including Cornell University and the Massachusetts Institute of Technology.

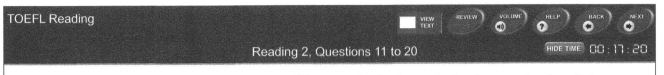

5. Although many land-grant universities are still known today for their agricultural roots, others have little agricultural identity and students are rarely from farm families. Today most of the land-grant colleges have expanded well beyond teaching only agriculture and mechanical arts and, therefore, are indistinguishable from other universities. The "colleges of agriculture" still in existence at land-grant universities resemble one another in their mission and curriculum. These universities continue to fulfill their democratic mandate for openness, accessibility, and service to people, and many of these institutions have joined the ranks of the nation's most distinguished public-research universities. Through the land-grant university heritage, millions of students in each state and territory of the US are able to study every academic discipline and explore fields far beyond the scope envisioned in the original land-grant mission.

Directions: Answer the questions.

11. The word "endow" in paragraph 1 is closest in meaning to

Ⓐ finance

Ⓑ name

Ⓒ inhabit

Ⓓ build

12. According to paragraph 1, it is NOT true that land-grant colleges were established in order to

Ⓐ respond to the Industrial Revolution

Ⓑ focus on a traditional liberal arts curriculum

Ⓒ include studies such as engineering

Ⓓ extend an education to the working class

13. The word "mandate" in paragraph 1 is closest in meaning to

Ⓐ authorization

Ⓑ jurisdiction

Ⓒ donation

Ⓓ bill

14. According to paragraph 2, which of the following is true?

Ⓐ The Morrill Act created the University of Michigan.

Ⓑ Farmers had wide access to higher education before 1862.

Ⓒ Some states already had public universities in 1862.

Ⓓ The Second Morrill Act was passed in response to 1862s.

15. The phrase "sail through" in paragraph 3 is closest in meaning to

Ⓐ circumnavigate

Ⓑ ignore completely

Ⓒ bypass entirely

Ⓓ pass easily

Go on to the next page ➜

16. The word "pursuit" in paragraph 4 is closest in meaning to

  (A) hunting

  (B) occupation

  (C) follow-up

  (D) inquiry

17. Which of the sentences below most clearly expresses important information in the highlighted sentence in paragraph 4? *Incorrect* choices change the meaning or leave out important information.

  (A) Some states share functions with other prestigious institutions.

  (B) Some state universities were the forerunners of land-grant universities.

  (C) In some states the land-grant universities are the flagship institutions.

  (D) In some states there are full-fledged research institutions.

18. Look at the four squares [■] that show where the following sentence could be added to paragraph 4.

  Most states chose to award land-grant status to public universities.

  Where would the sentence best fit?

  ⁴ [18A] ■ Over the decades, as the US economy grew and changed, so did the nature of demands for education and scientific pursuit. As more and more US citizens began to attend college, most colleges of agriculture were transformed into full-fledged universities. [18B] ■ In some states, like California, Maryland, Minnesota, and Wisconsin, land-grant universities have become the foremost public institutions of higher education and scientific research. In others, such as North Carolina, Michigan, and Oregon, higher education and research functions are shared with other prominent institutions. [18C] ■ Ultimately, most land-grant colleges became large public universities that offer a full spectrum of educational opportunities. [18D] ■ Only a very few land-grant colleges are private schools, including Cornell University and the Massachusetts Institute of Technology.

  (A) [18A]

  (B) [18B]

  (C) [18C]

  (D) [18D]

19. Which of the sentences below most clearly expresses important information in the highlighted sentences in paragraph 5? *Incorrect* choices change the meaning or leave out important information.

  (A) Although land-grant colleges differ, schools of agriculture are more alike.

  (B) Colleges of agriculture have a prominent place even today in college systems.

  (C) Universities are mandated today to continue teaching agriculture.

  (D) University expansion enabled colleges of agriculture to resemble one another.

20. **Directions:** Read the introductory sentence for a summary of the passage below. Complete the summary by choosing the THREE answer choices that include the key ideas in the passage. Some answer choices are incorrect because they include ideas that are not presented in the passage or are not significant in the passage. **This question is worth 2 points** (2 points for 3 correct answers, 1 point for 2 correct answers, and 0 points for 1 or 0 correct answers).

The passage discusses the American Land-Grant College System.

-
-
-

Choose 3 answers.

① Most states used the grants to establish agricultural and mechanical arts colleges.

② Many private colleges and universities became land-grant colleges.

③ The land-grant system helped extend higher education to working class families.

④ Land-grant colleges lost potential students to the Civil War.

⑤ Colleges of agriculture figure prominently in land-grant colleges today.

⑥ The system provided each state with 30,000 acres to establish a college or university.

STOP. This is the end of the Reading section for test-takers taking the TOEFL iBT test on the computer.

If you are preparing to take the Paper Edition of the test, continue to READING 3.

Go on to the next page →

READING 3

Read the passage.

Versatile Cotton

No one knows exactly how old cotton is. Scientists searching caves in Mexico found bits of cotton bolls and pieces of cotton cloth that proved to be at least 7,000 years old. They also found the cotton itself was much like that grown in North America today. Archaeologists have discovered remnants of cotton cloth more than 4,000 years old along the Peruvian coast. Approximately 3,000 years ago cotton was being grown, spun, and woven into cloth in the Indus Valley in Pakistan. At about the same time, natives of Egypt's Nile Valley were making and wearing cotton clothing. Arab merchants brought cotton cloth to Europe about A.D. 800. When Columbus landed in America in 1492, he found cotton growing in the Bahamian Islands. By A.D. 1500, the plant had reached the warm regions of the Americas, Eurasia, and Africa and was known throughout the world.

Cotton was first spun by machinery in England in 1730. The industrial revolution in England coupled with the 1793 American invention of the cotton gin, short for engine, which could do the work ten times faster than by hand, paved the way for the important place cotton holds in the world today. The gin made it possible to supply large quantities of cotton fiber to the fast-growing textile industry. Within ten years, the value of the US cotton crop rose from $150,000 to more than eight million dollars. In the 1850s a machine was invented to knock the hard hulls from the kernels of cottonseed, and so the cottonseed processing industry was born. In 1879 Ivory soap, made from the oil, was first produced. Around 1910 came America's first vegetable shortening, Crisco, which was made from cottonseed oil. Today, the world uses cottonseed oil in margarine, salad dressings, and cooking oils. Meal from the kernels is now made into fish bait, organic fertilizer, and feed for cattle. In the coming years, new uses will probably continue to be discovered for this multi-purpose plant.

Currently, cotton is the best-selling fiber throughout the world. Cotton comprises 61.5% of the total retail apparel and home furnishing market, aside from carpets, in the US. Most of the cotton that US mills spin and weave into cloth each year ends up as clothing. Cotton is frequently the fabric of choice as it absorbs color very well, and different textures can be achieved from different varieties of cotton. In addition to clothing, cotton is used in making such diverse items as book bindings, fish nets, handbags, coffee filters, lace, tents, curtains, and diapers.

Another attribute of cotton is its endurance. For this reason, it is an important component in medical supplies. Cotton is used for bandages and sutures because it will hold up in all kinds of environments. This durability also made it the preferred material for firefighting hoses. Fibers in the hoses would soak up water to prevent them from igniting. Today, however, fire hoses are usually made from synthetic materials that are cheaper and sturdier than cotton. In other environments, natural cotton is still the requested material for hoses; on US Navy ships the hoses are made of cotton because the sun tends to melt the synthetic, combustible materials. In addition, recent experiments have led scientists to think that cotton may be better for cleaning up oil spills than the synthetic material currently used.

Companies have come up with innovative uses of cotton. Recycled old denim jeans could be used for durable housing insulation. With Americans buying 450 million pairs of jeans annually, weighing in at roughly 1 kilo or 2.2 pounds per pair, they are being looked at as a great source of high-quality material. Cotton is often criticized for its water-intense production, but with jeans living a second life as insulation, jeans could continue to be a stylish yet green lifestyle choice. An Alabama company is attempting to turn the by-product from cotton ginning into high-quality mulch. While most other mulch, protective ground covering, is made from trees, this mulch is made using cotton gin trash. The result will reduce waste going to landfills, and mulch production will turn into a green industry itself. The all-natural mulch will reduce soil erosion on landscaping projects and should help grow healthy grass on lawns.

Refer to the passages below and answer the questions that follow.

Versatile Cotton

[1] No one knows exactly how old cotton is. Scientists searching caves in Mexico found bits of cotton bolls and pieces of cotton cloth that proved to be at least 7,000 years old. They also found the cotton itself was much like that grown in North America today. Archaeologists have discovered remnants of cotton cloth more than 4,000 years old along the Peruvian coast. Approximately 3,000 years ago cotton was being grown, spun, and woven into cloth in the Indus Valley in Pakistan. At about the same time, natives of Egypt's Nile Valley were making and wearing cotton clothing. Arab merchants brought cotton cloth to Europe about A.D. 800. When Columbus landed in America in 1492, he found cotton growing in the Bahamian Islands. By A.D. 1500, the plant had reached the warm regions of the Americas, Eurasia, and Africa and was known throughout the world.

Directions: Answers the questions.

21. With which of the following is the passage primarily concerned?

    (A) The increasing number of uses of cotton

    (B) The history of the cotton textile industry

    (C) The development of the edible cottonseed

    (D) The shift of cotton from a textile crop to a food crop

[2] Cotton was first spun by machinery in England in 1730. The industrial revolution in England coupled with the 1793 American invention of the cotton gin, short for engine, which could do the work ten times faster than by hand, paved the way for the important place cotton holds in the world today. The gin made it possible to supply large quantities of cotton fiber to the fast-growing textile industry. Within ten years, the value of the US cotton crop rose from $150,000 to more than eight million dollars. In the 1850s a machine was invented to knock the hard hulls from the kernels of cottonseed, and so the cottonseed processing industry was born. In 1879 Ivory soap, made from the oil, was first produced. Around 1910 came America's first vegetable shortening, Crisco, which was made from cottonseed oil. Today, the world uses cottonseed oil in margarine, salad dressings, and cooking oils. Meal from the kernels is now made into fish bait, organic fertilizer, and feed for cattle. In the coming years, new uses will probably continue to be discovered for this multi-purpose plant.

Go on to the next page ➜

22. How is paragraph 2 organized?

　Ⓐ categorically

　Ⓑ spatially

　Ⓒ sequentially

　Ⓓ chronologically

23. According to paragraph 2, the invention of the cotton gin was especially significant for which of the following reasons?

　Ⓐ It contributed to the Industrial Revolution.

　Ⓑ The textile industry was able to expand significantly.

　Ⓒ It created the cottonseed processing industry.

　Ⓓ Soaps and vegetable shortening resulted.

---

³ [24A] ■ Currently, cotton is the best-selling fiber throughout the world. Cotton comprises 61.5% of the total retail apparel and home furnishing market, aside from carpets, in the US [24B] ■ Most of the cotton that US mills spin and weave into cloth each year ends up as clothing. [24C] ■ Cotton is frequently the fabric of choice as it absorbs color very well, and different textures can be achieved from different varieties of cotton. [24D] ■ In addition to clothing, cotton is used in making such diverse items as book bindings, fish nets, handbags, coffee filters, lace, tents, curtains, and diapers.

---

24. Look at the four squares [■] that show where the following sentence could be added to paragraph 3.

Cotton is a component of many items other than clothing.

Where would the sentence best fit?

　Ⓐ [24A]

　Ⓑ [24B]

　Ⓒ [24C]

　Ⓓ [24D]

---

⁴ Another attribute of cotton is its endurance. For this reason, it is an important component in medical supplies. Cotton is used for bandages and sutures because it will hold up in all kinds of environments. This durability also made it the preferred material for firefighting hoses. Fibers in the hoses would soak up water to prevent them from igniting. Today, however, fire hoses are usually made from synthetic materials that are cheaper and sturdier than cotton. In other environments, natural cotton is still the requested material for hoses; on US Navy ships the hoses are made of cotton because the sun tends to melt the synthetic, combustible materials. In addition, recent experiments have led scientists to think that cotton may be better for cleaning up oil spills than the synthetic material currently used.

25. The word "durability" in paragraph 4 is closest in meaning to

(A) ignitability

(B) preference

(C) sturdiness

(D) medication

26. Which of the sentences below most clearly expresses important information in the highlighted sentence in paragraph 4? *Incorrect* choices change the meaning or leave out important information.

(A) The choice of artificial material for hoses is due to the cost and weakness of cotton.

(B) Although cotton is a better product, fire hoses are made from synthetic material.

(C) Cotton is no longer as durable as it once was.

(D) Fire hose prices have increased due to the cost of cotton.

27. The word "combustible" in paragraph 4 is closest in meaning to

(A) breakable

(B) operational

(C) flammable

(D) artificial

[5] Companies have come up with innovative uses of cotton. Recycled old denim jeans could be used for durable housing insulation. With Americans buying 450 million pairs of jeans annually, weighing in at roughly 1 kilo or 2.2 pounds per pair, they are being looked at as a great source of high-quality material. Cotton is often criticized for its water-intense production, but with jeans living a second life as insulation, jeans could continue to be a stylish yet green lifestyle choice. An Alabama company is attempting to turn the by-product from cotton ginning into high quality mulch. While most other mulch, protective ground covering, is made from trees, this mulch is made using cotton gin trash. The result will reduce waste going to landfills, and mulch production will turn into a green industry itself. The all-natural mulch will reduce soil erosion on landscaping projects and should help grow healthy grass on lawns.

28. The phrase "come up with" in paragraph 5 is closest in meaning to

(A) sought

(B) investigated

(C) devised

(D) attempted

Go on to the next page →

29. Match each description to the appropriate model on the right by placing a check mark (✓) in the correct boxes. **This question is worth 2 points** (2 points for 3 correct answers, 1 point for 2 correct answers, and 0 points for 1 or 0 correct answers).

	Organic fertilizer	Mulch	Housing insulation
By-product from cotton ginning			
Recycled old jeans			
Meal from cotton kernels			

30. **Directions:** An introductory sentence for a brief summary of the passage is provided below. Complete the summary by selecting the THREE answer options that express the most important ideas in the passage. Some sentences do not belong in the summary because they express ideas that are not presented in the passage or are minor ideas in the passage. This question is worth 2 points.

Humans have been using cotton to make things we need for at least 7,000 years.

-
-
-

Choose 3 answers.

① It took just two decades for the value of cotton to rise above eight million dollars.

② With the industrial revolution, people were able to process cotton more efficiently and make more products with the plant, such as soap and oil.

③ Cotton's qualities as fabric have made it popular in clothing industries and other industries.

④ Cotton is used in hospitals because it is able to absorb fluids, such as blood.

⑤ Even after its original use, products made from cotton can be re-used in a variety of ways.

⑥ Denim jeans can be recycled to make houses more energy efficient.

STOP. This is the end of the Reading section for the Paper Edition.

Listening Section

This section is the same for the computer-based TOEFL iBT test and the Paper Edition.

This section tests your ability to understand conversations and lectures in English. You can listen to each conversation and lecture only **one** time.

After each conversation or lecture, you will answer some questions. The questions usually ask about the main idea and supporting details or about a speaker's attitude or purpose. Answer the questions based on what the speakers say or imply.

You can take notes while you listen. The notes may help you answer the questions. You will NOT receive a score for your notes.

You will see the **audio icon** 🎧 in some questions. This means that you will hear a part of the question that does not appear on the test page.

Questions are worth 1 point. If a question is worth more than 1 point, specific directions will tell you how many points you can receive.

You will have approximately **36 minutes** to listen to the conversations and lectures and to answer the questions. You should answer each question even if your answer is only a guess. For this practice test, a useful guideline is to spend no more than 35 seconds to answer a question.

The Listening section is relevant for test-takers taking the computer-based version and the Paper Edition of the TOEFL iBT Test.

QUESTIONS

Questions 1–5

🎧 Listen to Track 16.

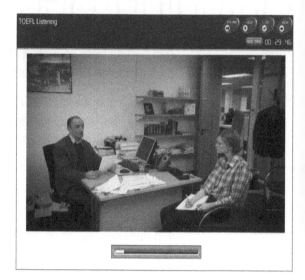

NOTES:

Directions: Answer the questions.

1. Why does the student go to see the professor?

    Ⓐ To get a recommendation for medical school

    Ⓑ To ask about changing advisors

    Ⓒ To find out how many required courses she has

    Ⓓ To consult about switching majors

2. What is stated about science prerequisites?

    Choose 2 answers.

    Ⓐ The student thinks they are more difficult than other subjects.

    Ⓑ She has seven or eight left to take.

    Ⓒ If she takes them, they will bring up her GPA.

    Ⓓ She has already taken many of them.

3. What incorrect assumption did the professor make?

    Ⓐ That premed courses are offered every semester

    Ⓑ That medical schools prefer science major applicants

    Ⓒ That the student had a different advisor

    Ⓓ That she wouldn't be able to complete all the coursework

4. What did the student say medical schools consider?

    Choose 3 answers.

    Ⓐ A student's GPA

    Ⓑ The entrance exam score

    Ⓒ Recommendations

    Ⓓ Having taken the prereqs

    Ⓔ Personal interview

5. What does the student say about the "What If?" link?

    Ⓐ She is not sure the professor knows about it.

    Ⓑ It told her how many courses she needs if she switches majors

    Ⓒ She can use it in place of conferring with an advisor

    Ⓓ It is a new program for business and history majors

Go on to the next page →

Questions 6–11

🎧 Listen to Track 17.

NOTES:

Directions: Answer the questions.

6. **What does the lecturer mainly discuss?**

   Ⓐ The role of the expert witness in court cases

   Ⓑ Why expert witnesses must take the stand

   Ⓒ The expense involved in hiring expert witnesses

   Ⓓ What to consider when choosing an expert witness

7. **Why does the professor mention that an expert witness must be someone the jury will understand?**

   Ⓐ Because expert witnesses do not usually talk with jurors

   Ⓑ Because jurors may not understand the language of experts

   Ⓒ Because expert witnesses need to be familiar with the jurors

   Ⓓ Because jurors need to get along with expert witnesses

8. **What does the professor NOT say about using doctors as expert witnesses?**

   Ⓐ The more impressive the credentials, the better.

   Ⓑ They must be working.

   Ⓒ It's preferable that they have published.

   Ⓓ They must have a state license.

9. **What does the lecturer say can be a problem of using a professional witness?**

   Ⓐ They may not have written anything.

   Ⓑ They can be expensive to hire.

   Ⓒ They may not understand the pressure in a cross-examination.

   Ⓓ It is better to hire one who has not published.

🎧 10. **Play Track 18 to listen again to part of the lecture. Then answer the question. Why does the professor say this?**

   Ⓐ Because he thinks the students can identify with juror reactions.

   Ⓑ Because he expects that the students will be on a jury one day.

   Ⓒ Because he is trying to stop the lecture for a minute.

   Ⓓ Because he wants them to imagine being an expert witness.

11. **What is stated in the lecture about being an expert witness?**

   Choose 2 answers.

   Ⓐ There are specific requirements that all witnesses must meet.

   Ⓑ It is a problem if the witness has written something that contradicts the testimony.

   Ⓒ The expert witness will charge twice as much as a normal hourly wage.

   Ⓓ Depending on the type of trial, a witness need not have advanced degrees.

Go on to the next page ➔

Questions 12–17

🎧 Listen to Track 19.

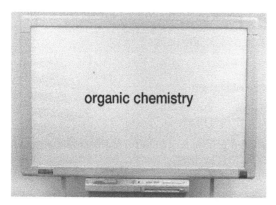

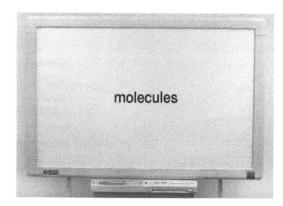

NOTES:

Directions: Answer the questions.

12. What does the professor mainly discuss?

(A) The syllabus of the inorganic chemistry course

(B) How inorganic chemistry differs from organic chemistry

(C) The basic chemical structure of organic molecules

(D) The substances taken for granted

13. According to the discussion, what questions can be answered by examining molecules?

Choose 2 answers.

(A) Why garlic smells

(B) What pills are made of

(C) Why we fill up our cars

(D) Why we need to exercise

14. What is NOT stated in the lecture about inorganic chemistry?

(A) Organic molecules constitute the building blocks of life.

(B) Organic chemistry studies carbon and its compounds.

(C) Molecules are made up of chemicals that regulate our bodies.

(D) There are different molecular compositions in the clothes we wear.

15. What does the professor say is the principal component of fats, sugars, and the nucleic acid compounds?

(A) organic substances

(B) natural fibers

(C) carbon

(D) proteins

16. Play Track 20 to listen again to part of the passage. Then answer the question. Why does the professor say this?

(A) He is presenting a specific example.

(B) He cannot remember any examples.

(C) He wants the students to name the industries.

(D) He is injecting a bit of humor into the discussion.

17. Which organic substance does the professor NOT mention as one that has improved the quality of life?

(A) gasoline

(B) medicine

(C) fats and sugars

(D) pesticides

Go on to the next page →

Questions 18–23

🎧 Listen to Track 21.

chewing gum

xylitol

NOTES:

Directions: Answer the questions.

18. What main point does the professor make about chewing gum?

   (A) More than 50 million hours of school are missed every year because of gum.

   (B) Children should chew xylitol gum in moderation.

   (C) Chewing xylitol gum increases saliva production.

   (D) Teeth can handle some gum chewing exposure to acids.

19. Play Track 22 to listen again to part of the passage. Then answer the question. Why does the professor say this?

   (A) To contrast with what happens in classrooms

   (B) To tell what she had to do when she was in school

   (C) To explain a reason why gum chewing was unacceptable

   (D) To let the students know they will have to clean their desks

20. In the talk, the professor describes the stages in cavity formulation. Summarize the sequence by putting the stages in the correct order. Number each stage 1, 2, 3, or 4.

   This question is worth 2 points (2 points for 3 correct answers, 1 point for 2 correct answers, and 0 points for 1 or 0 correct answers).

   _____ Demineralization occurs.

   _____ Saliva is overwhelmed.

   _____ Acids are produced.

   _____ Bacteria encounter sugar.

21. What does the professor say about chewing gum?

   Choose 3 answers.

   (A) Chewing gum of any kind increases saliva production.

   (B) Chewing sugar produces acids.

   (C) Chewing xylitol sweetened gum inhibits bacteria growth.

   (D) Chewing xylitol sweetened gum increases the acid level.

   (E) Chewing xylitol sweetened gum decreases saliva production.

22. According to the lecturer, why have school administrators NOT implemented gum chewing?

   (A) They do not want children to have ear infections.

   (B) They do not like children to blow bubbles in class.

   (C) They may not know about the international data.

   (D) They do not want to clean gum off of desks.

23. What does the professor suggest the optimal gum chewing regimen be?

   (A) 3 times daily, 3 to 5 minutes each time

   (B) 3 to 5 times daily, 3 minutes each time

   (C) 3 to 5 times daily, 5 minutes each time

   (D) 5 times daily, 3 to 5 minutes each time

Go on to the next page →

Questions 24–28

🎧 Listen to Track 23.

NOTES:

Directions: Answer the questions.

24. Why does the professor want to talk to Ali?

    (A) To find out if he eats lunch on campus

    (B) To make sure he has his paper back

    (C) To find out if he reviewed his paper

    (D) To recommend he goes to the writing center

25. How can the writing center help Ali?

    Choose 2 answers.

    (A) By reading the professor's comments

    (B) By looking at Ali's grammar mistakes

    (C) By seeing what kind of errors he makes regularly

    (D) By editing his essay line-by-line

26. How can Ali improve his introduction?

    Choose 2 answers.

    (A) By explaining why the topic is important

    (B) By giving his insights into the topic

    (C) By adding more information from his background reading

    (D) By giving more background information about what was happening at the time.

27. Play Track 24 to listen again to part of the passage. Then answer the question. Why does the professor say this?

    (A) She thinks Ali can do better with some help

    (B) Ali's mistakes are all minor

    (C) Ali's paper contains good ideas and supporting evidence

    (D) Ali read a lot of books

28. How can you make an appointment at the writing center?

    (A) By sending a text message

    (B) By going to see them

    (C) By asking a tutor to make an appointment for you

    (D) By writing a letter to them

STOP. This is the end of the Listening section.

Speaking Section

This section tests your ability to speak about different topics. You will answer four questions.

Question 1 asks you to make and defend a personal choice between two contrasting behaviors or courses of action.

Question 2 will include a reading and a listening passage. First, you will read a short passage which presents a campus-related issue. Then you will hear comments on the issue in the reading passage. Next you will summarize the speaker's opinion within the context of the reading passage.

Question 3 will also include a reading and a listening passage. First, you will read a short passage that broadly defines a term, process or idea from an academic subject. Then you will hear an excerpt from a lecture which provides examples and specific information to illustrate the term, process or idea from the reading passage. Next you will answer a question which asks you to combine and convey important information from the reading passage and the lecture excerpt.

Question 4 will include part of a lecture that explains a term or concept and gives concrete examples to illustrate that term or concept. The question asks you to summarize the lecture and demonstrate an understanding of the relationship between the examples and the overall topic.

While you read and listen, you can take notes that should help you answer the questions.

Listen carefully to the directions for each question. The preparation time begins right after you hear the question. You will be told when to begin to prepare and when to begin speaking.

The Speaking section is relevant for test-takers taking the computer-based version and the Paper Edition of the TOEFL iBT Test.

QUESTIONS

Track 25

1. You will be asked your opinion about a familiar topic. Listen to the question, and then prepare your response. You will have 15 seconds to prepare a response and 45 seconds to speak. You can take notes on the main points of a response.

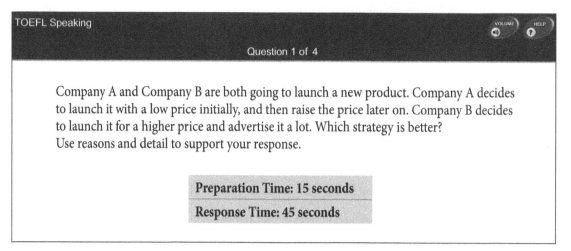

TOEFL Speaking

VOLUME   HELP

Question 1 of 4

Company A and Company B are both going to launch a new product. Company A decides to launch it with a low price initially, and then raise the price later on. Company B decides to launch it for a higher price and advertise it a lot. Which strategy is better?
Use reasons and detail to support your response.

Preparation Time: 15 seconds

Response Time: 45 seconds

NOTES:

Track 26

2. You will read a short passage and then listen to a conversation about the same topic. You will then answer a question about about them. You will have 45 seconds to read the passage. You can take notes on the main points of the reading passage.

Reading Time: 45 seconds

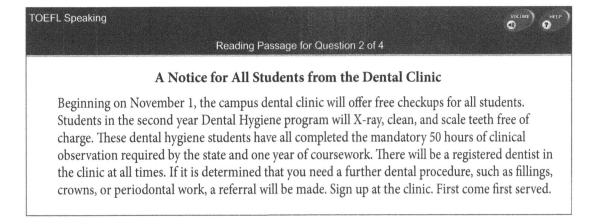

TOEFL Speaking

VOLUME   HELP

Reading Passage for Question 2 of 4

A Notice for All Students from the Dental Clinic

Beginning on November 1, the campus dental clinic will offer free checkups for all students. Students in the second year Dental Hygiene program will X-ray, clean, and scale teeth free of charge. These dental hygiene students have all completed the mandatory 50 hours of clinical observation required by the state and one year of coursework. There will be a registered dentist in the clinic at all times. If it is determined that you need a further dental procedure, such as fillings, crowns, or periodontal work, a referral will be made. Sign up at the clinic. First come first served.

Listen to two students talking. You can take notes on the main points of the conversation.

NOTES:

Now answer the following question:

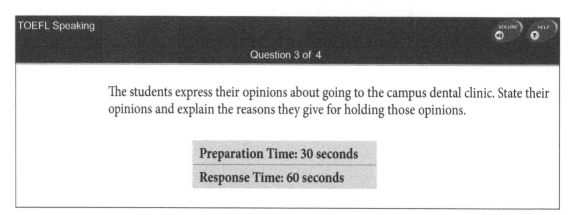

The students express their opinions about going to the campus dental clinic. State their opinions and explain the reasons they give for holding those opinions.

Preparation Time: 30 seconds

Response Time: 60 seconds

NOTES:

Track 27

3. You will read a short passage and then listen to part of a lecture about the same topic. You will then answer a question about them. You will have 45 seconds to read the passage. You can take notes on the main points of the reading passage.

Reading Time: 45 seconds

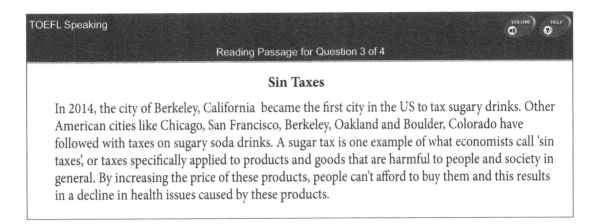

TOEFL Speaking   VOLUME   HELP

Reading Passage for Question 3 of 4

Sin Taxes

In 2014, the city of Berkeley, California became the first city in the US to tax sugary drinks. Other American cities like Chicago, San Francisco, Berkeley, Oakland and Boulder, Colorado have followed with taxes on sugary soda drinks. A sugar tax is one example of what economists call 'sin taxes', or taxes specifically applied to products and goods that are harmful to people and society in general. By increasing the price of these products, people can't afford to buy them and this results in a decline in health issues caused by these products.

Listen to the passage. You can take notes on the main points of the listening passage.

NOTES:

Go on to the next page →

Now answer the following question:

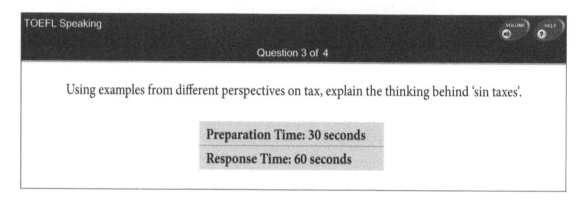

TOEFL Speaking

Question 3 of 4

Using examples from different perspectives on tax, explain the thinking behind 'sin taxes'.

Preparation Time: 30 seconds

Response Time: 60 seconds

Track 28

4. Listen to part of a lecture. You can take notes on the main points of the listening passage.

Now answer the following question:

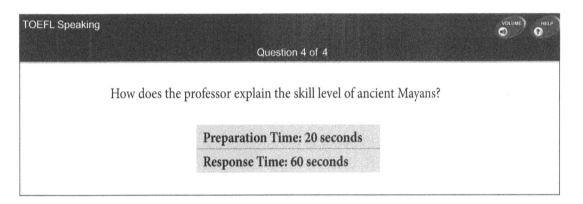

TOEFL Speaking

Question 4 of 4

How does the professor explain the skill level of ancient Mayans?

Preparation Time: 20 seconds

Response Time: 60 seconds

NOTES:

STOP. This is the end of the Speaking section.

Writing Section

This section tests your ability to use writing in an academic setting. There will be two writing tasks.

In the first writing task, the integrated writing task, you will read a passage and listen to a lecture where the speaker discusses the same topic from a different perspective. You will then write a summary. You may take notes on the reading and listening passages.

TOEFL iBT test on the computer

The second task on the computer-based TOEFL iBT test is the academic discussion task. In this task, you will write a response to the professor's question using the information in the texts and your own ideas.

TOEFL iBT Paper Edition

The second task on the Paper Edition of the TOEFL iBT test is the independent writing task. In this task, you will answer a question using your own background knowledge.

Integrated Writing Directions

For this task, you will read a passage about an academic topic, and then you will hear a lecture about the same topic. You can take notes on both.

Then you will read a question about the connection between the reading passage and the lecture. In your written response try to use information from both the passage and the lecture. You will **not** be asked for your own opinion. You can refer to the reading passage while you are writing.

You should plan on **3 minutes** to read the passage. Then listen to the lecture and give yourself **20 minutes** to plan and write your response. A successful response will be about 150 to 225 words. Your response will be judged on the quality of the writing and the correctness of the content.

QUESTION 1

Read the passage. On a piece of paper, take notes on the main points of the reading passage.

Reading Time: 3 minutes

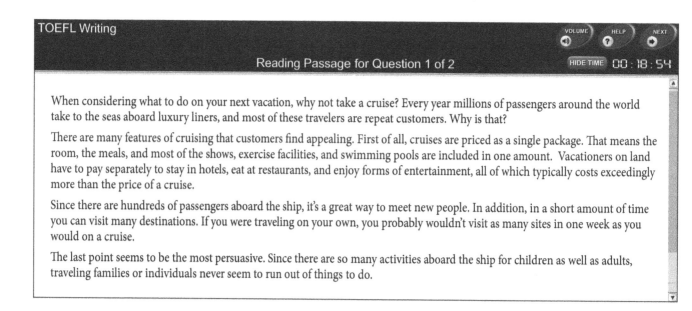

When considering what to do on your next vacation, why not take a cruise? Every year millions of passengers around the world take to the seas aboard luxury liners, and most of these travelers are repeat customers. Why is that?

There are many features of cruising that customers find appealing. First of all, cruises are priced as a single package. That means the room, the meals, and most of the shows, exercise facilities, and swimming pools are included in one amount. Vacationers on land have to pay separately to stay in hotels, eat at restaurants, and enjoy forms of entertainment, all of which typically costs exceedingly more than the price of a cruise.

Since there are hundreds of passengers aboard the ship, it's a great way to meet new people. In addition, in a short amount of time you can visit many destinations. If you were traveling on your own, you probably wouldn't visit as many sites in one week as you would on a cruise.

The last point seems to be the most persuasive. Since there are so many activities aboard the ship for children as well as adults, traveling families or individuals never seem to run out of things to do.

🎧 Play Track 29 to listen to part of a lecture in a hospitality class.

Now answer the following question:

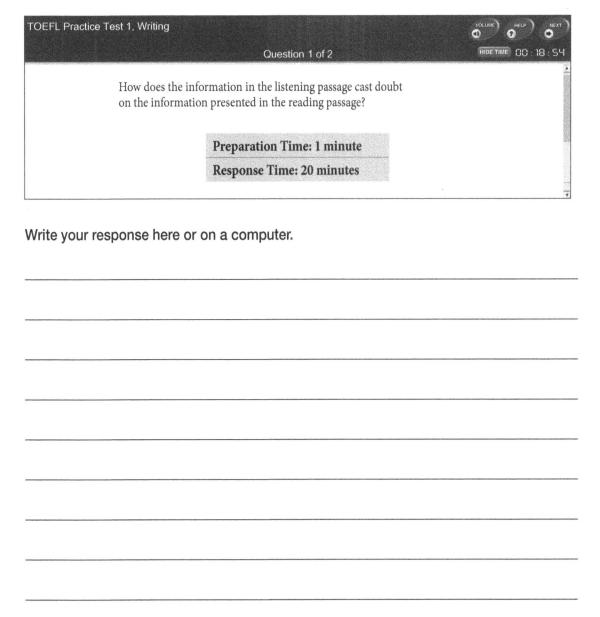

How does the information in the listening passage cast doubt on the information presented in the reading passage?

Preparation Time: 1 minute

Response Time: 20 minutes

Write your response here or on a computer.

_____

_____

_____

_____

_____

_____

_____

_____

Go on to the next page ➔

Writing for an Academic Discussion

For this task, you will read an online discussion. A professor has posted a question about a topic, and some classmates have responded with their ideas.

Write a response that contributes to the discussion. You will have **10 minutes** to write your response. It is important to use your own words in the response. Including memorized reasons or examples will result in a lower score.

QUESTION 2 for the computer-based TOEFL iBT Test

Your professor is teaching a class on education. Write a post responding to the professor's question.

In your response you should:
- express and support your opinion
- make a contribution to the discussion.

An effective response will contain at least 100 words.

Dr Sheena

We all know that there have been a lot of changes in education in the last few years. In this session, we'll be looking at how online learning has influenced the way university students study and spend time on and off campus. Are we studying more efficiently or losing something by not being in contact with other students. To get your thoughts on this topic, my question to you today is:

What has been the most important effect of online study for university students? Why? Should all university classes be taught online?

Carmen

In my opinion online study is much better and a more efficient way to learn. You can work at your own pace at a time that suits you and you can fit your education around your life – not the university timetable. In addition, there are so many subjects and topics related to your area of study that you can discover at a click – learning has become so much more interesting and exciting.

Cem

It's generally known that students use technology to learn informally through videos and online resources but this shouldn't be the way to study academic subjects at university. Isn't university about talking through issues and meeting other people, making connections and discussions?

_____

_____

_____

_____

_____

Go on to the next page ➔

94

FOR THE PAPER EDITION ONLY

Independent Writing Directions

For this task, you will write an essay that explains, supports, and states your opinion about an issue. You will have **30 minutes** to plan, write, and edit your essay. You can take notes on the main points of a response.

A successful response will be at least 300 words. Try to show that you can develop your ideas, organize your essay, and use language correctly to express your ideas. The essay will be judged on the quality of your writing.

QUESTION 2 for the Paper Edition

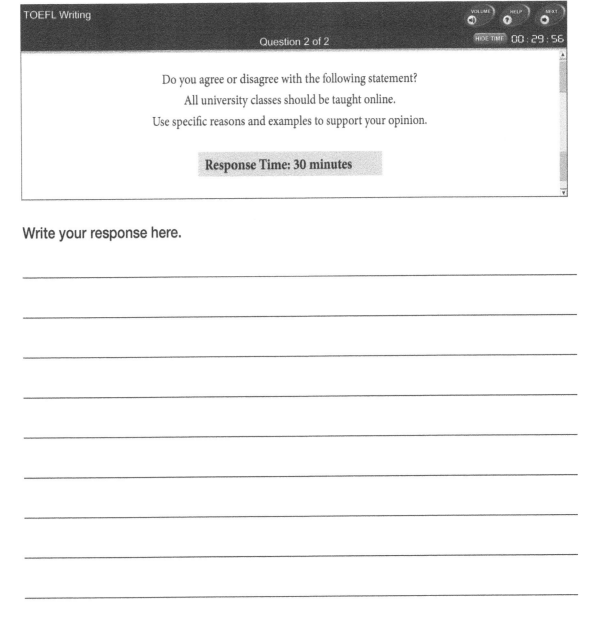

TOEFL Writing

VOLUME · HELP · NEXT

Question 2 of 2

HIDE TIME 00:29:56

Do you agree or disagree with the following statement?

All university classes should be taught online.

Use specific reasons and examples to support your opinion.

Response Time: 30 minutes

Write your response here.

_____

_____

_____

_____

_____

_____

_____

Go on to the next page →

Go on to the next page ➜

STOP. This is the end of the Writing section.

TOEFL iBT Practice Test 3

Reading Section

This section tests your ability to understand academic passages in English. The section is divided into separately timed parts.

Questions are worth 1 point except for the last question for each passage which is worth more than 1 point. The directions for the last questions explain how many points you can receive.

TOEFL iBT test on the computer

There are two reading passages in this section. You should plan to spend **18 minutes** reading each passage and answering the questions about it. You should take no more than **35 minutes** to complete the entire section.

Reading Section Timing Guide		
Passage	**Number of Questions**	**Time to Complete Test**
Passage 1	10	35 minutes
Passage 2	10	

The above information does not apply to the TOEFL iBT Paper Edition.

TOEFL iBT Paper Edition

There are three reading passages in this section in the TOEFL iBT Paper Edition. You should plan to spend **20 minutes** reading each passage answering the questions about it. You should take no more than **60 minutes** to complete the entire section.

Reading Section Timing Guide TOEFL iBT Paper Edition		
Passage	**Number of Questions**	**Time to Complete Test**
Passage 1	10	
Passage 2	10	60 minutes
Passage 3	10	

READING 1

Directions: Read the passage.

Lincoln Grows a Beard

1.   In 1860, both Abraham Lincoln and William H. Seward sought the presidency of the United States. The campaign was particularly fierce in New York. William H. Seward, the former governor of New York, had a good reputation as a statesman and well-respected businessman, whereas Lincoln, from Illinois, was less well known. New York had the largest population of any state in 1860, close to 4 million out of a total U.S. population of approximately 31 million. However, Lincoln had many supporters, including eleven-year-old Grace Bedell, from Westfield, New York, who proved to be one of Lincoln's most influential advocates. After listening to adult conversations about the candidates and looking at photographs of the two men, Grace believed that Lincoln could win the nomination by growing a full beard.

2.   It is almost impossible to think of the mid-nineteenth century without also thinking about male facial hair. Many if not most of the period's most famous figures sported facial hair of one variety or another, including goatees, mustaches, and most commonly beards. Aware of the general preference for facial hair, Grace reasoned that most ladies liked whiskers and would urge their husbands to vote for Lincoln if he had them. Less than a week before the election, Grace wrote Lincoln a letter. Lincoln, who had been a lifelong beardless man, received her letter on October fifteenth. The actual letter includes the following lines, "Dear Sir, My father has just come home from the fair and brought home your picture. I am a little girl only eleven years old but want you to be President of the United States very much so I hope you won't think me very bold to write to such a great man as you are. Have you any little girls about as large as I am? If so give them my love and tell her to write to me if you cannot answer this letter. I have four brothers and part of them will vote for you any way, and if you let your whiskers grow, I will try and get the rest of them to vote for you. You would look a great deal better for your face is so thin."

3.   Through the kindness of one of Lincoln's secretaries, Grace's letter reached him, touching him deeply. Although he feared that growing a beard so late in the campaign may seem a publicity stunt, he, nevertheless, answered Grace's letter. He responded saying, "Your very agreeable letter of the fifteenth is received. I regret the necessity of saying I had no daughters. I have three sons—one seventeen, one nine, and one seven years old. They, with their mother, constitute my whole family. As to the whiskers, having never worn any, do you not think people would call it a piece of silly affection if I were to begin now?" However, he changed his mind, and the rest is history. Perhaps Lincoln did win the election because of his newly-grown beard.

4.   Lincoln left Illinois fully bearded, bound for the White House on February 11, 1961. Along the way, he related the incident to a group of followers and said he would like to meet his young admirer. His train took him through New York State, stopping briefly in Westfield on February 16. The president-elect appeared on the train platform and called out for Grace, who eagerly awaited his arrival with her two sisters, Alice and Helen. The young girl was lifted up to meet the future president. Lincoln planted a kiss on her cheek saying, "You see, my dear, I let these whiskers grow for you. Perhaps you made me President."

5. In the early 1990s, Grace's original letter was offered for sale at a price of one million dollars. It is now housed in the Detroit Public Library. A private collector who wishes to remain anonymous owns Lincoln's return letter to Grace. In 2007 a researcher, Karen Needles, found a second letter to Lincoln. It was discovered in old Treasury Department documents at the National Archives. This letter, dated January 14, 1864, was a request for Lincoln's help as Grace was seeking employment in the Treasury Department. There is no record of any response by Lincoln; it probably never reached his desk.

Directions: Answer the questions.

1. According to paragraph 1, in 1860

  Ⓐ A the population of New York was nearly 31,000,000

  Ⓑ 4,000,000 people voted in the 1860 election

  Ⓒ Lincoln was the former governor of Illinois

  Ⓓ Lincoln had an eleven-year-old New York supporter

2. Why does the author mention that "New York had the largest population of any state in 1860"?

  Ⓐ To highlight the advantage Seward may have had

  Ⓑ To explain why Seward decided to run for president

  Ⓒ To clarify why the candidates were campaigning in New York

  Ⓓ To contrast the size of New York with the rest of the U.S.

3. Why does the author mention "goatees" in paragraph 2?

  Ⓐ To list an example of a type of facial hair

  Ⓑ To show the connection between human and animal hair

  Ⓒ To indicate the facial hair Lincoln sported

  Ⓓ To emphasize the least popular facial hair choice

4. According to paragraph 2, Grace suggests Lincoln grow a beard so that

  Ⓐ he will look older and kinder

  Ⓑ his face will look fuller

  Ⓒ he will look more like Seward

  Ⓓ he will resemble her brothers

5. The words "stunt" in paragraph 3 is closest in meaning to

  Ⓐ achievement

  Ⓑ stance

  Ⓒ opportunity

  Ⓓ trick

Go on to the next page →

6. The word "constitute" in paragraph 3 is closest in meaning to

  (A) legitimize

  (B) legalize

  (C) comprise

  (D) limit

7. Look at the four squares [■] that show where the following sentence could be added to paragraph 3.

  As a candidate for the presidency, Lincoln was inundated with hundreds of letters weekly and had neither the time nor the inclination to read them all.

  Where would the sentence best fit?

  ³ The [7A] ■ Through the kindness of one of Lincoln's secretaries, Grace's letter reached him, touching him deeply. Although he feared that growing a beard so late in the campaign may seem a publicity stunt, he, nevertheless, answered Grace's letter. [7B] ■ He responded saying, "Your very agreeable letter of the fifteenth is received. I regret the necessity of saying I had no daughters. I have three sons—one seventeen, one nine, and one seven years old. They, with their mother, constitute my whole family. As to the whiskers, having never worn any, do you not think people would call it a piece of silly affection if I were to begin now?" [7C] ■ However, he changed his mind, and the rest is history. Perhaps Lincoln did win the election because of his newly grown beard. [7D] ■

  (A) [7A]

  (B) [7B]

  (C) [7C]

  (D) [7D]

8. The author mentions "You see, my dear, I let these whiskers grow for you. Perhaps you made me President." in paragraph 4 in order to

  (A) provide an example of how Lincoln traveled with Grace

  (B) provide evidence that Lincoln enjoyed stopping along the route

  (C) provide support that Lincoln spoke to his constituents

  (D) provide proof that Lincoln acknowledged what Grace had done

9. Which of the sentences below best expresses the essential information in the highlighted sentence in paragraph 5? *Incorrect* choices change the meaning in important ways or leave out essential information.

  (A) Lincoln helped Grace in return for the help she had given him.

  (B) Grace hoped that Lincoln would assist her with a job she was seeking.

  (C) In 1864 Grace secured a job at the Treasury Department, thanks to Lincoln.

  (D) The 1864 letter documents Lincoln's efforts on behalf of Grace.

10. **Directions:** Read the introductory sentence for a brief summary of the passage below. Complete the summary by choosing the THREE answer choices that express the most important ideas in the passage. Some sentences do not belong in the summary because they express ideas that are not presented in the passage or are minor ideas in the passage. This question is worth 2 points.

The passage narrates how Lincoln decided to change his political image.

-
-
-

Choose 3 answers.

1. During the campaign, Lincoln toured the US by train to meet voters.
2. In the mid-nineteenth century, it was common for men to have facial hair.
3. Lincoln had a relatively small family.
4. Lincoln thought growing a beard might be seen as a stunt but still followed Grace's advice.
5. The fight to win the election in New York State was very close.
6. Lincoln's political rival had a photograph that showed him with a mustache.

READING 2

Directions: Read the passage.

Collecting Postage Stamps

1.   Generally speaking, the maxim "a thing of beauty is a joy forever" can apply to postage stamps as well as to
        other art forms. For this reason, a great deal of time, money, and trouble is expended by postal administrations
        around the world in selecting competent artists to design them. It has been noted that stamp collecting is the
        most expensive commodity in the world by weight. Although unique and attractive design is important in
        assessing the future prospects of a stamp, undoubtedly the determining factor is the number of stamps issued.
        The age-old law of supply and demand has to be taken into consideration. If, for example, China issued a
        commemorative stamp in an edition smaller than one million, it would automatically be a sound investment
        since there are around 20 million stamp collectors in China alone and many more abroad. On the other hand,
        one million copies of a commemorative stamp from the United Kingdom would be more than enough to
        supply all collectors from that country. In some cases, countries have to destroy unsold commemorative stamps
        after their period of validity.

2.   Postage-stamp collecting began at the same time that stamps were first issued, in the 1800s, and by 1860
        thousands of collectors and stamp dealers were appearing around the world as this new study and hobby spread
        across Europe, European colonies, the United States, and other parts of the world. The first postage stamp, the
        Penny Black, was issued by Britain in 1840 and pictured a young Queen Victoria. The stamps were produced
        without perforations. Consequently, they had to be cut from the sheet with scissors in order to be used. People
        started to collect stamps almost immediately. One of the earliest and most notable collectors was John Edward
        Gray. In 1862 Gray boasted that he "began to collect stamps shortly after the system was established and before
        it had become a rage."

3.   As the hobby and study of stamps expanded, stamp albums and stamp-related paraphernalia began to surface,
        and by the early 1880s, publishers like Stanley Gibbons made a business supplying collectors. While children
        and teenagers became avid stamp collectors in the 1860s and 1870s, many adults dismissed collecting as a
        childish pursuit. However, later, many of those same collectors as adults began to systematically study the
        available postage stamps and publish books about them. Stamp collecting is a less popular pursuit today than it
        was in the early twentieth century, but today it is estimated that more than 5 million people enjoy the hobby in
        the United States, while worldwide the estimated number of stamp collectors is around 60 million. Thousands
        of stamp dealers supply them with stamps along with stamp albums, catalogs, and other publications.
        Although the number of collectors today is smaller than in the past, stamp collecting remains a popular hobby
        throughout the world.

4.   One of the peculiarities of philately, or stamp collecting, is that so much attention and monetary importance
        is lavished on errors and imperfections. Paintings, jewelry, and antiques suffer considerably in value if their
        workmanship is faulty, but quite the reverse is true with stamps. Errors include stamps with inverted images.
        For example, one stamp from an 1870 French series was accidentally printed upside down. A 1918 U.S. airmail
        stamp, known as the Inverted Jenny, has an inverted airplane in the center. Both of these stamps are worth
        millions of dollars today. A 1932 stamp from the Philippines allegedly features Pagsanjan Falls, while actually

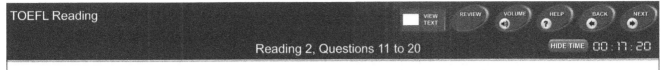

a fall from Yosemite, California, appears on the stamp. The most famous error is the 2010 American Statue of Liberty forever stamps, stamps that can be used even when the postage amount changes. The statue on the stamp is not one from the New York harbor but rather a copycat from a hotel on the Las Vegas strip. The error was not discovered for over a year and after ten and a half billion were produced, the largest run of an error in history. Some stamps have become legendary for their design, such as the first tri-color stamp produced in the Swiss canton of Basel in 1845 and the first triangular stamp issued in the Cape of Good Hope in 1853.

Directions: Answer the questions.

11. The word "them" in paragraph 1 refers to

    Ⓐ art forms

    Ⓑ postage stamps

    Ⓒ postal administrations

    Ⓓ competent artists

12. It is implied in paragraph 1 that

    Ⓐ The UK frequently overproduces commemorative stamps.

    Ⓑ It is not always easy to predict how many stamps to produce.

    Ⓒ Chinese stamps are collected both in China and abroad.

    Ⓓ China produces one million copies of each stamp.

13. The word "validity" in paragraph 1 is closest in meaning

    Ⓐ expiration

    Ⓑ commemoration

    Ⓒ supply

    Ⓓ legitimacy.

Go on to the next page →

14. Look at the four squares [■] that show where the following sentence could be added to paragraph 2.

Early stamps were sold in sheets, usually a hundred to a page.

Where would the sentence best fit?

² Postage-stamp collecting began at the same time that stamps were first issued, in the 1800s, and by 1860 thousands of collectors and stamp dealers were appearing around the world as this new study and hobby spread across Europe, European colonies, the United States, and other parts of the world. [24A] ■ The first postage stamp, the Penny Black, was issued by Britain in 1840 and pictured a young Queen Victoria. The stamps were produced without perforations. [24B] ■ Consequently they had to be cut from the sheet with scissors in order to be used. People started to collect stamps almost immediately. [24C] ■ One of the earliest and most notable collectors was John Edward Gray. In 1862 Gray boasted that he "began to collect stamps shortly after the system was established and before it had become a rage." [24D] ■

Ⓐ [24A]

Ⓑ [24B]

Ⓒ [24C]

Ⓓ [24D]

15. The word "rage" in paragraph 2 is closest in meaning to

Ⓐ fashion

Ⓑ problem

Ⓒ demand

Ⓓ necessity

16. The word "paraphernalia" in paragraph 3 is closest in meaning to

Ⓐ businesses

Ⓑ luggage

Ⓒ equipment

Ⓓ organizations

17. According to paragraph 3 it is NOT true that

Ⓐ more children and teens than adults began collecting stamps in the 1860s and 70s

Ⓑ as stamp collecting children and teens matured, they continued collecting stamps

Ⓒ stamp collecting was once more popular than it is nowadays

Ⓓ the number of stamp dealers has declined since the early twentieth century

18. The word "peculiarities" in paragraph 4 could best be replaced by

Ⓐ expenses

Ⓑ oddities

Ⓒ irregularities

Ⓓ wonders

19. The 2010 Statue of Liberty stamp and the 1932 Philippine fall stamp are examples of

   (A) inverted images
   (B) legendary designs
   (C) incorrect images
   (D) stamps without perforations

20. **Directions:** Read the introductory sentence for a brief summary of the passage below. Complete the summary by choosing the THREE answer choices that express the most important ideas in the passage. Some sentences do not belong in the summary because they express ideas that are not presented in the passage or are minor ideas in the passage. **This question is worth 2 points.**

   The passage discusses the history of stamps and collecting.

   -
   -
   -

   Choose 3 answers.

   (1) Philately supports many auxiliary businesses in addition to actual stamp collecting.
   (2) Although not as popular as it once was, there are still millions of stamp collectors.
   (3) Imperfections and errors make stamps more collectible.
   (4) John Edward Gray boasted about his stamp collection.
   (5) Initially stamps needed scissors to be cut because there were no perforations.
   (6) There are more collectors in China than in the UK.

STOP. This is the end of the Reading section for test-takers taking the TOEFL iBT test on the computer.

If you are preparing to take the Paper Edition of the test, continue to READING 3.

Go on to the next page ➜

READING 3

Read the passage.

Compulsory Voting

Compulsory voting is a system in which citizens must vote in elections or be present at a polling place on election day. If someone who is eligible to vote is not present, a fine may be levied, or the person must perform community service. If fines are unpaid or community service is not performed, jail time may result. In ancient Athens, it was the duty of every citizen to participate in decision making. An Athenian play from the fifth century BC depicts citizens who did not attend assembly being herded into the meeting place with a red-stained rope. Those with red on their clothes were fined.

Today there are 29 countries with compulsory voting. Of the 29, only 14 enforce the mandate. Of the 14, the requirements differ. For example, in Argentina, Brazil, and Peru only those over 18 and younger than 70 must vote. In Singapore, those 21 and over must vote. In Ecuador, it is compulsory for those between 18 and 65 and voluntary for those 16 to 18 and over 65. In Greece, if one does not vote, goods and services provided by public offices may be denied. Although voting may be compulsory, penalties for failing to vote are not always strictly enforced. One is excused in Argentina for sickness or being more than 500 kilometers away from one's designated voting place; however, if a Brazilian fails to vote without reason, certain restrictions will be placed on them, for example, restrictions on obtaining a passport. Bolivians who fail to vote cannot withdraw salaries from the bank for three months. In Turkey, a small fine is levied. Twelve countries have compulsory voting laws, but the laws are not enforced. They include Bulgaria, Costa Rica, Mexico, and Thailand. In the Dominican Republic and Egypt members of the military and police cannot vote. Belgian voters can vote in an embassy if they are abroad or can empower another voter to vote in their place.

Countries with compulsory voting generally hold elections on a Saturday or a Sunday or make the election day a national holiday to ensure that working people can fulfill their duty to cast their vote. If voters do not want to support any choice, they can cast blank ballots. Those in support of compulsory voting argue that candidates in this system must appeal to a general audience, rather than a targeted section of the nation. Under a non-compulsory voting system, if fewer people vote, then it is easier for smaller sectional interests and lobby groups to motivate particular constituencies and thereby control the outcome of the political process. Compulsory voting ensures a large voter turnout. A victorious candidate or party clearly represents a majority of the population, not just the politically motivated individuals who vote without obligation. In the United States 2020 presidential election, 67% of eligible voters voted, making it the highest voter turnout of the 21st century, according to the United States Census Bureau. But another way of looking at those statistics is to acknowledge that 33% of eligible voters did not vote. Those who support compulsory voting claim that this system better reflects the will of the people than voluntary voting does. With voluntary voting, they allege, the winner is the one who was more able to convince people to take time out of their day to cast a vote.

Voting is voluntary in the United States, and some support this practice. In the United States, they argue, a fundamental American right is freedom, so any compulsion, even voting, affects personal freedom. They point to the first amendment of the Constitution, freedom of speech, stating that freedom to speak necessarily includes the freedom not to speak, or in this case, not to vote. Others claim they have no interest in politics or no knowledge of the candidates. Someone who chooses not to vote may be well-informed but have no preference for a particular candidate. Some supporters of voluntary voting assert that low voter participation in a voluntary election is not necessarily an expression of voter dissatisfaction or apathy. It may be simply an expression of the citizenry's political will, indicating satisfaction with the political establishment. Whatever the reasons, there has never been a serious movement to make voting mandatory in the United States. Some contend that if the U.S. wants to increase voter turnout, it does not need to make voting mandatory, just change the voting day to Saturday or Sunday or make it a national holiday.

Refer to the passages below and answer the questions that follow.

Compulsory Voting

[1] Compulsory voting is a system in which citizens must vote in elections or be present at a polling place on election day. If someone who is eligible to vote is not present, a fine may be levied, or the person must perform community service. If fines are unpaid or community service is not performed, jail time may result. In ancient Athens, it was the duty of every citizen to participate in decision making. An Athenian play from the fifth century BC depicts citizens who did not attend assembly being herded into the meeting place with a red-stained rope. Those with red on their clothes were fined.

Directions: Answer the questions.

21. The word "levied" in paragraph 1 could best be replaced by

    Ⓐ collected

    Ⓑ targeted

    Ⓒ considered

    Ⓓ imposed

22. Why does the passage include the reference to Athens in paragraph 1?

    Ⓐ To present a concluding idea to the paragraph

    Ⓑ To explain why compulsory voting exists

    Ⓒ To compare and contrast community service and clothes dying

    Ⓓ To put citizenry participation in a historical context

Go on to the next page ➜

² Today there are 29 countries with compulsory voting. Of the 29, only 14 enforce the mandate. Of the 14, the requirements differ. For example, in Argentina, Brazil, and Peru only those over 18 and younger than 70 must vote. In Singapore, those 21 and over must vote. [23A] ■ In Ecuador it is compulsory for those between 18 and 65 and voluntary for those 16 to 18 and over 65. In Greece, if one does not vote, goods and services provided by public offices may be denied. Although voting may be compulsory, penalties for failing to vote are not always strictly enforced. [23B] ■ One is excused in Argentina for sickness or being more than 500 kilometers away from one's designated voting place; however, if a Brazilian fails to vote without reason, certain restrictions will be placed on them, for example, restrictions on obtaining a passport. Bolivians who fail to vote cannot withdraw salaries from the bank for three months. [23C] ■ In Turkey a small fine is levied. Twelve countries have compulsory voting laws, but the laws are not enforced. They include Bulgaria, Costa Rica, Mexico, and. In the Dominican Republic and Egypt members of the military and police cannot vote. Belgian voters can vote in an embassy if they are abroad or can empower another voter to vote in their place. [23D] ■.

23. Look at the four squares ■ that show where the following sentence could be added to paragraph 2.

Some countries even tax those who fail to vote.

Where would the sentence best fit?

Ⓐ [23A]

Ⓑ [23B]

Ⓒ [23C]

Ⓓ [23D]

³ Countries with compulsory voting generally hold elections on a Saturday or a Sunday or make the election day a national holiday to ensure that working people can fulfill their duty to cast their vote. If voters do not want to support any choice, they can cast blank ballots. Those in support of compulsory voting argue that candidates in this system must appeal to a general audience, rather than a targeted section of the nation. Under a non-compulsory voting system, if fewer people vote, then it is easier for smaller sectional interests and lobby groups to motivate particular constituencies and thereby control the outcome of the political process. Compulsory voting ensures a large voter turnout. A victorious candidate or party clearly represents a majority of the population, not just the politically motivated individuals who vote without obligation. In the United States 2020 presidential election, 67% of eligible voters voted, making it the highest voter turnout of the 21st century, according to the United States Census Bureau. But another way of looking at those statistics is to acknowledge that 33% of eligible voters did not vote. Those who support compulsory voting claim that this system better reflects the will of the people than voluntary voting does. With voluntary voting, they allege, the winner is the one who was more able to convince people to take time out of their day to cast a vote.

24. The word "cast" in paragraph 3 could best be replaced by

Ⓐ reject

Ⓑ elect

Ⓒ find

Ⓓ submit

25. The word "targeted" in paragraph 3 could best be replaced by.

    (A) purposeful

    (B) confined

    (C) defined

    (D) depleted

26. Which of the sentences below best expresses the essential information in the highlighted sentence in paragraph 3? *Incorrect* choices change the meaning in important ways or leave out essential information.

    (A) In a non-compulsory voting system, fewer people vote because of special interest and lobby groups.

    (B) In a compulsory voting system, lobby groups can exert influence and sway the election outcome.

    (C) Small particular interest and lobby groups have too much power in the current voting system.

    (D) When fewer vote in a voluntary system, it is easier for small groups with a particular agenda to influence the election.

⁴ Voting is voluntary in the United States, and some support this practice. In the United States, they argue, a fundamental American right is freedom, so any compulsion, even voting, affects personal freedom. They point to the first amendment of the Constitution, freedom of speech, stating that freedom to speak necessarily includes the freedom not to speak, or in this case, not to vote. Others claim they have no interest in politics or no knowledge of the candidates. Someone who chooses not to vote may be well-informed but have no preference for a particular candidate. Some supporters of voluntary voting assert that low voter participation in a voluntary election is not necessarily an expression of voter dissatisfaction or apathy. It may be simply an expression of the citizenry's political will, indicating satisfaction with the political establishment. Whatever the reasons, there has never been a serious movement to make voting mandatory in the United States. Some contend that if the U.S. wants to increase voter turnout, it does not need to make voting mandatory, just change the voting day to Saturday or Sunday or make it a national holiday.

27. The word "fundamental" in paragraph 4 could best be replaced by

    (A) radical

    (B) basic

    (C) primitive

    (D) controversial

28. According to paragraph 4, it is NOT true that some Americans support voluntary voting because

    (A) They believe they are guaranteed the freedom not to vote.

    (B) They have no preference for either candidate.

    (C) They are dissatisfied with the political establishment.

    (D) They have no interest in the political system.

Go on to the next page ➜

29. According to paragraph 4, what does the passage suggest would increase voter turnout in the U.S.?

Ⓐ Making voting mandatory

Ⓑ Making election day a holiday

Ⓒ Having a two-day election

Ⓓ Alternate Saturday and Sunday voting

30. **Directions:** An introductory sentence for a brief summary of the passage is provided below. Complete the summary by selecting the THREE answer options that express the most important ideas in the passage. Some sentences do not belong in the summary because they express ideas that are not presented in the passage or are minor ideas in the passage. This question is worth 2 points.

Compulsory voting is used by many countries around the world so that every eligible citizen votes in that country's elections.

- •

- •

- •

Choose 3 answers.

① To make sure people vote in countries with compulsory voting, different ways of enforcing this are used.

② Voters from countries with compulsory voting can ask someone they know to vote in their place.

③ Because compulsory voting means everyone has to vote, elections represent the politics of most of the people.

④ In countries with voluntary voting, the right not to vote is as important as the right to participate in elections.

⑤ In all countries with compulsory voting, weekends are given as holidays so that people can vote.

STOP. This is the end of the Reading section for the Paper Edition.

Listening Section

This section tests your ability to understand conversations and lectures in English. You can listen to each conversation and lecture only **one** time.

After each conversation or lecture, you will answer some questions. The questions usually ask about the main idea and supporting details or about a speaker's attitude or purpose. Answer the questions based on what the speakers say or imply.

You can take notes while you listen. The notes may help you answer the questions. You will NOT receive a score for your notes.

You will see the **audio icon** 🎧 in some questions. This means that you will hear a part of the question that does not appear on the test page.

Questions are worth 1 point. If a question is worth more than 1 point, specific directions will tell you how many points you can receive.

You will have approximately **36 minutes** to listen to the conversations and lectures and to answer the questions. You should answer each question even if your answer is only a guess. For this practice test, a useful guideline is to spend no more than 35 seconds to answer a question.

The Listening section is relevant for test-takers taking the computer-based version and the Paper Edition of the TOEFL iBT Test.

QUESTIONS

Questions 1–6

🎧 Listen to Track 30.

NOTES:

Directions: Answer the questions.

1. What does the lecturer mainly discuss?

    Ⓐ The population increase on Martha's Vineyard

    Ⓑ How Martha's Vineyard got its name

    Ⓒ The settlement of Martha's Vineyard

    Ⓓ The deaf population on Martha's Vineyard

2. Why does the lecturer most likely mention the Wampanoags?

    Ⓐ To discuss the farming and fishing heritage

    Ⓑ To question the population decline

    Ⓒ To give historical context to the settlement

    Ⓓ To explain the history of the deaf population

3. Why did the island name temporarily remove the apostrophe?

    Ⓐ Because a government agency tried to make spelling consistent

    Ⓑ Because it was easier to pronounce

    Ⓒ Because it was the name of the British explorer's mother-in-law and daughter

    Ⓓ Because only five U.S. location names have an apostrophe

4. How does the professor explain the high rate of island deafness?

    Ⓐ The use of Martha's Vineyard Sign Language encouraged deaf people to move to the island.

    Ⓑ The high rate of deaf and nondeaf marriages increased the deaf population.

    Ⓒ Deaf people could find work as farmers and fishermen on the island.

    Ⓓ The deaf population traces its hereditary deafness to one common ancestor.

5. Which of the following is NOT true about the island?

    Choose 2 answers.

    Ⓐ For almost two hundred years Martha's Vineyard's high rate of deafness was documented.

    Ⓑ As jobs in tourism increased so did the deaf population.

    Ⓒ Martha's Vineyard Sign Language is still used today.

    Ⓓ Martha's Vineyard is the eighth oldest surviving English place name in the US.

6. In the talk, the professor tells when various events occurred on the island. Number the events in the correct order. **This question is worth 2 points.**

    Number each event 1, 2, 3, or 4.

    _____ Celebrities and politicians visit and live on the island.

    _____ The tribe of Wampanoag dropped to 313 members.

    _____ Marriages between deaf and hearing spouses comprised 65% of all deaf marriages.

    _____The last person born into the sign language community died.

Questions 7–12

🎧 Listen to Track 31.

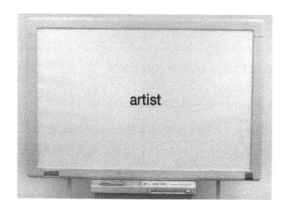

NOTES:

Directions: Answer the questions.

7. What does the lecturer mainly discuss?

    (A) Events leading up to Mary Cassatt's leaving home
    (B) The influences on the artistic life of Mary Cassatt
    (C) Why Mary Cassatt's father wanted her to stay in America
    (D) The life of a painter in nineteenth-century Paris

8. Why does the lecturer most likely mention Mary and her family living in Europe in the 1850s?

    (A) To imply that Mary may have been influenced by living there
    (B) To suggest that Mary made many artist friends while there
    (C) To hint that Mary decided to become an artist while there
    (D) To contrast the European and American lifestyles

9. What does the professor imply about the teachers and students at the Academy of Fine Arts?

    (A) They resented Cassatt's being so young.
    (B) Cassatt was a better artist than most of the students.
    (C) They were annoyed to have a female student.
    (D) Cassatt did not want to follow the curriculum.

10. Why did Cassatt use the name Mary Stevenson when she submitted to the Salon?

    (A) Females did not submit at that time.
    (B) She did not want her father to know about the submission.
    (C) She was afraid she would not be accepted.
    (D) Impressionist painters were not yet accepted by the Salon.

11. Which of the following did NOT happen to Cassatt?

    (A) Her paintings were destroyed in a Chicago fire.
    (B) With money from a Pittsburgh commission, she returned to Europe.
    (C) Her father refused to support her career financially.
    (D) Her career was more successful in America than in Europe.

12. In the talk, the professor tells when various events occurred in Cassatt's life. Number the events in the correct order. **This question is worth 2 points.**

    Number the events 1, 2, 3, or 4.

    _____ She begins private art lessons in the Louvre.
    _____ The Archbishop of Pittsburgh commissions her work
    _____ The Paris Salon accepts her paintings three years in a row.
    _____ Cassatt enrolls in Philadelphia's Pennsylvania Academy of the Fine Arts.

Go on to the next page →

Questions 13–17

🎧 Listen to Track 32.

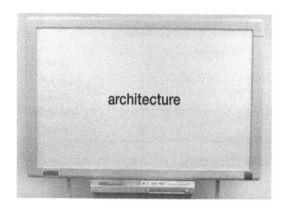

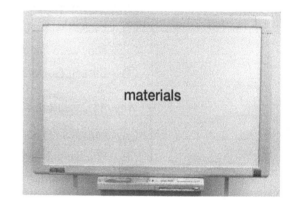

NOTES:

Directions: Answer the questions.

13. Why does the student want to talk to the professor?

   Ⓐ To tell her she is not an architecture major

   Ⓑ To clear up some confusion

   Ⓒ To find out what will be on the test

   Ⓓ To have the professor check her notes

🎧 14. Play Track 33 to listen again to part of the consultation. Then answer the question.

   Why does this professor say this?

   Ⓐ The review will start once the others arrive.

   Ⓑ No one else will be allowed at the review.

   Ⓒ The professor will give her something.

   Ⓓ The student will have a private session.

15. What confused the student about Wright's own home in Illinois?

   Ⓐ That it was built in the Prairie Style

   Ⓑ That its form is low and horizontal

   Ⓒ Its wood shingles are not Wright's usual material

   Ⓓ That it is built using cement and stucco

16. Check (✓) the boxes to show the location of the building material. **This question is worth 2 points.** Only THREE answers are correct.

   Check 3 boxes.

	California houses	Willit's House	Imperial Hotel
Soft lava			
Precast concrete blocks			
Wood and other materials as they appear in nature			

17. What is distinctive about the Imperial Hotel?

   Choose 3 answers.

   Ⓐ It survived earthquakes.

   Ⓑ It used outdoor porches and terraces.

   Ⓒ It was Wright's major Japanese project.

   Ⓓ It has a floating foundation.

   Ⓔ Its design inspired other Japanese buildings.

Go on to the next page ➔

Questions 18–23

🎧 Listen to Track 34.

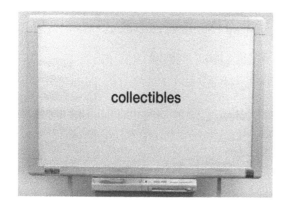

NOTES:

Directions: Answer the questions.

18. What does the professor mainly discuss in the lecture?

    (A) Buying Japanese tin toys

    (B) Three current collectibles

    (C) Fun with collectibles

    (D) Escaping from stocks and bonds

19. Which item is NOT mentioned as a suggested collectible?

    (A) ceramic vases

    (B) vintage motorcycles

    (C) celebrity autographs

    (D) original watches

20. What does the professor say is NOT a problem with buying collectibles?

    (A) Knowing the true market value of the item

    (B) Having to insure the item

    (C) Using the item while it's yours

    (D) Making sure the item is authentic

21. What does the professor say about collecting motorcycles?

    Choose 2 answers.

    (A) You can enjoy riding it while you have it.

    (B) A desirable one was recently bought for $275.

    (C) Some ones from the 1940s and 50s are more desirable.

    (D) Decide if you want to collect it or ride it.

🎧 22. Play Track 35 to listen again to part of the lecture. Then answer the question. Why does this professor say this?

    (A) She knows they will choose collectible buying as a profession.

    (B) She wants them to look for collectibles for her.

    (C) She assumes they will start buying collectibles.

    (D) She hopes they will be aware of collectibles.

23. What does the professor say about collecting autographs?

    Choose 2 answers.

    (A) She's lucky to have authentic Celtics' autographs.

    (B) Watch out for imitations.

    (C) Prices rise after a celebrity dies.

    (D) Celebrities are famous for only fifteen minutes.

Go on to the next page ➜

Questions 24–28

🎧 Listen to Track 36.

NOTES:

Directions: Answer the questions.

24. What will the department pay for?

    (A) Only the tickets for the conference

    (B) Only for living expenses

    (C) For the tickets for the conference and half of the travel expenses

    (D) For the tickets for the conference and half of the living expenses

25. Why does the professor want the posters soon?

    (A) To get the funding fixed

    (B) To show them to the committee organizing the conference

    (C) To organize the students so they can go to the conference

    (D) To meet the seminar deadline in one month

26. Why do the students think they have a chance of going to the conference?

    (A) The professor gave them ideas for a poster

    (B) They have nearly finished their posters

    (C) The professor gave them good feedback on their papers

    (D) The professor told them where to write their biodata

27. The lab assistant

    (A) can help produce a poster for them

    (B) can help develop the poster from their ideas

    (C) closed the lab before noon

    (D) can add visuals to make the poster impactful

28. Play Track 37 to listen again to part of the passage. Then answer the question. Why does the student say this?

    (A) He is inspired by the other student

    (B) The deadline for completing the work is soon

    (C) He doesn't have a lot of money

    (D) It will be great fun to go

STOP. This is the end of the Listening section.

Speaking Section

This section tests your ability to speak about different topics. You will answer four questions.

Question 1 asks you to make and defend a personal choice between two contrasting behaviors or courses of action.

Question 2 will include a reading and a listening passage. First, you will read a short passage that presents a campus-related issue. Then you will hear comments on the issue in the reading passage. Next, you will summarize the speaker's opinion within the context of the reading passage.

Question 3 will also include a reading and a listening passage. First, you will read a short passage that broadly defines a term, process, or idea from an academic subject. Then you will hear an excerpt from a lecture that provides examples and specific information to illustrate the term, process, or idea from the reading passage. Next, you will answer a question that asks you to combine and convey important information from the reading passage and the lecture excerpt.

Question 4 will include part of a lecture that explains a term or concept and gives concrete examples to illustrate that term or concept. The question asks you to summarize the lecture and demonstrate an understanding of the relationship between the examples and the overall topic.

While you read and listen, you can take notes that should help you answer the questions.

Listen carefully to the directions for each question. The preparation time begins right after you hear the question. You will be told when to begin to prepare and when to begin speaking.

The Speaking section is relevant for test-takers taking the computer-based version and the Paper Edition of the TOEFL iBT Test.

QUESTIONS

Track 38

1. You will be asked your opinion about a familiar topic. Listen to the question, and then prepare your response. You will have 15 seconds to prepare a response and 45 seconds to speak. You can take notes on the main points of a response.

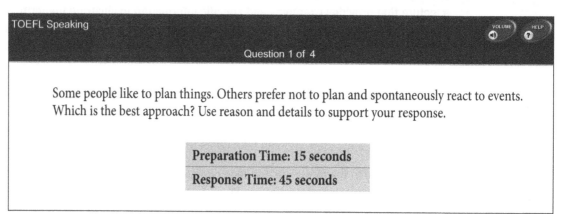

TOEFL Speaking

Question 1 of 4

Some people like to plan things. Others prefer not to plan and spontaneously react to events. Which is the best approach? Use reason and details to support your response.

> **Preparation Time: 15 seconds**
>
> **Response Time: 45 seconds**

NOTES:

Track 39

2. You will read a short passage and then listen to a conversation about the same topic. You will then answer a question about them. You will have 45 seconds to read the passage. You can take notes on the main points of the reading passage.

Reading Time: 45 seconds

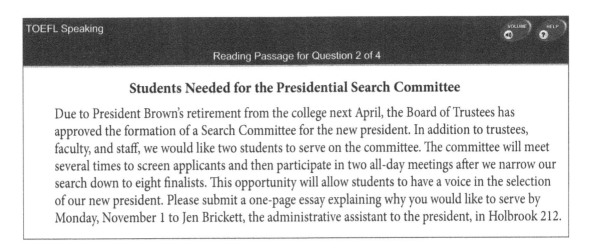

TOEFL Speaking   VOLUME   HELP

Reading Passage for Question 2 of 4

Students Needed for the Presidential Search Committee

Due to President Brown's retirement from the college next April, the Board of Trustees has approved the formation of a Search Committee for the new president. In addition to trustees, faculty, and staff, we would like two students to serve on the committee. The committee will meet several times to screen applicants and then participate in two all-day meetings after we narrow our search down to eight finalists. This opportunity will allow students to have a voice in the selection of our new president. Please submit a one-page essay explaining why you would like to serve by Monday, November 1 to Jen Brickett, the administrative assistant to the president, in Holbrook 212.

Listen to two students discuss the announcement. You can take notes on the main points of the conversation.

NOTES:

Now answer the following question:

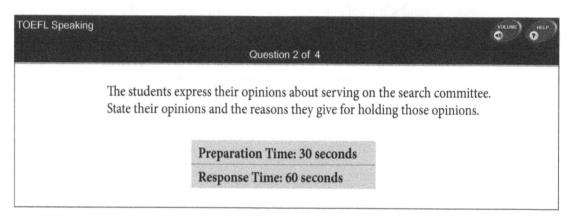

Track 40

3. You will read a short passage and then listen to part of a lecture about the same topic. You will then answer a question about them. You will have 45 seconds to read the passage. You can take notes on the main points of the reading passage.

Reading Time: 45 seconds

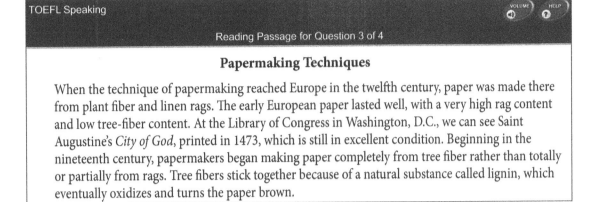

TOEFL Speaking

VOLUME   HELP

Reading Passage for Question 3 of 4

Papermaking Techniques

When the technique of papermaking reached Europe in the twelfth century, paper was made there from plant fiber and linen rags. The early European paper lasted well, with a very high rag content and low tree-fiber content. At the Library of Congress in Washington, D.C., we can see Saint Augustine's *City of God*, printed in 1473, which is still in excellent condition. Beginning in the nineteenth century, papermakers began making paper completely from tree fiber rather than totally or partially from rags. Tree fibers stick together because of a natural substance called lignin, which eventually oxidizes and turns the paper brown.

Listen to the passage. You can take notes on the main points of the listening passage.

NOTES:

Go on to the next page →

Now answer the following question:

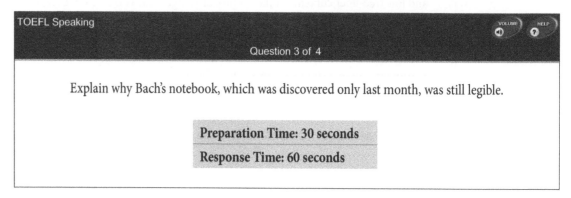

TOEFL Speaking

Question 3 of 4

Explain why Bach's notebook, which was discovered only last month, was still legible.

Preparation Time: 30 seconds

Response Time: 60 seconds

Track 41

4. You will listen to part of a lecture. You can take notes on the main points of the listening passage.

Now answer the following question:

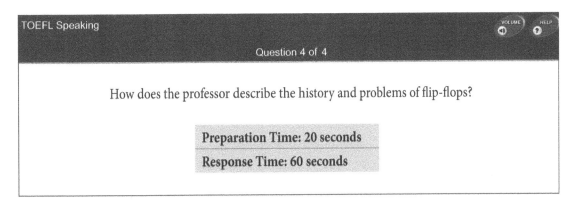

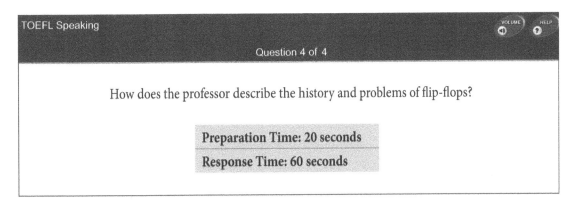
TOEFL Speaking

Question 4 of 4

How does the professor describe the history and problems of flip-flops?

Preparation Time: 20 seconds

Response Time: 60 seconds

NOTES:

STOP. This is the end of the Speaking section.

Writing Section

This section tests your ability to use writing in an academic setting. There will be two writing tasks.

In the first writing task, the integrated writing task, you will read a passage and listen to a lecture where a speaker discusses the same topic from a different perspective. You will then write a summary. You may take notes on the reading and listening passages.

TOEFL iBT test on the computer

The second task on the computer-based TOEFL iBT test is the academic discussion task. In this task, you will write a response to the professor's question using the information in the texts and your own ideas.

TOEFL iBT Paper Edition

The second task on the Paper Edition of the TOEFL iBT test is the independent writing task. In this task, you will answer a question using your own background knowledge.

Integrated Writing Directions

For this task, you will read a passage about an academic topic, and then you will hear a lecture about the same topic. You may take notes on both.

Then you will read a question about the connection between the reading passage and the lecture. In your written response try to use information from both the passage and the lecture. You will **not** be asked for your own opinion. You can refer to the reading passage while you are writing.

You should plan on **3 minutes** to read the passage. Then listen to the lecture and give yourself **20 minutes** to plan and write your response. A successful response will be about 150 to 225 words. Your response will be judged on the quality of the writing and the correctness of the content.

QUESTION 1

Read the passage. On a piece of paper, take notes on the main points of the reading passage.

Reading Time: 3 minutes

TOEFL Writing

Reading Passage for Question 1 of 2

HIDE TIME 00:18:54

A Good Night's Sleep

Research surrounding how to get a good night's sleep and what exactly constitutes a good night's sleep has proliferated around the world in the last decade. Along with the research, inconsistent and sometimes erroneous beliefs appear in print, even in medical journals. The first widely held belief is that some people function perfectly on only four hours of sleep a night. Legendary short sleepers, including former British Prime Minister Margaret Thatcher and former U.S. President Bill Clinton, don't necessarily do better on shorter sleep. "They're just not aware of how sleepy they are," claims Thomas Roth, PhD, a sleep researcher at Henry Ford Hospital in Detroit. Too little sleep is bad for your health and your image; it can make you ineffective, as it can impair performance, judgment, and attentiveness and it can even make you sick as it can weaken your immune system and cause obesity.

According to a Harvard Nurses' Health Study, female nurses who slept five hours or less a night were a third more likely to gain 33 pounds or more over 16 years than female nurses who slept seven hours.

Then there are problems associated with too much sleep, considered to be more than eight hours a night. Some studies have found that those who slept more than eight hours a night died younger than people who got between six and eight hours of sleep. However, those sleeping more than eight hours nightly may suffer from problems such as depression or uncontrolled diabetes that make them spend more time in bed. These health problems rather than the number of hours they spent in bed may be what contributed to them dying younger.

Another area of concern is napping. Many believe that this daytime sleep has great health benefits, including reduced stress and blood pressure. Nevertheless, numerous studies of nap benefits have led to conflicting conclusions. More research is needed to prove or disprove the benefits of napping.

🎧 Play Track 42 to listen to the passage.

Now answer the following question:

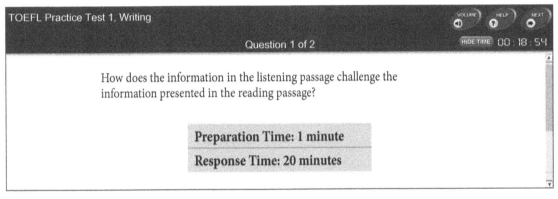

Write your response here or on a computer.

_____

_____

_____

_____

_____

_____

_____

_____

_____

Go on to the next page ➜

Writing for an Academic Discussion

For this task, you will read an online discussion. A professor has posted a question about a topic, and some classmates have responded with their ideas.

Write a response that contributes to the discussion. You will have **10 minutes** to write your response. It is important to use your own words in the response. Including memorized reasons or examples will result in a lower score.

QUESTION 2 for the computer-based TOEFL iBT Test

Your professor is teaching a class on tourism. Write a post responding to the professor's question.

In your response you should:

- express and support your opinion
- make a contribution to the discussion.

An effective response will contain at least 100 words.

Dr Yu

The old saying goes *travel broadens the mind*, and there is some evidence to show that travelling and living in new countries actually improves us as individuals. Travelling can help our confidence but also improve our thinking ability. But are these good enough reasons to leave home or is it better to spend time with friends and family. Let me know your opinion.

Is it better to travel and experience new environments or should we spend time with people who are close to us?

Rene

I can't say I agree. I know a lot of people who go abroad to live or study or work and they all say that home is the best place. People are better when they feel safe and secure and not in a new stressful place. In addition, there is so much you can learn from home, why do you need to travel?

Arjun

You've got a point Rene, but people need to push themselves in order to learn about themselves, and travel is the best way to learn new languages and experience new cultures. Meeting new people can be exciting and interesting, learning how to adapt can broaden our outlook and add to our social skills.

_____

_____

_____

_____

FOR THE PAPER EDITION ONLY

Independent Writing Directions

For this task, you will write an essay that explains, supports, and states your opinion about an issue. You will have **30 minutes** to plan, write, and edit your essay. You can take notes on the main points of a response.

A successful response will be at least 300 words. Try to show that you can develop your ideas, organize your essay, and use language correctly to express your ideas. The essay will be judged on the quality of your writing.

QUESTION 2 for the Paper Edition

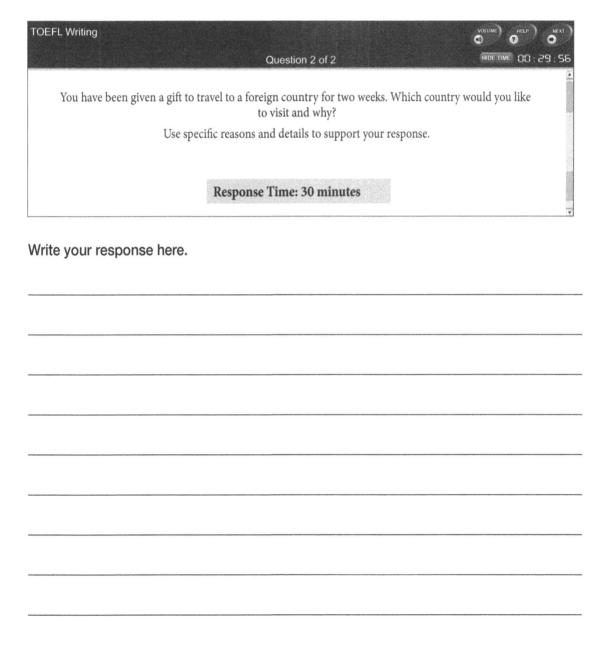

TOEFL Writing

Question 2 of 2

HIDE TIME 00 : 29 : 56

You have been given a gift to travel to a foreign country for two weeks. Which country would you like to visit and why?

Use specific reasons and details to support your response.

Response Time: 30 minutes

Write your response here.

STOP. This is the end of the Writing section.

TOEFL iBT Practice Test 4

TOEFL iBT Practice Test 4

Reading Section

This section tests your ability to understand academic passages in English. The section is divided into separately timed parts.

Questions are worth 1 point except for the last question for each passage which is worth more than 1 point. The directions for the last questions explain how many points you can receive.

TOEFL iBT test on the computer

There are two reading passages in this section. You should plan to spend **18 minutes** reading each passage and answering the questions about it. You should take no more than **35 minutes** to complete the entire section.

Reading Section Timing Guide		
Passage	Number of Questions	Time to Complete Test
Passage 1	10	35 minutes
Passage 2	10	

The above information does not apply to the TOEFL iBT Paper Edition.

TOEFL iBT Paper Edition

There are three reading passages in this section in the TOEFL iBT Paper Edition. You should plan to spend **20 minutes** reading each passage answering the questions about it. You should take no more than **60 minutes** to complete the entire section.

Reading Section Timing Guide TOEFL iBT Paper Edition		
Passage	Number of Questions	Time to Complete Test
Passage 1	10	
Passage 2	10	60 minutes
Passage 3	10	

READING 1

Directions: Read the passage.

The House Finch

1.   The house finch, a sparrow-like bird native to western North America, originally lived in the wild in the western United States and Mexico. In the seventeenth and eighteenth centuries, house finches made their homes in canyons and deserts, avoiding both forests and grassy regions without trees. Today, house finches can be found all over the United States, thanks to humans who changed the course of the birds' development. A highly social bird, the house finch is rarely seen alone outside of the breeding season and may form flocks as large as several hundred birds. During courtship, males sometimes feed females in a display that begins with the female gently picking at his bill and fluttering her wings. The red head and breast of a male house finch comes from pigments contained in its food. The more pigment in the food, the redder the male. That is why people sometimes see orange or yellowish male house finches. Females prefer to mate with the reddest male they can find. House finches feed their nestlings exclusively on plant foods, a fairly rare occurrence in the bird world. Many of the birds that are vegetarians as adults still find animal food to keep their fast-growing youth supplied with protein. The long, twittering sound of both the male and female can now be heard in most of the neighborhoods of the continental United States.

2.   House finches first became popular as domestic birds in the United States in the nineteenth century, when they were shipped from California to Hawaii, most likely as pets, sometime before 1870. The population of these beautiful red and yellow birds, with their stunning singing voices, quickly spread to the other Hawaiian Islands. By 1901 they had become abundant on all the major Hawaiian Islands. Starting around this time, house finches, sold as "Hollywood Finches" in major East Coast cities like Boston and New York, were spread around the country because of market demand.

3.   The trade in house finches should have halted with the passage of the Migratory Bird Treaty Act of 1916, a federal law making it unlawful to hunt, capture, or sell over 800 species of migratory birds, including the sale of house finches as pets. The Act, enacted in an era when bird species were threatened by the commercial trade in birds and bird feathers, was one of the first federal environmental laws. However, it was not until the summer of 1939 that the government finally began cracking down on the illegal sale of wild songbirds, including the so-called "Hollywood Finches" in New York City. Before they knew about the change in policy, some pet store owners had gone to Los Angeles to obtain finches to sell in New York. Upon their return to New York with their "Hollywood" birds, instead of paying hefty fines, they irresponsibly released a few captive house finches on Long Island in order to avoid prosecution when confronted by law enforcement.

4.   During the 1940s and 1950s, the population was mainly confined to New York City. The small population struggled for survival for many years, establishing a small breeding enclave. However, by the 1950s the finches ended up surviving in the wild streets of metropolitan areas, nesting among the urban skyscrapers. By the 1960s the range of the house finch rapidly expanded from New York City, breeding new populations as the birds' nesting sites started spreading, likely due to attempts to attract these birds to backyard bird feeders. Amazingly, 20 years later, house finches could be found throughout the U.S. and southern Canada. Their total number in North America is estimated at more than a billion birds, with a substantial percentage east of the Mississippi River. The wild populations of East Coast house finches, descendants of the trapped California birds, provide an interesting case study of adaptation to the environment.

Directions: Answer the questions.

1. It is NOT true according to paragraph 1 that
   - (A) house finches may be red, yellow, or orange
   - (B) house finches exclusively nest in canyons and deserts
   - (C) both male and female house finches emit sounds
   - (D) male house finches become red from what they eat

2. It can be inferred from paragraph 1 that
   - (A) most birds are not vegetarians
   - (B) orange and yellow house finches do not mate
   - (C) as house finches become adults, they eat animal food
   - (D) young house finches find their own food

3. The word "stunning" in paragraph 2 is closest in meaning to
   - (A) attractive
   - (B) impressive
   - (C) attacking
   - (D) shrill

4. The word "abundant" in paragraph 2 is closest in meaning to
   - (A) hunted
   - (B) scarce
   - (C) plentiful
   - (D) visible

5. According to paragraph 3, the Migratory Bird Treaty Act
   - (A) attempted to improve the environment
   - (B) tried to recover bird feathers
   - (C) was not enforced for several decades
   - (D) aimed to protect endangered species

6. It can be inferred from paragraph 3 that marketing "Hollywood Finches"
   - (A) signified authenticity
   - (B) established their origin
   - (C) had a glamorous appeal
   - (D) legitimized their nationality

7. The phrase "cracking down on" in paragraph 3 is closest in meaning to
   - (A) reporting
   - (B) restraining
   - (C) supervising
   - (D) undermining

Go on to the next page →

8. It can be inferred from paragraph 3 that house finches were trapped in Los Angeles

- (A) to avoid prosecution
- (B) to avoid paying hefty fines
- (C) to comply with the Migratory Bird Treaty Act
- (D) to be sold in New York City

9. Look at the four squares [■] that show where the following sentence could be added to paragraph 4.

The birds experienced exponential growth in the wild because of the species' high fertility rate, which had decreased in captivity.

Where would the sentence best fit?

⁴ 4 [9A] ■ During the 1940s and 1950s, the population was mainly confined to New York City. [9B] ■ The small population struggled for survival for many years, establishing a small breeding enclave. However, by the 1950s the finches ended up surviving in the wild streets of metropolitan areas, nesting among the urban skyscrapers. By the 1960s the range of the House finch rapidly expanded from New York City, breeding new populations as the birds' nesting sites started spreading, likely due to attempts to attract these birds to backyard bird feeders as well as the availability of food. [9C] ■ Amazingly, 20 years later, house finches could be found throughout the U.S. and southern Canada. Their total number in North America is estimated at more than a billion birds, with a substantial percentage east of the Mississippi River. The wild populations of East Coast House finches, descendants of the trapped California birds, provide an interesting case study of adaptation to the environment. [9D] ■

- (A) [9A]
- (B) [9B]
- (C) [9C]
- (D) [9D]

10. **Directions:** An introductory sentence for a brief summary of the passage is provided below. Complete the summary by selecting the THREE answer choices that express the most important ideas in the passage. Some sentences do not belong in the summary because they express ideas that are not presented in the passage or are minor ideas in the passage. **This question is worth 2 points.**

The passage discusses the adaptation of the house finch.

- •
- •
- •

Choose 3 to complete the summary.

① In cities like Boston, "Hollywood Finches" were once in demand.

② Because house finches were released into the wild, they number more than a billion today.

③ The sale of house finch feathers prompted passage of the Migratory Bird Treaty Act.

④ Although at one time house finches were domestic caged birds, today these birds are found in the wild.

⑤ Ironically, the Migratory Bird Treaty Act was directly responsible for the birds' proliferation.

⑥ At one time house finches lived only on the Hawaiian Islands.

Go on to the next page ➜

READING 2

Directions: Read the passage.

Lie Detector Tests

1.   Lie detector tests have become a popular cultural icon—from crime dramas to comedies to advertisements—the picture of a polygraph pen wildly gyrating on a moving chart is a readily recognized symbol. However, as psychologist Leonard Saxe has argued, the idea that one can detect a person's veracity by monitoring physiological changes is more myth than reality. Even the term "lie detector," used to refer to polygraph testing, is a misnomer. So-called "lie detection" involves inferring deception through analysis of physiological responses to a structured series of questions that may vary whenever the test is administered.

2.   Lie detectors record a person's physiological reactions to certain questions. Basically, the instrument records four physiological activities. Originally, a moving roll of graph paper recorded these reactions. Today a computer enters the assessments from three instruments. One is a device wrapped around a subject's chest and stomach to record the rate and depth of breathing. The second is a blood pressure cuff placed on the subject's arm to measure heartbeat and trace changes in blood pressure. The third are electrodes placed on the subject's fingertips that measure changes in the electrical resistance of the skin and can indicate subtle sweating. The recording instrument and questioning techniques are used only during a part of the polygraph examination. A typical examination includes a pretest phase during which the technique is explained, and each test question reviewed. The pretest interview is designed to ensure that subjects understand the questions and to induce a subject's concern about being deceptive. Polygraph examinations often include a procedure called a "stimulation test," which is a demonstration of the instrument's accuracy in detecting deception.

3.   Several questioning techniques are commonly used in polygraph tests. The most widely used test format for subjects in criminal investigations is the Control Question Test (CQT). The CQT compares responses to "relevant" questions (e.g., "Did you rob the bank?"), with those of "control" questions. The control questions are designed to control for the effect of the generally threatening nature of relevant questions. Control questions concern misdeeds that are similar to those being investigated, but refer to the subject's past and are usually broad in scope; for example, "Have you ever gotten someone else in trouble for something you did?" A person who is telling the truth is assumed to fear control questions more than relevant questions. This is because control questions are designed to arouse a subject's concern about their past truthfulness, while relevant questions ask about a crime they know they did not commit. The accuracy (i.e., validity) of polygraph testing has long been controversial. An underlying problem is theoretical: There is no evidence that any pattern of physiological reactions is unique to deception. An honest person may be nervous when answering truthfully and a dishonest person may be composed. In that sense, a lie detector might be better called a fear detector.

4.   Polygraph testing has generated considerable scientific and public controversy. Most psychologists and other scientists agree that there is little basis for the validity of polygraph tests. Courts, including the United States Supreme Court, have repeatedly rejected the use of polygraph evidence because of its inherent unreliability. Nevertheless, polygraph testing continues to be used in non-judicial settings, often to screen personnel, but sometimes to try to assess the truthfulness of suspects and witnesses. Polygraph tests are also sometimes used by individuals seeking to convince others of their innocence and, in a narrow range of circumstances, by private agencies and corporations. For now, although the idea of a lie detector may be comforting, the most practical advice is to remain skeptical about any conclusion extracted from a polygraph.

Directions: Answer the questions.

11. The word "icon" in paragraph 1 could best be replaced by

    (A) prank   (C) stereotype

    (B) appearance   (D) symbol

12. It is implied in paragraph 1 that

    (A) The popularity of lie detector tests is on the rise.

    (B) Polygraph testing can detect a person's veracity.

    (C) Whenever administered, lie detector tests need to vary.

    (D) Although popular, lie detectors are not reliable.

13. The word "so-called" in paragraph 1 could best be replaced by

    (A) supposed

    (B) nicknamed

    (C) respected

    (D) known

14. It is NOT true according to paragraph 2 that

    (A) three different devices are placed on the subject.

    (B) the moving roll of graph paper has been replaced by a computer.

    (C) questioning the subject is done throughout the test.

    (D) the questions are reviewed in advance.

15. Which of the sentences below best expresses the essential information in the highlighted sentence in paragraph 2? *Incorrect* choices change the meaning in important ways or leave out essential information.

    (A) By explaining the procedure to the test takers before the test, the subjects are induced to be deceptive.

    (B) Test takers need to understand what will transpire in case they choose to be deceptive.

    (C) The purpose of the interview is to explain the procedure and encourage test takers to be honest.

    (D) During the pretest stage of the procedure, test takers are concerned about being truthful.

Go on to the next page →

16. Look at the four squares ■ that show where the following sentence could be added to paragraph 2.

The subjects cannot claim that their physiological reactions were caused by a surprising or upsetting question.

Where would the sentence best fit?

² Lie detectors record a person's physiological reactions to certain questions. Basically, the instrument records four physiological activities. Originally a moving roll of graph paper recorded these reactions. Today a computer enters the assessments from three instruments. [16A] ■ One is a device wrapped around a subject's chest and stomach to record the rate and depth of breathing. The second is a blood pressure cuff placed on the subject's arm to measure heartbeat and trace changes in blood pressure. The third are electrodes placed on the subject's fingertips that measure changes in the electrical resistance of the skin and can indicate subtle sweating. The recording instrument and questioning techniques are used only during a part of the polygraph examination. A typical examination includes a pretest phase during which the technique is explained and each test question reviewed. [16B] ■ The pretest interview is designed to ensure that subjects understand the questions and to induce a subject's concern about being deceptive. [16C] ■ Polygraph examinations often include a procedure called a "stimulation test," which is a demonstration of the instrument's accuracy in detecting deception. [16D] ■

Ⓐ [16A]

Ⓑ [16B]

Ⓒ [16C]

Ⓓ [16D]

17. According to paragraph 3, which of the following is stated about people who have not committed a crime?

Ⓐ If they did not commit the crime, they have nothing to fear from the questions.

Ⓑ They fear control questions more because they ask questions not about the crime.

Ⓒ Their truthfulness will be a cause for concern while answering relevant questions.

Ⓓ They have no reason to be nervous because they know they did not commit a crime.

18. According to paragraph 3, the attitude of the author toward lie detector tests is

Ⓐ disbelieving

Ⓑ amused

Ⓒ confused

Ⓓ supportive

19. It is implied in the passage that

Ⓐ lie detector tests have become a useful tool in the workplace

Ⓑ the judicial system will be reexamining lie detector usage

Ⓒ there may be some limited usefulness in using lie detectors

Ⓓ those who are guilty of a crime request their usage

20. **Directions:** An introductory sentence for a brief summary of the passage is provided below. Complete the summary by selecting the THREE answer choices that express the most important ideas in the passage. Some sentences do not belong in the summary because they express ideas that are not presented in the passage or are minor ideas in the passage. **This question is worth 2 points.**

The passage discusses the validity of lie detector tests.

-
-
-

Choose 3 answers.

1. Lie detector tests are frequently seen in movies and on TV.
2. Today a computer records the reactions.
3. Because there is no scientific proof of the device's reliability, it is not allowed in U.S. courts.
4. A person's truthfulness can be measured physiologically.
5. A lie detector test might be better called a fear detector.
6. Three instruments measure the body's physiological reactions to a series of questions.

STOP. This is the end of the Reading section for test-takers taking the TOEFL iBT test on the computer.

If you are preparing to take the Paper Edition of the test, continue to READING 3.

Go on to the next page ➔

READING 3

Read the passage.

This section is for the Paper Edition only.

We are the Imposters

Even though they are at the top of their game, some people often get a sneaky feeling that they do not deserve their success. They doubt their abilities so much that they sometimes believe their success is down to chance, good luck, or some other coincidence. Worse still, they worry that, despite their achievements, they could be found to be an imposter who should not be successful. Unfortunately, these kinds of feelings happen to many of us. It is estimated that around 70% of people experience these feelings during their lifetime. Labeled *imposter syndrome* (IS), it is the perception that you do not deserve your achievements.

Initially identified by researcher Dr. Pauline Clance, from her research into high-achieving professional women, IS is experienced by a wide variety of people no matter their gender, occupation, or culture. When a task is given to a person with imposter syndrome, they will display anxiety-related behavior. Typically, at work, a person with IS either over-prepares or delays performing the task, at which time they go into a period of intense work to complete the task. After finishing, their feelings of achievement do not last and often they will not accept positive feedback about how well they have performed, usually saying the success was due to luck or coincidence rather than themselves. This failure to own their success reinforces their pattern of thinking they are not responsible for their successes.

As seen, anyone can experience IS. Because it is difficult to identify, research into IS has focused on personality and character traits. The first characteristic closely associated with IS is perfectionism (when someone sets high and often unrealistic goals). Studies found that people with IS had a higher concern about their mistakes, great dissatisfaction with their performance, and high levels of self-criticism. The second feature is the need to be special or the best in comparison with other people in their area of work. However, when people with IS meet other people with the same skills as them, they think they are not special and dismiss their talents as being inadequate. The third characteristic is evident when people with IS are given a task: they experience fear of failure and feelings of embarrassment if they make mistakes. For this reason, they tend to overwork. The fourth trait is that they have difficulty accepting their successes, deny their competence, and often attribute their achievements to external factors. Finally, people with IS may feel guilty because they are successful and therefore different.

The causes of IS are not entirely known. Although it has been attributed to personality characteristics such as anxiety and perfectionism, other studies have associated it with early problems in the family or childhood memories of dealing with success or failure. In 1985, Dr. Clance said her studies showed that there were common factors leading to IS. Within the family, there was the idea that their talents are special compared with other family members but also messages that success requires little effort. Importantly, there was a lack of positive praise. A later study found that high levels of family control, tension, and conflict, as well as confusing messages about achievement also contributed.

Go on to the next page ➜

The connection between IS and psychological problems such as depression is well known (although it is unlikely to lead to serious depression). Unfortunately, it can lead to a cycle of imposter syndrome—when people with imposter feelings succeed, they believe that their success was due to their overwork and perfectionism and rely on this for their next success, not their innate skills. There are ways to help, though. Sharing feelings with peers can help people recognize their progress and stop comparisons with other people. So can being realistic about their limits—what they can and cannot do, what they are good and less good at, and where they can improve. Most people with IS need help to change how they think about their achievements and Dr. Clance urges people with IS to stop trying for perfection and recognize that doing a task well enough is something to celebrate.

Refer to the passages below and answer the questions that follow.

We are the Imposters

[1] Even though they are at the top of their game, some people often get a sneaky feeling that they do not deserve their success. They doubt their abilities so much that they sometimes believe their success is down to chance, good luck, or some other coincidence. Worse still, they worry that, despite their achievements, they could be found out to be a fraud or an imposter who should not be successful. Unfortunately, these kinds of feelings happen to many of us. It is estimated that around 70% of people experience these feelings during their lifetime. Labeled "imposter syndrome" (IS), it is the perception that you do not deserve your achievements.

Directions: Answer the questions.

21. The phrase "at the top of their game" in paragraph 1 could best be replaced by

    (A) the best days of their lives

    (B) feeling slightly silly

    (C) in very good health

    (D) very successful

22. According to paragraph 1, the feeling of "imposter syndrome"

    (A) only happens to people who achieve highly

    (B) is very common

    (C) is experienced by people who gain success through luck

    (D) is experienced by frauds and imposters

Go on to the next page →

² Initially identified by researcher Dr. Pauline Clance, from her research into high-achieving professional women, IS is experienced by a wide variety of people no matter their gender, occupation, or culture. [23A] ■ When a task is given to a person with imposter syndrome, they will display anxiety-related behavior. [23B] ■ Typically, at work, a person with IS either over-prepares or delays performing the task, at which time they go into a period of intense work to complete the task. After finishing, their feelings of achievement do not last and often they will not accept positive feedback about how well they have performed, usually saying the success was due to luck or coincidence rather than themselves. [23C] ■ This failure to own their success reinforces their pattern of thinking they are not responsible for their successes. [23D] ■

23. Look at the four squares [■] that show where the following sentence could be added to paragraph 2.

This fact can affect the way they do their work.

Where would the sentence best fit?

(A) [23A]

(B) [23B]

(C) [23C]

(D) [23D]

24. The word "coincidence" in paragraph 2 could best be replaced by

(A) negativity

(B) opportunity

(C) misfortune

(D) chance

³ As seen, anyone can experience IS. Because it is difficult to identify, research into IS has focused on personality and character traits. The first characteristic closely associated with IS is perfectionism (when someone sets high and often unrealistic goals). Studies found that people with IS had a higher concern about their mistakes, great dissatisfaction with their performance, and high levels of self-criticism. The second feature is the need to be special or the best in comparison with other people in their area of work. However, when people with IS meet other people with the same skills as them, they think they are not special and dismiss their talents as being inadequate. The third characteristic is evident when people with IS are given a task: they experience fear of failure and feelings of embarrassment if they make mistakes. For this reason, they tend to overwork. The fourth trait is that they have difficulty accepting their successes, deny their competence, and often attribute their achievements to external factors. Finally, people with IS may feel guilty because they are successful and therefore different.

25. Why do people with imposter syndrome tend to work too much?

(A) Because they are afraid of other people

(B) Because they want to succeed and not be embarrassed

(C) Because they know that they frequently make mistakes

(D) Because they like having tasks given to them

Go on to the next page ➜

[4] The causes of IS are not entirely known. Although it has been attributed to personality characteristics such as anxiety and perfectionism, other studies have associated it with early problems in the family or childhood memories of dealing with success or failure. In 1985, Dr. Clance said her studies showed that there were common factors leading to IS. Within the family, there was the idea that their talents are special compared with other family members but also messages that success requires little effort. Importantly, there was a lack of positive praise. A later study found that high levels of family control, tension, and conflict, as well as confusing messages about achievement also contributed.

26. The word "their" in paragraph 4 refers to

   (A) Dr. Clance's studies

   (B) common factors leading to a person having imposter syndrome

   (C) people with imposter syndrome

   (D) other family members

27. Which of the sentences below best expresses the essential information in the highlighted sentence in paragraph 3? *Incorrect* choices change the meaning in important ways or leave out essential information.

   (A) People who experience imposter syndrome were not praised by their parents in childhood

   (B) There were too many positive comments from their parents

   (C) There was not enough discipline in their family when they were growing up

   (D) Positive approval is a key factor in developing imposter syndrome

[5] The connection between IS and psychological problems such as depression is well known (although it is unlikely to lead to serious depression). Unfortunately, it can lead to a cycle of imposter syndrome—when people with imposter feelings succeed, they believe that their success was due to their overwork and perfectionism and rely on this for their next success, not their innate skills. There are ways to help, though. Sharing feelings with peers can help people to recognize their progress and stop comparisons with other people. So can being realistic about their limits—what they can and cannot do, what they are good and less good at, and where they can improve. Most people with IS need help to change how they think about their achievements and Dr. Clance urges people with IS to stop trying for perfection and recognize that doing a task well enough is something to celebrate.

28. According to paragraph 5, what can imposter syndrome lead to?

   (A) A repetition of the same pattern of actions

   (B) Serious psychological problems

   (C) A point where it cannot be treated

   (D) Overwork and perfectionism

Go on to the next page →

29. According to paragraph 5, which thing DOES NOT help people with imposter syndrome?

   Ⓐ Talking to friends

   Ⓑ Knowing what you are good and not good at

   Ⓒ Stopping trying to be perfect in everything you do

   Ⓓ Comparing yourself with other people

30. **Directions:** An introductory sentence for a brief summary of the passage is provided below. Complete the summary by selecting the THREE answer options that express the most important ideas in the passage. Some sentences do not belong in the summary because they express ideas that are not presented in the passage or are minor ideas in the passage. This question is worth 2 points.

Imposter syndrome happens when a successful person feels that they do not deserve their success.

-

-

-

Choose 3 answers.

⓵ People with imposter syndrome also suffer from depression.

⓶ Dr Pauline Clance was the first person to experience imposter syndrome.

⓷ A range of people experience imposter syndrome and this may be shown in anxious or unconfident behavior.

⓸ There are many characteristics associated with the syndrome, including a desire to do things perfectly, being a high achiever and a fear of mistakes.

⓹ Many causes of imposter syndrome have been traced to a person's upbringing and family background.

⓺ Imposter syndrome is mainly experienced by high-achieving women.

STOP. This is the end of the Reading section for the Paper Edition.

Listening Section

This section tests your ability to understand conversations and lectures in English. You can listen to each conversation and lecture only **one** time.

After each conversation or lecture, you will answer some questions. The questions usually ask about the main idea and supporting details or about a speaker's attitude or purpose. Answer the questions based on what the speakers say or imply.

You can take notes while you listen. The notes may help you answer the questions. You will NOT receive a score for your notes.

You will see the **audio icon** 🎧 in some questions. This means that you will hear a part of the question that does not appear on the test page.

Questions are worth 1 point. If a question is worth more than 1 point, specific directions will tell you how many points you can receive.

You will have approximately **36 minutes** to listen to the conversations and lectures and to answer the questions. You should answer each question even if your answer is only a guess. For this practice test, a useful guideline is to spend no more than 35 seconds to answer a question.

The Listening section is relevant for test-takers taking the computer-based version and the Paper Edition of the TOEFL iBT Test.

QUESTIONS

Questions 1–5

🎧 Listen to Track 43.

NOTES:

Directions: Answer the questions.

1. Why does the student go to see the dean?

   (A) To learn what the club budget is

   (B) To find out if Professor Roberto will be their advisor

   (C) To see if they can perform *West Side Story*

   (D) To get permission to set up a drama club

2. According to the student, how would the club get major funding?

   (A) From the campus club allowance

   (B) From admission fees for the plays

   (C) From an outside source, such as a grant

   (D) From the seed money for the first play

3. What does the student say about a dedicated space?

   (A) He would like to use half of the old gym.

   (B) Finding a dedicated space will be impossible.

   (C) Holbrook Hall would work since it has no function.

   (D) Any space where they could put a stage is fine.

4. What does the dean say about the club request?

   (A) He should see if the trustees will donate money.

   (B) His request will be at the top of the list.

   (C) She has to wait and see who else petitions.

   (D) The small yearly allowance will not suffice.

5. What does the dean say the student needs to submit?

   (A) The time and place of the performances

   (B) The name of the play they'll be performing

   (C) The names of at least ten club members

   (D) The names of the students in the drama class

Go on to the next page →

Questions 6–11

🎧 Listen to Track 44.

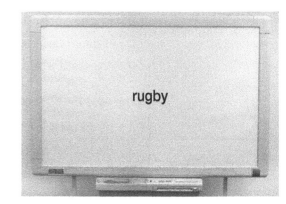

NOTES:

Directions: Answer the questions.

6. How is the information in the passage organized?

    (A) The steps in the process are outlined.

    (B) The topic is explained through an extended example.

    (C) The professor compares and contrasts the topic.

    (D) The causes are explained and developed.

7. Play Track 45 to listen again to part of the passage. Then answer the question.

    Why does the professor say this?

    (A) He is listing the elements of soccer.

    (B) He is contrasting the first game with that of today.

    (C) He is contrasting soccer and football.

    (D) He is giving specifics of comparison.

8. According to the discussion, what was different about how Harvard and McGill preferred to play in 1875?

    (A) Harvard preferred to run while holding the ball.

    (B) McGill's game more closely resembled rugby.

    (C) McGill wanted to kick the ball while advancing.

    (D) Harvard wanted to tackle the opposing players.

9. According to the passage, what is said about the comparison of soccer to football?
Choose 2 answers.

    (A) They are both played with 11 players.

    (B) They both consider tackling to be integral to the game.

    (C) Both soccer and football derive from rugby.

    (D) Football resembles rugby more than it resembles soccer.

10. According to the passage, what contributions did Walter Camp make to football?
Choose 2 answers.

    (A) He established the first university team west of Pennsylvania.

    (B) He reduced the size of the playing field.

    (C) He lowered the number of players from 15 to 11.

    (D) He increased the number of university teams to 43.

11. What can be inferred about those young men who played soccer but didn't attend high school or college.

    (A) Because they liked the game so much, they decided to attend college.

    (B) Their games were not as competitive as those played at college.

    (C) Their games had more players on the teams than those at colleges.

    (D) Their rivalries increased the popularity of the sport.

Go on to the next page →

Questions 12–17

🎧 Listen to Track 46.

NOTES:

Directions: Answer the questions.

12. What does the professor mainly discuss in the lecture?

    Ⓐ The role of Frederick Tudor in building iceboxes

    Ⓑ Utilizing ice in the refrigeration process

    Ⓒ Events leading up to drinking iced tea

    Ⓓ Home ice delivery by horse and buggy

13. Why does the professor most likely mention his grandparents.

    Ⓐ To honor their memory

    Ⓑ To personalize the topic

    Ⓒ To connect them with Tudor

    Ⓓ To insert an element of humor

14. What is stated in the lecture about Frederic Tudor?
    Choose 2 answers.

    Ⓐ He traveled to India.   Ⓑ He was from Boston.

    Ⓒ He became known as the Ice King.   Ⓓ His slabs of ice were for export only.

15. Match each description to the appropriate model on the right by placing a check mark (✓) in the correct boxes. **This question is worth 2 points.**

	Cheaper models	More expensive models	Refrigeration models
Used spigots for draining ice water from a catch pan			
Used electricity instead of ice			
Used a drip pan that was placed under the box			

🎧 16. Play Track 47 to listen again to part of the discussion. Then answer the question.

How does the professor feel about the stories

    Ⓐ They delighted him.   Ⓑ He was bored by them.

    Ⓒ He was embarrassed by them.   Ⓓ They became old.

17. In the talk, the professor describes the states in the history of refrigeration. Summarize the sequence by putting the stages in the correct order. Number each stage 1, 2, 3, or 4.
    This question is worth 2 points.

    _____ Tudor sent ice ships from Boston to Calcutta.

    _____ Refrigeration began using electricity.

    _____ Tudor and Wyeth perfected an ice-cutting machine.

    _____ The icebox became a domestic necessity.

Go on to the next page ➜

Questions 18–22

🎧 Listen to Track 48.

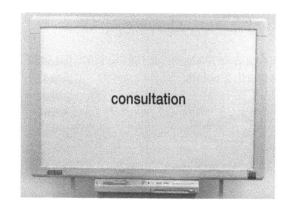

NOTES:

Directions: Answer the questions.

18. Why does the student go to see the professor?

    (A) To resolve some confusion

    (B) To get some help with an assignment

    (C) To discuss something from the text

    (D) To improve his writing

19. Which fallacies or defective proofs did they review?

    Choose 2 answers.

    (A) Red Herring Fallacy

    (B) Post Sequitur

    (C) Myth of the Average

    (D) Post Hoc

20. According to the professor, why would an athlete wear the same socks every game?

    (A) That is what athletes usually do to make one event follow the next.

    (B) It's an example of the red herring fallacy.

    (C) If she won a game wearing those socks, she'll need to wear them to win.

    (D) She would want to try to win by getting the opponents off their game.

21. Play Track 49 to listen again to part of the passage. Then answer the question. What does the professor mean when she says this?

    (A) "Can you hear what I'm saying to you?"

    (B) "Does what I said seem like a good idea?"

    (C) "Should I speak a little louder?".

    (D) "Can you sound them out for me?"

22. According to the professor, which fallacy or defective proof occurs when the speaker tries to distract the listener with irrelevant material

    (A) Post Hoc

    (B) Myth of the Mean

    (C) Non-Sequitur

    (D) Red Herring Fallacy

Go on to the next page →

Questions 23–29

🎧 Listen to Track 50.

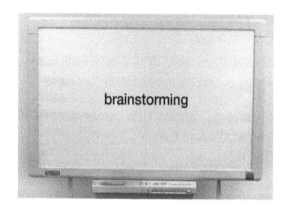

NOTES:

Directions: Answer the questions.

23. What is the talk mainly about?
    - (A) Misconceptions about the superiority of group work
    - (B) Why working in groups outperform individuals working alone
    - (C) The benefits of brainstorming
    - (D) Why companies want their employees to work in groups

24. According to the professor, how did brainstorming evolve?
    - (A) From researchers in the 1950s
    - (B) From advertising executives
    - (C) From companies around the world
    - (D) From team member suggestions

25. According to the lecture, what are the key features of brainstorming?

    Choose 2 answers.

    - (A) Group members generate a single idea
    - (B) Individuals increase creativity working alone
    - (C) Group members build on each other's ideas
    - (D) Members generate as many ideas as possible

26. According to the professor, what does the research into brainstorming groups reveal?
    - (A) That brainstorming groups don't perform as well as independent individuals
    - (B) That creative people feed off each other's thinking processes and create energy
    - (C) That by working in groups people come up with more and better ideas
    - (D) That companies should encourage everyone to be a team player

27. What does the professor claim are the benefits of working in groups?

    Choose 2 answers.

    - (A) Working in teams will outperform working individually.
    - (B) People believe they are the star of the team.
    - (C) Working in groups satisfies belonging needs.
    - (D) Most of the time performance improves.

28. What does the professor imply business managers should do?
    - (A) Let individuals believe they each are crucial team members.
    - (B) Forget about teamwork and promote individuality.
    - (C) Explain to employees that group work is not really effective.
    - (D) Encourage group work even if productivity does not really improve.

STOP. This is the end of the Listening section.

Speaking Section

This section tests your ability to speak about different topics. You will answer four questions.

Question 1 asks you to make and defend a personal choice between two contrasting behaviors or courses of action.

Question 2 will include a reading and a listening passage. First, you will read a short passage which presents a campus-related issue. Then you will hear comments on the issue in the reading passage. Next, you will summarize the speaker's opinion within the context of the reading passage.

Question 3 will also include a reading and a listening passage. First, you will read a short passage that broadly defines a term, process, or idea from an academic subject. Then you will hear an excerpt from a lecture which provides examples and specific information to illustrate the term, process, or idea from the reading passage. Next, you will answer a question which asks you to combine and convey important information from the reading passage and the lecture excerpt.

Question 4 will include part of a lecture that explains a term or concept and gives concrete examples to illustrate that term or concept. The question asks you to summarize the lecture and demonstrate an understanding of the relationship between the examples and the overall topic.

While you read and listen, you can take notes that should help you answer the questions.

Listen carefully to the directions for each question. The preparation time begins right after you hear the question. You will be told when to begin to prepare and when to begin speaking.

The Speaking section is relevant for test-takers taking the computer-based version and the Paper Edition of the TOEFL iBT Test.

QUESTIONS

Track 51

1. You will be asked your opinion about a familiar topic. Listen to the question, and then prepare your response. You will have 15 seconds to prepare a response and 45 seconds to speak. You can take notes on the main points of a response.

Play Track 51 to hear question 1.

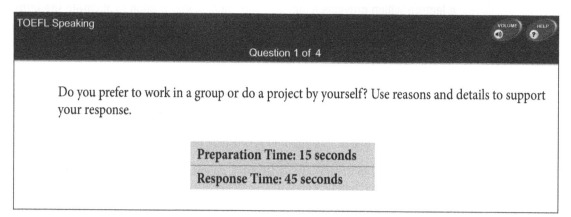

TOEFL Speaking   VOLUME   HELP

Question 1 of 4

Do you prefer to work in a group or do a project by yourself? Use reasons and details to support your response.

> Preparation Time: 15 seconds
>
> Response Time: 45 seconds

NOTES:

Track 52

2. You will read a short passage and then listen to a conversation about the same topic. You will then answer a question about them. You will have 45 seconds to read the passage. You can take notes on the main points of the reading passage.

Reading Time: 45 seconds

TOEFL Speaking

Reading Passage for Question 2 of 4

Summer Storage Announcement

In response to student requests, the college will be offering a summer storage option for personal items. For a fee of 25 dollars for a medium-sized box and 50 dollars for a large box, student items can be stored in the basement of Green Hall. This site is securely locked and will be patrolled by campus security on a regular basis. For those of you traveling a great distance or those who do not wish to bring home winter, bulky, or other items not needed over the summer, this arrangement should suit your needs. The box sizes are currently on display in the lobby of Green Hall. Boxes can be dropped off after final exams on May 10 and will be available for pickup on August 31.

Listen to two students discuss the announcement. You can take notes on the main points of the conversation.

NOTES:

Go on to the next page ➜

Now answer the following question:

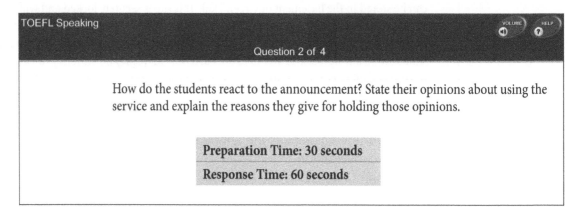

TOEFL Speaking

Question 2 of 4

How do the students react to the announcement? State their opinions about using the service and explain the reasons they give for holding those opinions.

Preparation Time: 30 seconds

Response Time: 60 seconds

NOTES:

Track 53

3. You will read a short passage and then listen to part of a lecture about the same topic. You will then answer a question about them. You will have 45 seconds to read the passage. You can take notes on the main points of the reading passage.

Reading Time: 45 seconds

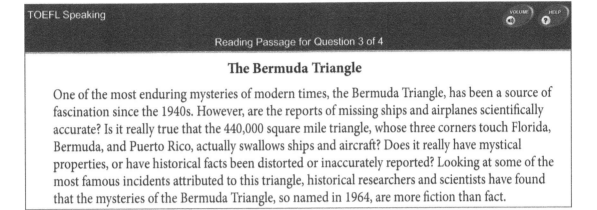

TOEFL Speaking

Reading Passage for Question 3 of 4

The Bermuda Triangle

One of the most enduring mysteries of modern times, the Bermuda Triangle, has been a source of fascination since the 1940s. However, are the reports of missing ships and airplanes scientifically accurate? Is it really true that the 440,000 square mile triangle, whose three corners touch Florida, Bermuda, and Puerto Rico, actually swallows ships and aircraft? Does it really have mystical properties, or have historical facts been distorted or inaccurately reported? Looking at some of the most famous incidents attributed to this triangle, historical researchers and scientists have found that the mysteries of the Bermuda Triangle, so named in 1964, are more fiction than fact.

Listen to the passage. You can take notes on the main points of the listening passage.

NOTES:

Now answer the following question:

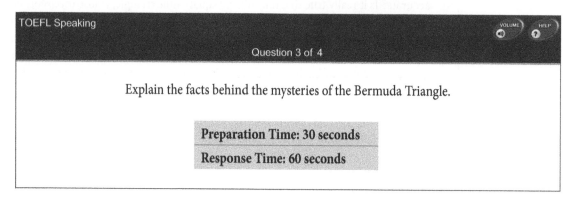

TOEFL Speaking

Question 3 of 4

Explain the facts behind the mysteries of the Bermuda Triangle.

Preparation Time: 30 seconds

Response Time: 60 seconds

NOTES:

Track 54

4. You will listen to part of a lecture. You can take notes on the main points of the listening passage.

Now answer the following question:

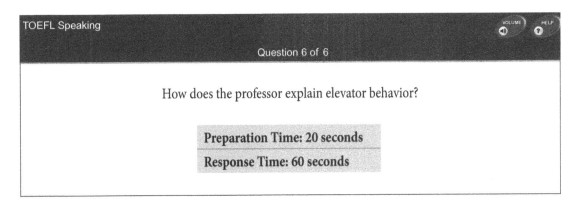

How does the professor explain elevator behavior?

Preparation Time: 20 seconds

Response Time: 60 seconds

NOTES:

STOP. This is the end of the Speaking section.

Writing Section

This section tests your ability to use writing in an academic setting. There will be two writing tasks.

In the first writing task, the integrated writing task, you will read a passage and listen to a lecture. You will then answer a question based on the reading passage and the lecture.

TOEFL iBT test on the computer

The second task on the computer-based TOEFL iBT test is the academic discussion task. In this task, you will write a response to the professor's question using the information in the texts and your own ideas.

TOEFL iBT Paper Edition

The second task on the Paper Edition of the TOEFL iBT test is the independent writing task. In this task, you will answer a question using your own background knowledge.

Integrated Writing Directions

For this task, you will read a passage about an academic topic, and then you will hear a lecture about the same topic. You may take notes on both.

Then you will read a question about the connection between the reading passage and the lecture. In your written response try to use information from both the passage and the lecture. You will **not** be asked for your own opinion. You can refer to the reading passage while you are writing.

You should plan on **3 minutes** to read the passage. Then listen to the lecture and give yourself **20 minutes** to plan and write your response. A successful response will be about 150 to 225 words. Your response will be judged on the quality of the writing and the correctness of the content.

QUESTION 1

Read the passage. On a piece of paper, take notes on the main points of the reading passage.

> **Reading Time: 3 minutes**

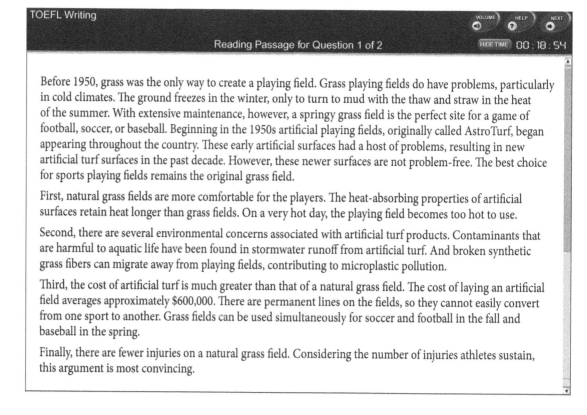

TOEFL Writing

VOLUME   HELP   NEXT

Reading Passage for Question 1 of 2

HIDE TIME   00 : 18 : 54

Before 1950, grass was the only way to create a playing field. Grass playing fields do have problems, particularly in cold climates. The ground freezes in the winter, only to turn to mud with the thaw and straw in the heat of the summer. With extensive maintenance, however, a springy grass field is the perfect site for a game of football, soccer, or baseball. Beginning in the 1950s artificial playing fields, originally called AstroTurf, began appearing throughout the country. These early artificial surfaces had a host of problems, resulting in new artificial turf surfaces in the past decade. However, these newer surfaces are not problem-free. The best choice for sports playing fields remains the original grass field.

First, natural grass fields are more comfortable for the players. The heat-absorbing properties of artificial surfaces retain heat longer than grass fields. On a very hot day, the playing field becomes too hot to use.

Second, there are several environmental concerns associated with artificial turf products. Contaminants that are harmful to aquatic life have been found in stormwater runoff from artificial turf. And broken synthetic grass fibers can migrate away from playing fields, contributing to microplastic pollution.

Third, the cost of artificial turf is much greater than that of a natural grass field. The cost of laying an artificial field averages approximately $600,000. There are permanent lines on the fields, so they cannot easily convert from one sport to another. Grass fields can be used simultaneously for soccer and football in the fall and baseball in the spring.

Finally, there are fewer injuries on a natural grass field. Considering the number of injuries athletes sustain, this argument is most convincing.

🎧 Play Track 55 to listen to the passage.

Now answer the following question:

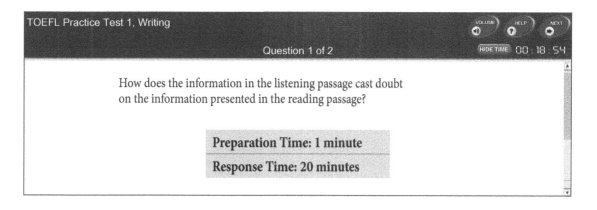

Write your response here or on a computer.

_____

_____

_____

_____

_____

_____

_____

_____

Go on to the next page ➔

Writing for an Academic Discussion

For this task, you will read an online discussion. A professor has posted a question about a topic, and some classmates have responded with their ideas.

Write a response that contributes to the discussion. You will have **10 minutes** to write your response. It is important to use your own words in the response. Including memorized reasons or examples will result in a lower score.

QUESTION 2 for the computer-based TOEFL iBT Test

Your professor is teaching a class on ethics. Write a post responding to the professor's question.

In your response you should:

- express and support your opinion
- make a contribution to the discussion.

An effective response will contain at least 100 words.

Professor Georgina

Before a new beauty product, agricultural chemical, cleaning product or drug goes onto the market for human use, we have to be sure that it won't cause harm or death to the user. Living animals have been used for years to test their reactions to new products, often causing them injury or death in place of humans. How do you feel about this? To get your opinions and thoughts I'd like to ask you

Should animals be used for drug testing or is the practice cruel and unnecessary?

Abiodun

I feel very strongly that we shouldn't use animals to test drugs. Like the professor said, it's cruel and there are new ways to test products now. In addition, animal biology is so different to human biology that we can't be sure the results are transferable.

Piotr

Actually, I agree with Abiodun, it's not a great way to test drugs but unfortunately it's the best we have got. We can't test drugs directly on humans and we need to know what the effects could be. Animal testing has saved thousands of lives and scientists need it to develop safe drugs.

_____

_____

_____

_____

_____

_____

Go on to the next page ➜

FOR THE PAPER EDITION ONLY

Independent Writing Directions

For this task, you will write an essay that explains, supports, and states your opinion about an issue. You will have **30 minutes** to plan, write, and edit your essay. You can take notes on the main points of a response.

A successful response will be at least 300 words. Try to show that you can develop your ideas, organize your essay, and use language correctly to express your ideas. The essay will be judged on the quality of your writing.

QUESTION 2 for the Paper Edition

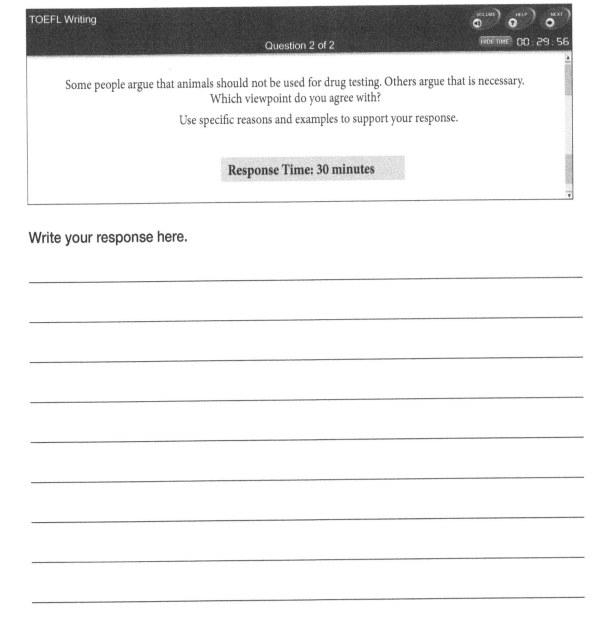

| TOEFL Writing | VOLUME | HELP | NEXT |
| Question 2 of 2 | | | HIDE TIME 00:29:56 |

Some people argue that animals should not be used for drug testing. Others argue that is necessary. Which viewpoint do you agree with?

Use specific reasons and examples to support your response.

Response Time: 30 minutes

Write your response here.

_____

_____

_____

_____

_____

_____

_____

Go on to the next page →

Go on to the next page →

STOP. This is the end of the Writing section.

Guide to the TOEFL iBT® Test

The Guide to the TOEFL iBT® Test shows you strategies for success as you prepare for the exam. This detailed guide breaks down every section of the test so you know what to expect. Included are detailed descriptions of each of the four test sections, so you will know what you need to do in order to prepare and succeed on the TOEFL iBT test. Information is presented in easy-to-read charts and tables that you can refer to as you study.

The guide also presents ways to overcomes common challenges with helpful solutions for you to implement as part of your preparation.

Tips for Success

Make a plan to succeed, and start by following these tips:

» **Register for the test early**. Check the application deadlines for the universities you are applying to. Make sure that you register to take the test well before the deadline to ensure that your scores arrive on time. For information on how to register, see page 209 of this book.

» **Learn the score requirements for the universities you want to apply to**. Degree programs that have minimum score requirements typically post them on their websites.

» **Start to study early.** The more you practice, the more you will improve your skills. Give yourself at least one month to review the materials and complete <u>all</u> of the practice activities in this book. Spend at least one hour a day studying and don't give up. Remember, by using this book, you are on your way to high scores on the TOEFL iBT test!

» **Time yourself** when you complete the exercises and practice tests.

» **Complete the exercises** on the page. Also, don't be afraid to make your own notes on the page. For example, writing down the definitions to words you don't know on the page will help you remember them later on.

» In the reading sections, read the passages as many times as you need to in order to understand the concepts taught in this book.

» In the listening sections, listen to the passages as many times as you need to in order to get used to the speed.

» In the writing sections and the speaking sections, return to the prompts and try to come up with new responses. Practice until creating responses within the time limits becomes easy for you.

Taking the TOEFL iBT® Test

What is the TOEFL iBT® Test?

The TOEFL iBT® Test accurately measures how well you can read, listen, speak, and write in English in a college or university classroom. It helps you stand out confidently and it comes with a clear advantage—colleges and universities know you are ready to succeed and communicate in English.

The TOEFL iBT® Test is offered in three different ways, so you can choose the testing option that best suits your needs and preferences:

» TOEFL iBT Test: Test on a computer at an authorized test center.

» TOEFL iBT Home Edition: Test on a computer at home.

» TOEFL iBT Paper Edition: Test in two sessions—Reading, Listening, and Writing on paper at an authorized test center, and Speaking on a computer at home. This is available in select countries.

The TOEFL iBT® Test (Computer-based test at a Test Center)

You will have just under two hours to complete the TOEFL iBT® Test. The test has four sections:

» Reading measures your ability to understand academic reading material written in English: 35 minutes; 20 questions

» Listening measures your ability to understand spoken English as it is used in colleges and universities: 36 minutes; 28 questions

» Speaking measures your ability to speak English in an academic context: 16 minutes; four tasks

» Writing measures your ability to write in English in a way that is appropriate for college and university coursework: 29 minutes; two tasks

The test emphasizes integrated skills and helps you confirm that you are ready to communicate your ideas about what you will read and listen to in English in your academic courses. Integrated tasks require you to combine more than one skill. You'll be asked to:

» Read, listen, then speak in response to a question

» Listen and then speak in response to a question

» Read, listen, then write in response to a question

Each section of the test has a time limit. If you finish a section early, you can go on to the next section, but you can't go back to a section you have already completed or for which time has been called. However, you can go back to previous passages—within the Reading section only—during the time for that section.

You should work quickly but carefully on the Reading and Listening section questions. Some questions are more difficult than others, but try to answer every one to the best of your ability. If you're not sure of the answer to a question, make the best guess you can.

The questions in the Speaking and Writing sections are each separately timed. Try to answer every one of these questions as completely as possible in the time allowed. Respond only on the assigned topic. If you respond on a different topic, your response will not be scored.

The TOEFL iBT® Test (Home Edition)

The TOEFL iBT Test Home Edition is the same TOEFL iBT® Test you would take at a test center—just taken from the privacy of your own home or in a secure location and monitored online by a human proctor—offered everywhere that the TOEFL iBT® Test is normally available. Prior to registering for the Home Edition, be sure you review and meet the At Home Testing and Equipment and Environment requirements; refer to the website for additional information at https://www.ets.org/toefl/test-takers/ibt/about/testing-options.html. You are required to have your computer scanned for a system check and for any software that may be used for an unfair advantage.

The at-home test is identical in content, format, and on-screen experience to the test taken at a test center and is offered around the clock, four days a week.

The TOEFL iBT® Test (Paper Edition)

You can take the TOEFL iBT® Test on paper in select countries if you prefer that testing format.

The Paper Edition is given in two testing sessions.

> » The Reading, Listening and Writing sections are taken on paper at an ETS-authorized test center.

> » The Speaking section is taken at home in a separate session monitored online by a human proctor, within three days of the test center appointment.

Because the Speaking section is administered at home, make sure you meet the necessary Equipment and Environment requirements before you register. Refer to the website for additional information at https://www.ets.org/toefl/test-takers/ibt/about/testing-options.html

You will have three hours to complete the TOEFL iBT® Paper Edition. The test has four sections:

> » Reading measures your ability to understand academic reading material written in English: 54–72 minutes; 30–40 questions

> » Listening measures your ability to understand spoken English as it is used in colleges and universities: 41–57 minutes; 28–39 questions

> » Writing measures your ability to write in English in a way that is appropriate for college and university coursework: 50 minutes; two tasks

> » Speaking measures your ability to speak English in an academic context: 17 minutes; four tasks

The test emphasizes integrated skills and helps you confirm that you are ready to communicate your ideas about what you will read and listen to in English in your academic courses. Integrated tasks require you to combine more than one skill. You'll be asked to:

> » Read, listen, then speak in response to a question

> » Listen and then speak in response to a question

> » Read, listen, then write in response to a question

The test you take may include extra questions in the Reading or Listening section that do not count toward your score. This means that on the day of the test you will see extra passages and questions in either the Reading section or Listening section. These questions are often new questions that are being tested. Even though these questions are not graded, you will have no way of knowing which section or questions are experimental, so it is very important that you try your best on all of the sections and all of the questions in the test.

Each section of the test has a time limit. If you finish a section early, you can go on to the next section, but you can't go back to a section you have already completed or for which time has been called. However, you can go back to previous passages—within the Reading section only—during the time for that section.

There is a mandatory 10-minute break between the Listening section and the Speaking section. You should work quickly but carefully on the Reading and Listening section questions. Some questions are more difficult than others, but try to answer every one to the best of your ability. If you're not sure of the answer to a question, make the best guess you can.

The questions in the Speaking and Writing sections are each separately timed. Try to answer every one of these questions as completely as possible in the time allowed. Respond only on the assigned topic. If you respond on a different topic, your response will not be scored.

Overview of the TOEFL iBT® Test

Here is some more information about the content of the TOEFL iBT® Test. The test is divided into four timed parts: Reading, Listening, Speaking, and Writing. Each section tests key skills that you will need in order to succeed as a student at an English-speaking university.

Reading Section

The reading section is the first section on the test. It measures your reading comprehension abilities by presenting you with a series of academic passages. Then, you will answer a set of questions based on each reading passage. The questions in this section test your ability to:

» identify the main idea.

» understand the main details.

» make inferences.

» understand the organizational structure of the passage.

» use context clues to determine the definitions of key words.

There are two, three or four academic reading passages per reading section, depending on which version of the test you are taking. Each passage is between 600 and 750 words long. After each reading passage you will answer a set of questions. There are ten questions per passage. In the reading section, you are allowed to go back to previously answered questions in the section to review or change your answers. For more information on the reading section, see *Skills for the TOEFL iBT® Test: Reading and Writing.*

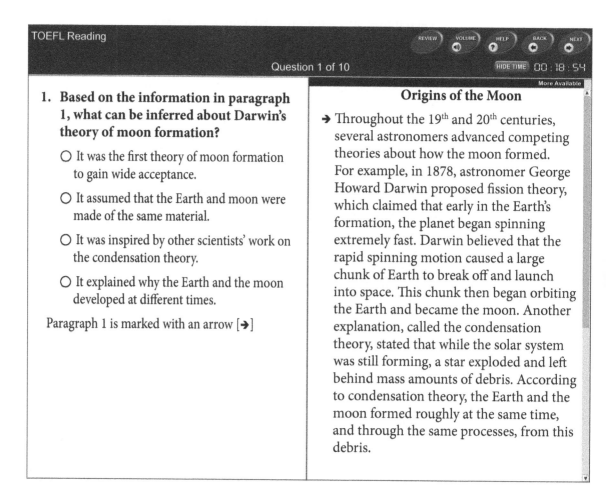

Listening Section

The listening section is the second section on the test. In order to evaluate your listening comprehension abilities, you will first listen to a lecture or conversation through your headphones. Then, you will answer a set of questions based on each listening passage. The questions in this section will test your ability to:

» identify the main idea or purpose of the listening passage.

» understand the main details.

» make inferences.

» identify the speaker's purpose.

There are five listening passages per listening section in the computer-based version of the TOEFL iBT test, and five or seven listening passages in the Paper Edition. Each listening passage is between three and five minutes long. After each listening passage, you will answer a set of questions. There are five or six questions per passage. In the listening section, you are <u>not</u> allowed to review questions that you have answered previously. For more information on the listening section, see *Skills for the TOEFL iBT® Test: Listening and Speaking*.

Speaking Section

The speaking section is the third section on the test, unless you are taking the Paper Edition. In this section, you will speak into the microphone your responses to a variety of tasks. The tasks test a number of speaking abilities, including:

» giving opinions.

» understanding and responding to questions in the classroom.

» participating in discussions on academic subjects.

» synthesizing (combining) information from two sources.

» reporting the opinions of others.

» interacting with university employees.

There are four speaking tasks in the speaking section: one independent task and three integrated tasks.

Each item requires different skills, including reading, listening and speaking; listening and speaking; and speaking only. For more information on the speaking section, see *Skills for the TOEFL iBT® Test: Listening and Speaking*.

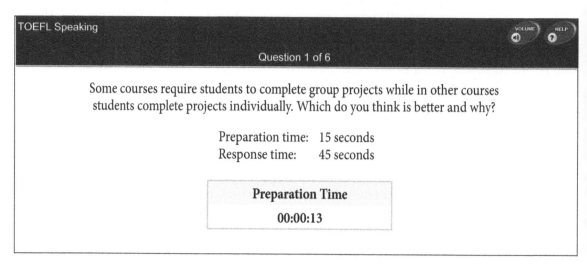

Writing Section

The writing section is the fourth section on the test (or third section if you are taking the Paper Edition). In this section, you will type or write your responses for each item. The tasks measure your ability to:

» plan and organize an essay.

» develop a written response by using examples or specific details.

» use a variety of grammatical structures and vocabulary.

» use correct spelling and punctuation.

There are two writing tasks in the writing section: the first task is the integrated writing task.

TOEFL iBT test on the computer

The second task on the computer-based TOEFL iBT test is the academic discussion task. In this task, you will write a response to the professor's question using the information in the posts and your own ideas.

TOEFL iBT Paper Edition

The second task on the Paper Edition of the TOEFL iBT test is the independent writing task. In this task, you will answer a question using your own background knowledge.

For more information on the writing section, see *Skills for the TOEFL iBT® Test: Reading and Writing*.

TOEFL iBT® Test Computer
QUICK GUIDE: Based / Home Edition

Section	Tasks	Timing
Reading Section	Reading Passages: 2 Number of Questions: 20	**Total Section Time: 35 minutes**
Listening Section	Listening Passages: 5 3 Lectures 2 Conversations Number of Questions: 28	**Total Section Time: 36 minutes**
Speaking Section	Number of Questions: 4 1 Independent 3 Integrated	**Total Section Time: 16 minutes**
Writing Section	Number of Tasks: 2 1 Integrated 1 Academic Discussion	Integrated Task: 19 minutes Academic Discussion Task: 10 minutes **Total Section Time: 29 minutes**

QUICK GUIDE: TOEFL iBT® Test Paper Edition

Section	Tasks	Timing
Reading Section	Reading Passages: 3 or 4 Number of Questions: 30 questions if the test comprises 3 reading passages, or 40 questions if the test comprises 4 reading passages	54 minutes if the test comprises 3 reading passages, or 72 minutes if the text comprises 4 reading passages. **Total Section Time: 54–72 minutes**

Listening Section	Listening Passages: 5 or 7
	
	    3 or 4 Lectures
	
	    2 or 3 Conversations
	
	Number of Questions:
	
	28 questions if the test comprises 5 listening passages, or
	
	39 questions if the test comprises 7 listening passages
		41 minutes if the test comprises 5 listening passages, or
		
		57 minutes if the test comprises 7 listening passages.
		
		Total Section Time: 41–57 minutes

	10-Minute Break	

Writing Section	Number of Tasks: 2
	
	    1 Integrated
	
	    1 Independent
		Integrated Task: 20 minutes
		Independent Task: 30 minutes
		
		Total Section Time: 50 minutes

Speaking Section	Number of Questions: 4
	
	    1 Independent
	
	    3 Integrated
		Total Section Time: 17 minutes

Other Points for Test-Takers to Bear in Mind

Computer Keyboard

TOEFL iBT test centers use a standard English-language (QWERTY) computer keyboard. QWERTY takes its name from the first six letters in the third row of the keyboard. If you haven't used this type of keyboard before, try to practice on one before taking the test. At some test centers the common keyboard used in that location is configured to QWERTY and a template is provided to each test taker to help locate the few keys that are in a different location.

Alternate Format Materials

If you need test preparation materials in an alternate format, please contact ETS Disability Services directly.

Test Takers with Disabilities or Health-related Needs

» Testing accommodations are available for test takers with disabilities or health-related needs who meet ETS requirements. If you are requesting accommodations, you must have them approved before you can register for the test.

» If seeking accommodations, submit your request as early as possible. Documentation review takes approximately four to six weeks once your request and completed paperwork have been received at ETS.

Registration

There are a number of ways to register for the TOEFL iBT® Test. The easiest way to register is through your ETS account. You can also register by phone or by mail, using the TOEFL iBT Registration Form (PDF).

Before you can register, you'll need to create an ETS account, if you don't already have one. You can do this online at www.ets.org/mytoefl or with the TOEFL® Official App.

Be sure that the spelling of the name you use when you register exactly matches the name printed on the ID document you'll bring to the test center. Read the specific requirements for your location, if any, and have your ID ready when you register for the test.

Your ETS Account

Online or via the TOEFL® Official App

» You will need to create an ETS account, if you don't already have one. You can do this online, via the TOEFL® Official App or by phone.

» Whichever way you create your account, be sure to complete all the required sections. The information you provide will be kept completely confidential.

» Confirm your profile—you'll see a confirmation page showing all the information you submitted.

» Once you enter your name and date of birth, you can't change those fields. Make sure the information you enter exactly matches the identification (ID) document you will bring with you to the test center.

By phone

» You can register by phone using a credit/debit card, or an electronic check (e-check) in U.S. dollars.

» Regular phone registration closes seven full days before the test date. Late phone registration closes at 5pm, local test center time, on the day before your test appointment. If you register after the regular seven-day deadline, you'll be charged a late fee.

» Check the registration form at www.ets.org/s/toefl/pdf/iBT_reg_form.pdf to see what other information you will need when you call.

By mail

» You can register by mail with the test registration form, which is available for download at www.ets.org/s/toefl/pdf/iBT_reg_form.pdf.

» Enter all the information on the form.

» Include credit/debit card information, or a check or money order in U.S. dollars. Mail the completed form to the address shown on the form. The form must be received at least four weeks before your earliest test date choice.

» You will be assigned a test date, time and location (test center only) based on the information you provide on the form.

Important Things to Know When You Register

» Information regarding test center and test date availability is subject to change. The most current information regarding test centers, dates and other registration information is available through your ETS account.

» Not all test centers are open on all test dates.

» When you select a date range and general location, you will see a list of test centers in that area. If you are looking for a specific center that is not listed, try a different date range.

» During registration, you can select up to four free score recipients. See "Choosing Score Recipients" on the next page.

» Register early; test dates can fill up quickly.

» Take the test as soon as possible so your scores will be received in time to be considered with your application(s).

» Registration is not transferable. You can't let someone else use your test appointment.

» Walk-in registration is not available.

» Return to your ETS account the day before your test to check your appointment details, either online or via the app. Changes may have been made, such as a different building or start time.

Test Dates

The TOEFL iBT® Test is offered up to six days a week around the world at authorized test centers or from home. When you register, you'll select the TOEFL iBT testing option that suits your needs and preferences: at a test center, at home, or on paper. Test dates are available in your ETS account. Not all test dates are available in all locations.

The TOEFL iBT Paper Edition requires two appointments that must be made together when registering. For the Reading, Listening, and Writing sections of the Paper Edition, appointments are available up to two dates per month at an authorized test center. The Speaking section is taken at home in a separate session within three days of the test center appointment.

Test Locations

The most current information regarding test center locations is in your ETS account. Test centers are added frequently, and information on seat availability is subject to change without notice.

The at-home test is offered everywhere that the TOEFL iBT® Test is normally available.

The TOEFL iBT Paper Edition will initially be offered in select locations; please refer to the website for additional information at https://www.ets.org/toefl/test-takers/ibt/about/testing-options.html.

Registration Deadlines

» Test dates can fill up quickly, so early registration is recommended to get your preferred test location and date. Registration opens approximately six months before the test date.

» Regular online registration closes seven full days before the test date. Late phone registration closes at 5pm, local test center time, on the day before your test appointment. Late online registration closes two days before the test date. For example, if the test date you want is a Saturday, the last day you can register is Thursday. If you register after the regular seven-day deadline, you'll be charged a late fee.

Scoring

Choosing Score Recipients

» You can select up to four score recipients (the designated institutions who will receive your scores) for free at any time until 10pm local test center time on the day before your test appointment. After that time, you'll be charged a fee for sending score reports.

» Recipients can't be added, changed or deleted after the 10pm deadline.

» You can't select your score recipients at the test center.

Understanding Your TOEFL iBT Test Scores

Once you've completed your TOEFL iBT test, you'll receive four scaled section scores and a total score.

Each section has a score range of 0–30. These are added together for a total score of 0–120.

Each skill has four or five proficiency levels, so where your score falls within that range tells you your proficiency for that skill.

Skill	Level
Reading	Advanced (24–30)
	High-Intermediate (18–23)
	Low-Intermediate (4–17)
	Below Low-Intermediate (0–3)
Listening	Advanced (22–30)
	High-Intermediate (17–21)
	Low-Intermediate (9–16)
	Below Low-Intermediate (0–8)
Speaking	Advanced (25–30)
	High-Intermediate (20–24)
	Low-Intermediate (16–19)
	Basic (10–15)
	Below Basic (0–9)
Writing	Advanced (24–30)
	High-Intermediate (17–23)
	Low-Intermediate (13–16)
	Basic (7–12)
	Below Basic (0–6)

MyBest® Scores

Since 2019, the TOEFL publishers have also been offering a new feature called MyBest® scores (or superscores), which show your best overall performance by combining your highest section scores from all test dates within the last two years. This means you may be able to meet score requirements for your institution with fewer tests and meet your goals sooner.

All TOEFL iBT score reports show both your traditional scores from your selected test date and your MyBest scores. An increasing number of universities and other institutions accept MyBest scores. We recommend that you check with institutions directly to confirm their TOEFL score requirements.

If you take the TOEFL iBT Paper Edition, the MyBest scores section will only include your scores from Paper Edition tests. It won't include your scores from tests taken at a test center or from home (TOEFL iBT Home Edition).

How is the Test Scored?

TOEFL iBT tests are only scored by a centralized scoring network, never at the test center. The Reading and Listening sections are scored by computer. The Speaking and Writing sections are scored by a combination of automated AI scoring and multiple highly trained human raters. For more information, see the TOEFL website.

Getting Your TOEFL iBT Test Scores

Your scores will be available in your ETS account. How soon they'll be available depends on how you took the test:

Taken at a test center: 4–8 days after your test date

TOEFL iBT Home Edition: 4–8 days after your test date

TOEFL iBT Paper Edition: 11–13 business days after your test date

Your scores are valid for two years. You can download and print a PDF copy of your score report. PDF score reports are ready for download two days after you receive your scores electronically through your ETS account.

When your designated score recipients will receive your scores depends on how you took the test and what method of score delivery they use.

On Test Day

This information applies if you're taking the TOEFL iBT® Test or the TOEFL iBT Paper Edition (Reading, Listening, and Writing sections).

Before Your Test Session

Before your test appointment, there are a few important things you should do:

» Verify your test location and reporting time. Test locations and reporting times can sometimes change. Check your ETS account 24 hours before your test.

» Check your ID document. You won't be admitted to the test center without proper documentation. Be sure the name you used when you registered exactly matches the name on your ID document.

» Review the general guidelines and the testing room guidelines.

» Dress comfortably and come prepared for varying room temperatures. If you need to remove an item of clothing during the test, such as a sweater, you will be instructed to place it in the storage area provided by the test center. If there is no storage area available, the item can be hung on the back of your chair. If you leave the testing room to go to the storage area, this will be treated as an unscheduled break, and you will be required to sign out of the testing room and sign back in upon your return to the testing room and show your ID. The test clock does not stop during any unscheduled breaks.

Overview of the Reading Section

The reading section is the first part of the TOEFL iBT test. It tests your comprehension of written English by presenting you with a series of reading passages and then asking you a set of questions based on each one.

QUICK GUIDE: TOEFL iBT® Computer Test

Definition	The reading section tests your ability to understand written academic English. The section includes different types of reading passages that are based on a variety of academic subjects.
Targeted Skills	• In order to do well on the reading section, you must be able to: • understand basic academic vocabulary in context. • quickly scan a written passage and understand its main ideas and supporting details. • understand how information is organized. • understand inferences, relationships, paraphrases, and the purpose of a passage. • answer questions within the given time.
The Reading Passages	The reading section includes two reading passages. Each passage is usually 650–700 words long. Each passage will appear on your screen and remain there while you answer the questions based on that passage. There are three different types of passages in the reading section: expository, argumentative, and historical. In addition, each passage is arranged according to a particular organizational style, which include compare and contrast, cause and effect, problem and solution, theory and support, and classification. For more information about passage types and organizational styles, see page 214.
Questions	There are ten questions per reading passage. The questions are multiple choice and can usually be classified as one of the following question types: • Detail • Vocabulary • Referent • Sentence Summary/Simplification • Negative Fact • Passage/Prose Summary • Function • Insert A Sentence/Text • Inference
Timing	You will have **35 minutes** to read and answer the questions for a set of two reading passages.

PAPER EDITION: Please note that, in the Paper Edition of the TOEFL iBT test, the testing company ETS may include extra sample material. This sample material is not scored. However, since you will not know which passages are sample materials, you should try your best on all of the passages.

This means that the Paper Edition of the Reading section could be 30–40 questions, and you will be given 54–72 minutes to complete the Reading section of the Paper Edition.

For information on the Paper Edition of the test, please see page 208.

Reading Section: Passage Types

In the reading section, you will be presented with reading passages that are similar to texts that a student may encounter at a North American university. The topics for the reading passages are drawn from a wide range of academic subjects, including the following:

- anthropology
- archaeology
- art history
- astronomy
- botany
- biology
- education

- engineering
- environmental science
- geography
- geology
- history
- literature
- marketing

- music
- paleontology
- photography
- psychology
- sociology
- urban studies

There are three types of passages in the reading section: expository, argumentative, and historical. Typically, a reading section will consist of at least one of each passage type.

Passage Type	Definition	Sample Topics
Expository	Provides a general explanation of a topic	• Types of Camouflage • Adaptations of Deep Sea Fish • Important Traditions of the Bambara Culture
Argumentative	Provides a point of view and gives several reasons to support that point of view	• Evidence of Contact Between Pacific Cultures and Indigenous Americans • Recuperation Theory vs. Circadian Theory of Sleep • How Non-Native Species Hurt Local Habitats
Historical	Focuses on past events	• History of the Telescope • The Effects of the Norman Conquest • Journalism and Social Change in the Twentieth Century

Organizational Styles

Each passage will usually feature a specific organizational style. An organizational style describes how the ideas in a passage are arranged.

Common Organizational Styles of Reading Passages	
Organizational Style	Description
Classification	Describes two or three different categories of something
Compare / Contrast	Discusses similarities and differences between two or more things
Cause / Effect	Discusses similarities and differences between two or more things
Theory / Support	Presents a theory and provides support for it
Problem / Solution	Presents a problem and discusses solutions

Challenges and Solutions

» **CHALLENGE 1: "I don't know a lot of the words that I see in the passages or in the questions."**

SOLUTION: Expand your vocabulary. There are several tools that you can use to increase your vocabulary. For one, there are several word lists available that present the most common words found in academic settings. The Academic Word List, developed by Averil Coxhead, is a list of 570 words that are commonly included in introductory college texts. Getting to know these words will likely help you perform better on the test and prepare you for entering English-language courses.

SOLUTION: Use a learner's dictionary when you study. Dictionaries such as the *Collins Cobuild Advanced Dictionary* offer clear definitions, sample sentences, grammar, illustrations, and photographs to help you expand your knowledge and use of everyday and academic vocabulary. In this book, you will find definitions for challenging or unfamiliar words, much like you would in the TOEFL iBT reading passages. These definitions come from the *Collins Cobuild Advanced Dictionary*.

SOLUTION: Use context clues. Context clues are the words and phrases that surround key words. Using these clues will help you determine the meanings of unfamiliar words. The author may use a number of strategies to provide context clues for key words, including giving examples of the key word, contrasting the meaning of the key word with an opposite idea, or giving an indirect definition of a key word. To practice finding and using context clues, try reading a 300-word excerpt from a newspaper or a college textbook. Pay attention to the strategies that the authors use to help you figure out the definitions of difficult words.

Strategies for Using Context Clues		
Strategy	**Key Words**	**Example**
Pay attention to **examples** that appear near the highlighted word. If you are familiar with the examples, you can use them to determine the meaning of the highlighted word.	such as including consists of this includes like	The photographs show banal activities, like going to the grocery store or doing household chores.
Look for key words that signal a **contrast** from a previous idea. If you know the meanings of the words from surrounding sentences, you'll know that the highlighted word has an opposite meaning.	Unlike X . . . On the other hand, X . . . While . . . But . . . However . . .	Unlike most mammals, few of which are venomous, the platypus produces a **noxious** substance that can cause extreme pain in humans.
Look for **indirect definitions** of terms in the sentences that surround the highlighted word. These definitions may include an easier synonym of the highlighted word or information that helps clarify its meaning.	and meaning that	In the southwestern United States, the sunflower is ubiquitous, and it is difficult to find a garden that doesn't include the plant.

SOLUTION: Learn how to look at word parts, like prefixes and suffixes, to determine the meanings of unknown words. Many English words are formed through the use of prefixes, which go at the beginnings of words, and suffixes, which go on the ends of words. By learning the meanings of common English prefixes and suffixes, you will be able to guess the definitions of unknown words.

» **CHALLENGE 2: "I often run out of time before completing all of the questions."**

SOLUTION: Use skimming and scanning skills to find the answers to the questions. Skimming is when you quickly read a passage, paying attention only to the most important ideas. By skimming, you can often identify the key ideas that many questions are based on in a short amount of time. This way, you can avoid running out of time during the test.

In order to skim effectively, make sure you know where to find the most important ideas. Regardless of the different organizational styles for passages, important ideas often appear in the same places. See the table below for information on where to find a passage's most important ideas.

Part of the Passage	Skimming Strategy
Introduction	• Read **the last two–three lines** in the introductory paragraph. These lines will typically describe the main idea of the passage.
Body Paragraphs	• Read **the first two–three lines** in the body paragraphs. These sentences will describe the main ideas of the paragraphs. • Read **the last two–three lines** in the body paragraphs. These lines will often explain how each paragraph relates to the main idea of the passage. These lines will also help you understand how the body paragraphs are related to one another.

Scanning is when you read the passage quickly in order to find specific key words or ideas. After you've read a question and its answer options, you should make note of any key words or ideas, like names, terms, or numbers, that will help you answer the question. Then, scan the passage, looking specifically for those key words.

Remember, you don't need to understand every word perfectly while you skim or scan a passage. The most important part is to find the information you need in order to answer the questions quickly and correctly.

To practice skimming and scanning, find an article with 600–700 words in a college textbook. First, skim the article and write down the most important ideas on a piece of scrap paper. Then, try scanning the article for key words and dates. The more you practice skimming and scanning, the faster and more accurate you will get, so try to practice every day.

SOLUTION: Pay attention to the on-screen clock. This clock displays how much time you have left in the section. While you work on the questions, be sure to glance at the clock. On the reading section, you are able to return to unanswered questions later, so be sure to take advantage of this feature. If you take more than two minutes on a question, skip it and return to it later. This will help you avoid getting stuck on one question and wasting your time.

» **CHALLENGE 3: "The passages are often complicated and confusing—sometimes I get lost as I'm reading them."**

SOLUTION: Understand the basic organizational styles found on the reading section of the TOEFL iBT test. If you lose concentration or become confused while you are reading, you just have to think about how the passage is structured in order to get back on track. See the table below for the most common organizational structures of the reading passages and how the information in these passages is often arranged.

	Classification	Compare / Contrast	Cause / Effect	Problem / Solution	Theory / Support
Introduction	Introduces what will be classified in the passage	Introduces two ideas, things, or events	Introduces an event or process	Introduces a problem	Introduces a theory
Body Paragraphs	Present 2–3 **different types or features** of the subject being classified	The first body paragraph describes several **features of the first subject.** In the following paragraphs, the author presents **corresponding features of the second subject**, pointing out how these are **similar to or different from** those of the first subject.	The first body paragraph describes 1–2 **causes** for an event or process. Then, the author describes the **effects**, or consequences, of the causes.	Provide 2–3 **solutions** to the problem	Provide 2–3 **pieces of evidence** to support the theory

To practice, read each of the passages in this book. See if you can identify the organizational structure of each passage. Make note of how the body paragraphs are organized.

SOLUTION: Look for transition language as you read. Transition language includes words and phrases that are used to connect the ideas in different sentences. For example, some transition words signal the introduction of a new topic (e.g., "Another example of X is . . ."), while others signal a process or sequence of events (e.g., "First . . ."). Transition words often appear at the beginning of a new paragraph, though they can appear in the middle part of a paragraph as well. By paying attention to transition words and how they are used, you can get a better sense of what is happening in the passage. In turn, this will help you avoid becoming confused by the information in the passage.

» **CHALLENGE 4: "There's too much information to remember!"**

Solution: Don't worry about remembering every detail from the passage. In the reading section, the passages will <u>always</u> appear on the right side of the screen while you answer the questions. The paragraph that the question is based on will be marked with an arrow [→], and you will be able to scroll through the paragraph as you answer the question in order to find any information you may need.

SOLUTION: On your scrap paper, create a quick outline of the passage. Just because you have access to the passage while you answer the questions doesn't mean that it's not helpful to write down notes in certain instances. For example, while you skim the passage, you can create a quick outline of the basic points in the reading. You should try to use abbreviation strategies so you don't spend too much time writing your outline. Then, you can use this outline as a quick reference while you answer the questions. The outline does not need to contain all of the details from the passage, but it should contain the main ideas, which can be helpful when answering nearly all of the question types. See below for a sample outline for a reading passage.

■ Fossey
- studied and protected the mountain gorilla
- started a new approach to conservation
- worked in Rwanda
- established research centre
■ Threats
- hunters
- loss of habitat
- tourism
■ Fossey's work
- saved the gorillas from extinction
- began 'active conservationism'
- supported local population
- showed humans and natural world can work
  together

Note that while the outline is very brief, it still contains the most important ideas from the passage. Furthermore, the outline reflects the basic organization of the passage, which would be especially helpful for passage/prose summary questions. Regardless of what question type you are working on, by writing this information down, you may find that you understand the basic ideas of the passage better and remember them more clearly.

SOLUTION: Write down key words and ideas as you read the questions and answer options. Some people find it helpful to highlight key words while they read. However, on the day of the test, you will <u>not</u> be able to highlight any portion of the text on the computer screen. Instead, you can use your notepaper to write down any key words that will help you remember important ideas from the questions or the answer options. Then, you can refer to your list of key words and quickly scan for them in the reading passage.

» **CHALLENGE 5: "I have a hard time telling the difference between major supporting details and minor facts."**

SOLUTION: Try to understand the role of the details in the passage. By understanding how the details that you are confused about relate to the ideas in the passage, you will be able to sort the major details from the minor ideas. Use the steps in the table below to start understanding the roles of details in a passage.

Steps For Differentiating Between Major Supporting Details and Minor Facts	
Step 1	Skim the first paragraph to find the topic sentence. Topic sentences are sentences that express the main topic of a passage or paragraph. Regardless of the passage type or organizational style of a passage, each reading passage will have a major point that it is trying to make. The introduction will usually provide a brief background of the main topic and then present a topic sentence that summarizes the main point of the passage.
Step 2	Skim the body paragraphs to find the topic sentence for each paragraph. The topic sentences are usually located within the first two or three lines of the body paragraphs. By locating the topic sentences, you can start to understand what the main argument of the passage is and how the author has organized the flow of ideas.
Step 3	Once you've located the topic sentences and the main point of the passage is clear to you, quickly review the details that you are unsure about. Again, when you review details, make sure you scan the passage for the key words associated with those details in order to save time.
Step 4	When you read a sentence containing a detail you are unsure about, ask yourself the following question: If you were to leave out that particular detail, would the main point of the passage be weakened? If the answer is yes, the detail in question is probably a major detail. On the other hand, if leaving out the detail would <u>not</u> majorly change or weaken the main point of the passage, then the detail is a minor fact.

» CHALLENGE 6: "None of the answer options 'feels' right."

SOLUTION: Familiarize yourself with the question types and the skills required to answer each one. On the reading section, there are ten possible question types. By learning which skills each question type tests, you will better understand what to look for in a correct answer, which should help improve your intuition about the correct answers.

SOLUTION: Understand how correct answer options are created. While the correct answers on the reading section will vary in many ways, remember that one common feature of correct answer options is the rewording of key information. A correct answer option will <u>always</u> contain key information that you've read in the passage. However, the information is typically mixed up so that the correct answer option doesn't use the exact wording from the reading. In other words, the correct answer option will include paraphrased information from the reading passage. Information in answer options may be paraphrased by:

- changing out key words (i.e., using synonyms).
- including general information about a concept that is described in detail in the passage.
- changing the voice of the information from active to passive (or vice versa). The passive voice is formed by using the verb *be* + past participle.

SOLUTION: Use a process of elimination. A process of elimination involves reading each answer option carefully and eliminating options that are incorrect. Typically, you can eliminate answer options that contain:

- information that contradicts the facts and details presented in the passage.
- information that does <u>not</u> answer the question.
- the exact wording from the passage. Remember, the correct answer typically paraphrases information from the passage, so an answer option that includes the same wording is probably incorrect.

SOLUTION: Skip questions you are unsure about. Remember, you are allowed to return to previous questions on the reading section. However, you have only limited time to answer all of the questions in this section. For some people, it's easier to answer difficult questions once they've had some time to think about them. So if you find that you're spending too much time on one question and you aren't certain of the answer, move on to the next question or the next passage. You may find that it's easier to answer a difficult question when you return to it later.

Overview of the Listening Section

The listening section is the second part of the TOEFL iBT test. It tests your ability to understand spoken English by presenting you with a series of listening passages and then asking you a set of questions based on each listening passage.

QUICK GUIDE: TOEFL iBT® Computer Test

Definition	The listening section tests your comprehension of English lectures and conversations. The section includes different types of listening passages spoken by native speakers. Some passages are about academic topics, while others are about experiences that a student may encounter on campus.
Targeted Skills	In order to do well on the listening section, you must be able to: • understand basic academic vocabulary. • identify a speaker's meaning based on intonation and tone. • take good notes. • answer questions within the given time.
The Listening Passages	The listening section consists of five listening passages, which you hear through your headset. There are three different types of passages in the listening section: academic lectures, office hours conversations, and service encounter conversations (for more information about passage types, see pages 223–224). Each passage is between three and five minutes long, and you will hear each passage only once.
Questions	There are five or six questions per listening passage. After an academic lecture, you will answer six questions. After office hours and service conversations, you will answer five questions. The questions usually fall into the following categories: • Main Idea • Function • Detail • Attitude • Purpose • Organization • Inference • Connecting content
Timing	The clock will <u>not</u> run while you are listening to the passages. In other words, no time will be deducted while you are listening to the lectures / conversations. The entire section, including listening time, takes approximately **36 minutes** to complete.

PAPER EDITION: Please note that, in the Paper Edition of the TOEFL iBT test, the testing company ETS may include extra sample material. This sample material is not scored. However, since you will not know which passages are sample materials, you should try your best on all of the passages.

This means that the Paper Edition of the Listening section could be 28–39 questions, and you will be given 41–57 minutes to complete the Listening section of the Paper Edition.

For information on the Paper Edition of the test, please see page 208.

Listening Section

On-Screen Tools for the computer test

In the listening section, the information on the computer screen is slightly different than in other parts of the test. Study the sample screen below to familiarize yourself with the on-screen tools for the listening section.

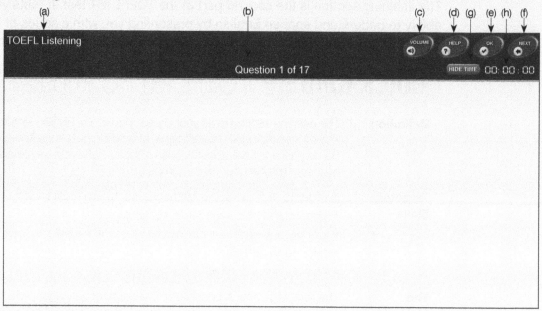

(a) indicates what **section of the test** you are currently working on

(b) shows how many of the **questions** you have **completed** in the section

(c) allows you to **adjust the volume** of the listening passages. When you click on this button, you will be able to move a slider up or down to increase or decrease the volume.

(d) allows you to **get important information** about the section. Keep in mind that the clock will continue to count down if you click on this button.

(e) is used to **confirm your answer**. You will make your answer choice on the screen and then click on this button to proceed to the next question (see *f*). Remember, once you go to the next question, you cannot go back to previous questions.

(f) is used to **move on to the next question**. You cannot proceed until you have confirmed your answer choice by clicking on the "OK" button (see *e*).

(g) allows you to hide / view the countdown clock

(h) shows how much time is left to answer the questions

Please note that the on-screen tools in your test may not be exactly like the ones above.

Listening Section: Passage Types

In the listening section, there are three types of listening passages: office hours conversations, service encounter conversations, and academic lectures. Each passage type differs in terms of content.

Office Hours Conversations   Office hours conversations typically focus on topics that may come up in a conversation between a student and a professor. In North American universities, office hours are a set time during which professors meet with students in order to answer questions or discuss school-related matters.

The office hours conversations on the TOEFL iBT test last between four and five minutes. Topics vary and may include:

- discussions of paper topics or assignments.
- inquiries for more information on or clarification of a concept introduced in class.
- requests for letters of recommendation or career advice.

Service Encounters   Meanwhile, service encounter conversations deal with issues that a student at a North American university may experience in a number of on-campus situations. Service encounter passages are conversations that occur between a university student and an employee of the university. The employee may work in any of the following departments:

- housing
- student life
- registrar
- financial aid
- campus security
- career services
- library

The service encounter conversations on the TOEFL iBT test last between three and five minutes. The topics of service encounter conversations are not academic; rather, they deal with issues that a student may experience while at a university. Sample topics of service encounter passages include:

- getting a new roommate
- joining a club
- adding or dropping a class
- learning about scholarships
- reporting a lost item
- advice for finding an on-campus job
- reserving a book at the library

Academic Lectures   Finally, academic lectures focus on academic topics that draw from a variety of academic subjects. These listening passages are similar to lectures given by professors that students might encounter in university classrooms. The topics for academic lectures are drawn from a wide range of academic subjects, including:

- anthropology
- archaeology
- art history
- astronomy
- biology
- botany
- education
- engineering
- environmental science
- geography
- geology
- history
- literature
- music
- paleontology
- photography
- psychology
- sociology
- urban studies

There are three academic lectures in the listening section of the computer-based TOEFL iBT test. The academic lectures can be further classified into three types: professors' lectures, integrated lectures, and in-class discussions. The main distinction between each type is the amount of student interaction. See the table below for more information on each type of academic lecture.

Professors' Lectures	Integrated Lectures	In-class Discussions
Professor talks 100% of the time.	Professor talks 75% of the time. Students may ask questions or provide brief answers to the professor's questions, but the bulk of the content is spoken by the professor.	Professor and two students have roughly the same amount of talking time. In this type of discussion, students often address each other in addition to speaking to the professor.

PAPER EDITION: In the Paper Edition of the TOEFL iBT test, there are three to four academic lectures in the listening section.

Challenges and Solutions

» **CHALLENGE 1: "I don't know a lot of the words that I hear in the audio recordings or see in the questions."**

SOLUTION: Expand your vocabulary. The TOEFL iBT test content focuses mainly on academic contexts. There are several word lists available that present the most common words found in academic settings. The Academic Word List (AWL), developed by Averil Coxhead, is a list of 570 words that are commonly included in introductory college texts. Getting to know these words will likely help you perform better on the test and prepare for entering English-language courses.

SOLUTION: Listen for definitions when you hear a word you don't know. When a specific term is introduced, the professor will <u>always</u> define the word in the lecture.

SOLUTION: Use the context, words, or phrases around unknown words in the recording, questions, or answer options to help you figure out meaning. In the listening section, speakers will often provide a number of meaning clues for the definitions of key terms. See the table below for common ways that speakers give context clues for key terms. To practice, try listening to English-language news programs or podcasts. Announcers often make the meaning of new terms clear by using these types of clues. Remember that you can often slow video and audio material down when listening online or using your player app.

Ways of Giving Context Clues			
Repetition	**Rewording**	**Definition Signposts**	**Giving Examples**
The speaker will repeat a key term several times in the same paragraph.	The speaker will often reword a phrase so that the meaning of a term is clearer. A rewording often includes the following phrases: • *By that, I mean . . .* • *What I'm talking about here is . . .* • *In other words . . .*	Speakers use certain terms to introduce a definition, including: • *This refers to . . .* • *This means . . .* • *That's a . . .* • *I think a definition is in order here.*	In order to clarify a definition, speakers will give examples. Listen for the following phrases for examples: • *like* • *such as* • *you know*
Example	**Example**	**Example**	**Example**
Animals use <u>camouflage</u> to protect themselves from predators. An animal might blend in with the background, and that's <u>camouflage</u>.	*Why do companies <u>vet</u> new hires? I mean, why do they <u>perform background checks and check out the potential employee's history</u>?*	*It's a matter of agency. <u>I think a definition is in order here.</u> Agency is people's ability to make choices that will influence their futures.*	*Engaging in <u>recreational activities, such as running or playing an instrument</u>, has been shown to reduce stress levels.*

» **CHALLENGE 2: "I get lost as I listen to lecture portions of the listening test."**

SOLUTION: The lectures in the listening section of the TOEFL iBT test are typically between three and five minutes long. Sometimes it's difficult to stay focused throughout the test. One way to avoid problems with this is to learn the organizational structure of TOEFL iBT listening passages. If you understand how each passage is generally structured, you will be able to better predict what type of information will be included in the lecture and where this information will appear in the lecture. If you lose concentration while listening, you just have to think about how the passage is structured in order to get back on track. Note that nearly all of the academic lectures in the TOEFL iBT listening section follow one of the following common organizational structures:

- definition
- pros and cons (advantages and disadvantages)
- cause and effect
- theory / support
- compare and contrast
- process
- classification

To practice, try listening to some of the lectures on the audio for this book. See if you can identify what types of structures they are.

SOLUTION: Listen for signposts. A signpost is a word or phrase that is used to signal a specific type of information in a listening passage. For example, some signposts signal the introduction of a new topic (*On another note . . .*), while others signal the definition of a key term (e.g., *By that, I mean . . .*). By listening for signposts, you can get a better sense of what is happening in the lecture, which will help you become focused again. To practice, listen to a recording of a lecture from this book and write down all the signpost words you hear. Then, check your notes against the script. How many did you notice?

SOLUTION: Recognize what information is important and what is not. During a listening passage, speakers often digress, or talk about information that is not directly related to the main topic of the lecture or conversation. If you get lost while you are listening, recognizing digressions will help you refocus on the important information. See the table below for words and expressions that are often used to introduce digressions.

Expressions that Signal Digressions
Now, this won't be on the test, but it's interesting to think about.
You don't have to write this down, but consider that . . .
Just as an aside, I want you all to know that . . .
This is only somewhat related, but . . .
It doesn't really make a difference to what we're discussing today, but don't you think that . . . ?
Don't let this confuse you, because it doesn't really apply to what we're talking about today.
This may be oversimplified, but for the purposes of today's lecture, it's really all you need to know about X.

» **CHALLENGE 3: "I don't always understand the conversations in the audio recordings—there's so much back and forth and corrections and other stuff."**

SOLUTION: Like written English, spoken English is vital to communication. However, unlike written language, spoken language is more informal and includes interruptions, mispronunciations, repetition, clarifications, pauses, intonation changes to make a point, etc. The listening passages on the TOEFL iBT test are authentic-sounding lectures and conversations and include many common features of spoken language.

Try listening to the audio passages in this book and notice features like interruptions, misspeaks, and repetitions. These features are included in order to make the listening passages sound more natural. By noting and understanding how speakers use these features, you will become more accustomed to the flow of the listening passages on the TOEFL iBT test.

Common Features of Spoken English			
	Interruptions	**Misspeaks / Corrections**	**Repetition**
Examples	*Pardon me . . .*	*Now, their meaning is entirely explicit—or rather, entirely implicit.*	*OK, this is important.*
	Wait, but what about . . . ?		*Let me say that again.*
	A: So you're a junior and— *B: A senior, actually.*	*Another difference between the two animals is that salamanders—sorry, I mean lizards—can live in a much drier environment.*	*Did you get that?*

Common Features of Spoken English		
Interruptions	**Misspeaks / Corrections**	**Repetition**
Typically, if someone interrupts another person, the information is important. For example, a person might interrupt the other speaker to give correct or updated information.	When a speaker misspeaks, be sure to write down the correction, since answer options for detail questions are often based on these.	Repeated information is often tested on the TOEFL iBT test. If you hear repeated information, write it down in your notes.

(Notes)

SOLUTION: Get used to the flow of native English by exposing yourself to as much natural English as possible. The more exposure you have to native English speech, the more you'll understand the native English used on the TOEFL iBT test. Ways for increasing your exposure to spoken English include:

- watching TV shows or movies. The TV shows don't have to be educational—comedies and dramas include great examples of natural spoken English. While you watch, note how people often interrupt others, correct themselves after making a mistake, or quickly change topics. If you find this difficult, try watching movies with subtitles. Listening can be easier when you can read to check understanding.

- joining an English-language speaking club. You might find that your university, local library, or community center has one. By joining, you will not only be able to practice speaking English, you will also have the opportunity to hear native speakers and take part in natural conversations.

» **CHALLENGE 4: "There's too much information to remember!"**

SOLUTION: During the TOEFL iBT test, you will listen to the passage first and then see the questions one at a time. The listening passages may include a lot of information, but remember that you are allowed to take notes during this portion of the test. Because of this, it's important to develop your note-taking skills. Taking notes during the lectures / conversations will force you to listen carefully and help you remember important information that you'll need to answer the questions. Of course, you won't be able to write down <u>all</u> that you hear, but using the following note-taking strategies will help you write down the most important information.

- Use abbreviations. You won't have enough time to write everything out, so be sure to use shorter forms whenever possible. Also, use abbreviations that make sense to you—it won't help you if you write something down but don't remember what it means. See the table below for tips for abbreviations. Then, practice writing down things you hear using abbreviations, but remember to be sure you understand what they mean!

Abbreviation Tip	Examples
Use numerals instead of writing out numbers.	one, two, three, etc. → 1, 2, 3, etc.
Leave the vowels out of words.	conversation, forest, novel → cnvrstn, frst, nvl
Use symbols instead of words.	Jane and Jack → Jane + Jack Jane or Jack → Jane / Jack everyone except Jack → everyone -Jack the numbers increased → the #s ↑ eight hundred dollars → $800 fifty percent → 50% at → @

Abbreviation Tip	Examples	
Use common abbreviations.	without → w/o	because → b/c
	within → w/in	before → b4
	approximately → approx.	example → ex.
	et cetera → etc.	regarding → re.

- During the lectures, some key words might appear on whiteboards—just like the kind you see in classrooms—on your screen. Write down terms that appear on the whiteboard. While you usually won't be tested on the definition of these terms, they may be related to important ideas, so having them in your notes will be useful.

- Make note of information that is emphasized by the speaker. Be sure to mark in your notes which speaker made the comments. Speakers often emphasize information by changing their tone. In other cases, information may be emphasized by the amount of time that is spent talking about one subject. In either case, be sure to underline that information in your notes so you know that it was emphasized.

- Organize your notes as you write. It can be very helpful to write down the following words and use them as headings:

  - Main Idea
  - Detail 1
  - Support
  - Detail 2
  - Support

  Then, if you leave room beneath each of the above points, you can write down supporting details under them later. By organizing your notes well, you will be able to look at them and understand how the lecture / conversation was organized. Furthermore, it might be helpful to keep a log of the notes you take while doing the activities in this book. Later, you can review them and look for ways to better organize your notes.

» **CHALLENGE 5: "I don't always understand the speakers. Sometimes they talk too fast."**

SOLUTION: The speakers in the listening passages on the TOEFL iBT test are native speakers of English. Differences in pronunciation and speed reflect the way that native speakers of English actually talk. There are many common English reductions that you may hear on the TOEFL iBT test. Reductions are shortened forms of certain word combinations that omit sounds or blend two or more words. Reductions are very common in the listening passages of the TOEFL iBT test, so make sure you know how they are formed. Study the table below for common reductions. You can practice by listening to audio passages from this book and noticing the reductions. Are some harder than others to understand? Focus on them, and listen as many times as it takes for the meanings to become clear.

Common Reductions in the Listening Section

Who did you go to the movies with?	→ *Whodja go to the movies with?*
What did you do that for?	→ *Whatdja do that for?*
When did you finish?	→ *Whendja finish?*
Where did you get those shoes?	→ *Wheredja get those shoes?*
How did you do on the test?	→ *Howdja do on the test?*
How have you been doing?	→ *Howvya been doing?*
Don't you like him?	→ *Doncha like 'im?*
Did you talk to her?	→ *Didja talk to 'er?*
What are you going to do?	→ *What are you gonna do?*
How about this one?	→ *How 'bout this one?*
I'm trying to finish my homework.	→ *I'm tryna finish my homework.*
A lot of people were there.	→ *Alotta people were there.*
I don't know.	→ *I dunno.*
I've got to go now.	→ *I've gotta go now.*
Could you help me with this?	→ *Couldja help me with this?*

SOLUTION: Download some English-language podcasts or radio programs that you can store on your computer. At first, practice listening to only a minute or two of the program at a time. As your comprehension improves, increase the listening time to seven minutes, the maximum time limit for any one TOEFL iBT listening passage. When you listen, focus on understanding the speakers' pronunciation throughout the entire program. Listen to the programs as many times as you need to until you understand the main ideas.

SOLUTION: If possible, purchase a digital recording device with variable-speed playback capabilities. Using a variable-speed digital recorder, you can record English-language radio broadcasts, television shows, and podcasts. At first, you can play back this media at a slow speed. As your comprehension level increases, you can increase the playback speed until you are listening to the broadcasts at their original speed.

» **CHALLENGE 6: "None of the answer options 'feels' right. It's as if the lecture and the answer options are not related."**

SOLUTION: The writers of the TOEFL iBT test are looking to see if you can understand and interpret what is said, how it is said, and what it may or may not mean. Therefore, it's important to understand how correct answer options are created so you will be able to identify the correct option more easily. One extremely common feature of correct answer options on the TOEFL iBT test is the rewording of key information. Basically, a correct answer option will <u>always</u> contain key words that you've heard in the lecture / conversation. However, the correct answer option typically mixes up the information and doesn't contain the exact wording from the listening passage. In other words, the correct answer option will include paraphrased information from the listening passage. Information in answer options may be paraphrased by:

- changing out key content words (using synonyms).
- including general information about a concept that is described in detail in the listening.
- changing the voice of the information from passive to active (or vice versa) in the answer option (e.g., *The boy <u>hit</u> the ball.* vs. *The ball <u>was hit</u> by the boy.*). The passive voice is formed by using a form of the verb *be* + past participle.

Study the table on the next page for specific examples of how paraphrasing may be used on the TOEFL iBT test. If you want to practice, after you complete an activity in this book, try to identify the paraphrase types used in some of the answer options. This may help you improve your ability to recognize correct and incorrect answers.

Paraphrase Type	You'll Hear This in the Lecture:	You'll See a Question Like This:	You'll See Answer Options Like This:
Changes to Content Words	*The bengal scampered swiftly.*	How did the tiger run?	Fast (✓) Slowly (✗)
Specific to General	*OK, you'll just need to tell me your mailing address, date of birth, and student ID number.*	What does the clerk ask for?	Some personal information (✓) A change of address form (✗)
Voice Changes	*The make up exam was given by the TA on Friday.*	What happened at the end of the week?	The students retook the test. (✓) The TA took the test again. (✗)

(✓) correct answer option
(✗) incorrect answer option

SOLUTION: Use a process of elimination. Read each answer option carefully and draw a line through those that contain:

- information that states the opposite of the facts and details presented in the passage.
- information that does <u>not</u> answer the question.
- the exact wording from the passage. Remember, the correct answer typically paraphrases information from the passage, so an answer option that includes the same wording is probably incorrect.

SOLUTION: Don't spend too much time answering any one question. If you aren't certain of an answer, select whatever answer option you feel is the most appealing and move on to the next question.

Overview of the Speaking Section

The speaking section tests your ability to speak English by presenting you with a variety of tasks. During this section, you will wear a headset. The headphones of the headset are noise-canceling, which means that you will not be able to hear noise around you, including the other test-takers giving their responses while you are working on the section. The headset is also equipped with a microphone that you can adjust so that your spoken responses can be digitally recorded.

QUICK GUIDE: TOEFL iBT® Test

Definition	The speaking section tests your ability to understand written and spoken English and respond to questions appropriately. For each question, you will be presented with a specific task that may test the following skills: reading, listening and speaking, listening and speaking, and speaking only.
Targeted Skills	In order to do well on the speaking section, you must be able to: • understand and respond to questions. • express your opinion about a subject. • report the ideas and / or opinions of other people. • summarize the main idea of a listening passage. • combine information from different sources. • answer questions within the given time.
The Questions	The speaking section includes four distinct questions. The first question is an independent question, and the remaining three are integrated tasks.
Timing	The time that you have to prepare and respond to each question varies by question type. See the list below for the order in which the questions appear on the test and the preparation and response times for each question type.

Question Type	Preparation	Response
1. Paired Choice	15 seconds	45 seconds
2. Campus Matters	30 seconds	60 seconds
3. Academic Reading and Lecture	30 seconds	60 seconds
4. Academic Summary	20 seconds	60 seconds

The entire section takes approximately **16 minutes** to complete.

Please note that the computer version and Paper Edition of the TOEFL iBT test are the same. The speaking section is the third part of the TOEFL iBT computer-based test and the Home Edition of the TOEFL iBT test.

If you are taking the Paper Edition of the TOEFL iBT test, the Speaking test is taken at home in a separate session monitored online by a human proctor, within three days of the test center appointment.

Speaking Section

On-screen Tools for the computer test

You will see a number of on-screen tools during the speaking section. Study the sample screen below to familiarize yourself with the on-screen tools for the speaking section.

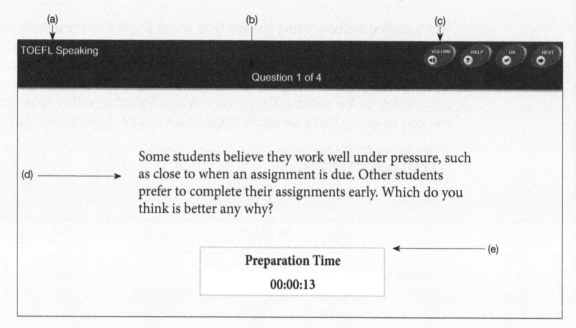

(a) indicates what **section of the test** you are currently working on

(b) shows how many of the **questions** you have **completed** in the section

(c) allows you to **adjust the volume** of the listening passages. When you click on this button, you will be able to move a slider up or down in order to increase or decrease the volume.

(d) shows you the prompt on the screen. You will also hear the narrator reading the prompt through the headphones.

(e) shows how much time you have left to prepare. During your response time, the on-screen clock will show how much time you have left to respond.

Please note that the on-screen tools in your test may not be exactly like the ones above.

Speaking Section: Item Types

In the speaking section, there are two types of items: an independent question and integrated questions. The main difference between the item types is the skills involved in answering them. One involves speaking only, another involves listening and speaking, while others still involve a combination of listening, reading, and speaking.

Independent Task: The first question (Paired Choice question) is an independent task. For this question, you will be asked a short question about general topics.

Independent Task
Question 1

Skill: Speaking Only

You will be presented with two options. You will state the option that you prefer and provide support based on your personal experiences. Again, you do not need any specific academic knowledge.

Integrated Tasks: The remaining three questions in the speaking section are integrated tasks. These tasks require you to use a combination of skills in order to answer the questions.

Integrated Tasks	
Questions 2 and 3	Question 4
Skills: Reading / Listening / Speaking	**Skills: Listening / Speaking**
First, you will read a text. Then, you will hear a listening passage on the same topic of the text. The question will involve combining information from the text and the listening passage.	First, you will hear a listening passage. Then, you will answer a question that is based on the listening passage. In your response, you will have to summarize the information from the listening passage.

Speaking Section: Scoring: The responses that you give on the speaking section are digitally recorded and sent to ETS, where they are scored by human raters. Three raters will review each response and give it a rating of 1–4, with 4 being the highest score possible. The 3 ratings are added together, and the sum is converted to a score that falls on the 0–30 score range.

When scoring your responses, the raters will listen to the entire response and assign you a rating based on your overall skill. This means that it's possible to make a few mistakes and still receive a top score as long as your overall response fulfills the general scoring criteria described below.

Scoring Category	What Raters Will Be Looking For
Delivery	• You don't speak too fast or too slowly. • You make use of all of the allowed time when you give your response. • Your language is easy to understand.
Language Usage	• You use proper grammar in your response. • You use varied vocabulary. • You are able to produce complex sentence structures in English.
Topic Development	• You stay on topic for the duration of your response. • Your response is well organized and easy to understand. • You provide sufficient support for your response. • You clearly show the relationships between your ideas.

Please note that raters don't expect your response to be perfect. For example, some pronunciation and / or intonation mistakes are OK as long as you can still be understood.

Challenges and Solutions

» **CHALLENGE 1: "I don't know what to say when I give my answers."**

SOLUTION: Learn exactly what ETS is looking for in an answer. While the scoring criteria vary slightly according to the question, there are some general features that every response on the speaking section should include. Look at the scoring guide on pages 233–234 for a general overview of how your responses will be scored. The explanations for each question in *Skills for the TOEFL iBT® Test: Listening and Speaking* also provide a more detailed guide as to what you should include in your responses. Knowing ahead of time exactly what information you will be expected to give for each question will give you a general idea of what to say on the day of the test.

SOLUTION: Quickly write a bare-bones outline of your response. Depending on the question, you will have between 15 and 30 seconds to prepare your response. You should use this time to quickly prepare an outline of your response. Don't bother writing out the entire response; rather, you should focus on writing down a few words to help you remember and organize the key parts of your response. This will serve as a guide for you when you start speaking and help keep you from freezing during the response time.

Also, remember that the preparation time won't start until after the narrator has finished reading the question. Since the question also appears on your screen, you can earn some extra time to prepare by reading the question yourself and starting to write your outline as soon as you have read and understood the question. Finally, remember that people tend to lose focus when they feel nervous. By preparing an outline, you will feel more confident when you give your response, which will keep you from rambling.

SOLUTION: Use the templates found in the Get Set sections of this book to organize your answers. For each question type, there is specific information that you must include in your response. By understanding what information you need to include for each question type, you will have a better idea of what you need to say during the response time.

Templates by Question Type

Question 1
Restatement of the Prompt
Topic Sentence
    Key Point 1
        Personal Details
    Key Point 2
        Personal Details

Question 2
Proposed Change
    Reason 1 for Change
    Reason 2 for Change
Student's Opinion
    Reason 1 for Opinion
        Supporting Details
    Reason 2 for Opinion
        Supporting Details

Question 3
Reading and Lecture Topic
    Relationship Between Sources
Key Point 1 from Reading
    Support from Lecture
Key Point 2 from Reading
    Support from Lecture

Question 4
Main Topic of Lecture
    Key Point 1
        Supporting Details
    Key Point 2
        Supporting Details

» **CHALLENGE 2: "I always run out of time and end up getting cut off before presenting all my information."**

SOLUTION: Time yourself when you practice for questions in the speaking section. There are many practice speaking items provided in this book. A good strategy for preparing for the speaking section is to use a clock to time yourself when you complete the practice sections. The following chart shows how much time to give yourself for each question.

Response Times by Question	
Question 1 Paired Choice **45 seconds**	**Question 2** Campus Matters **60 seconds**
Question 3 Academic Reading and Lecture **60 seconds**	**Question 4** Academic Summary **60 seconds**

By timing yourself while you practice, you will learn how to pace yourself when giving your responses. That way, you won't speak too fast (or too slowly) and you will be able to give a complete response during the allotted time.

SOLUTION: Use the on-screen tools to help you determine how much time you have left. When you give a response in the speaking section, you will see a clock on your computer screen that will count down how much time you have left to respond. While you are speaking your answer into the microphone, check the clock to determine whether you will have enough time to finish your response. If you see that you have only a little time left, try to speed up, but not so much that your speech is difficult to understand.

SOLUTION: Focus on quality and not quantity. The raters are not concerned with how much information you can provide in the given time. Rather, they want to know if you can give a response that adequately answers the question. If you organize your response using the templates provided in this book, you are sure to provide all of the information that raters are looking for in a top-scoring response—and none of the extra information that will waste your given response time.

An added advantage of using the templates to organize your responses is that they will help you reduce the number of fillers you use while you give your response. Fillers are words or sounds that speakers use to get extra time while they think of what to say next. In English, common fillers include *um*, *uh*, and *like*. When you organize your response before you start speaking, you won't need to use fillers to think of what you will say next. This will help you save time when you give your response.

» **CHALLENGE 3: "I'm scared to speak. It's not common to give opinions in my country."**

SOLUTION: Know which questions in the speaking section require you to express opinions. Some questions require you to give your opinion, while others ask you to describe the opinions of other people. Knowing this information will help you prepare before you take the test. Use the table below to help you know when and how to use opinion language.

Question	Whose Opinion Will You Give?	Expressions You Can Use in Your Response
Question 1: Paired Choice	Give <u>your own opinion</u> about which of the two provided options is best.	• *While some people think that X, I personally believe that . . .* • *I know that some people feel differently, but it's my opinion that . . .* • *I realize that not everybody will agree, but I think that . . .* • *Of the two choices given, I strongly believe that . . .* • *Other people might disagree, but my view is that . . .*
Question 2: Campus Matters	Give the opinion of <u>one student in the conversation</u>. One student in the conversation will either strongly agree or disagree with the campus matter. Do <u>not</u> give your own opinion for this task!	• *The woman feels that . . .* • *The man in the conversation thinks X is a good / bad idea.* • *The woman says she supports / opposes . . .* • *In the man's opinion, X is a good / bad plan . . .* • *The woman's view is that X is positive / negative . . .*

Each question type in the speaking section is addressed in detail and includes more opinion language for specific question types.

SOLUTION: Be aware that there are no right or wrong opinions on the TOEFL iBT test. In other words, you are <u>not</u> being graded based on your opinions themselves. What's really important is how well you support your opinion in your response. For questions that require you to give your own opinion, try to determine which opinion would be easiest to support. If you think of it this way, you will feel more confident about speaking your opinions because you will know that you can support them. Also, remember that giving an opinion on the TOEFL iBT test is just part of a task—it's not an activity that exposes you or your personal feelings.

» **CHALLENGE 4: "I forget most of the information given in the reading passages and audio recordings as I'm giving my response."**

SOLUTION: Know what to expect. Three of the four tasks in the speaking section are integrated tasks. This means that they require listening / speaking skills or a combination of reading / listening / speaking skills. Although you can't know exactly which topics will appear on the test, by studying in this book the descriptions of each question type, you will understand how the reading and listening passages are organized and what type of information is typically included in them. This knowledge might help you fill in the gaps or guess the general ideas of the information you've forgotten.

For example, imagine that you are on question 2 (Campus Matters) on the test and you can't remember what the conversation was about. If you know that the speakers in Campus Matters questions <u>always</u> talk about a problem that one of the speakers is having, it might help you remember other details, too.

SOLUTION: Take notes! While you read or listen, you should be sure to write down important information that you can use in your response. How do you know what information is important? If you're familiar with all of the question types, you'll know what information you'll be expected to include in your responses. Study the table below for the basic information you should be writing down for each question type.

Question	Skills	What You Should Write Down
Question 2: Campus Matters	Reading / Listening	<u>Reading</u> • Proposed change • Two reasons for change <u>Listening (Conversation)</u> • Student's opinion of change • Two reasons for that opinion
Question 3: Academic Reading and Lecture	Reading / Listening	<u>Reading</u> • Main idea • Two key points <u>Listening (Lecture)</u> • Two supporting details for topic from reading
Question 4: Academic Lecture	Listening	• Main topic of lecture • Two key points

» **CHALLENGE 5: "On the integrated tasks, I never have enough time to finish reading the reading passage before the audio recording begins."**

SOLUTION: Be prepared to begin reading the passages for Questions 2 and 3 as soon as they appear on the screen. On the day of the test, the reading passage will appear on the screen while the narrator introduces the passage. Don't wait until the narrator finishes speaking to begin reading. By beginning to read while the narrator is still speaking, you will gain a few extra seconds to read the passage.

SOLUTION: Use the on-screen tools to help you keep track of how much time you have. Remember, when the narrator finishes introducing the reading topic, the clock on the screen will begin counting down the time. As you read, look at the clock to see how much time you have left. You may need to read faster or scan for details (see below) if you are running out of time.

SOLUTION: Time yourself while you read excerpts from textbooks and on-campus notices. The practice readings should be about 100 words each, and you should give yourself 45 seconds to read each one. If you practice reading the same types of texts that appear on the test, you're more likely to improve your reading speed.

To find texts like those that appear on Campus Matters questions, try visiting student-life sections of university websites. These sites are likely to have announcements about campus events or notices that are similar to those that appear on the test.

To find texts like those on Academic Reading and Lecture questions, look through introductory textbooks. Be sure to look for subjects that commonly appear on the TOEFL iBT test, including biology, botany, marketing, sociology, and psychology.

SOLUTION: Practice scanning texts for major details. In some cases, you will not have time to read all of the text that is provided on the test. If you don't think you will be able to finish reading in the time you have left, you will need to scan the rest of the reading for important details. This means quickly looking for important details that will help you create a strong response. Look for the signposts below to help you quickly find the key points and supporting details while you scan.

Key Points Signposts	Supporting Details Signposts
The first / second reason . . .	For example . . .
Another example of . . .	According to . . .
Furthermore . . .	A recent survey shows . . .
In addition . . .	To illustrate . . .
Other ways that . . .	For instance . . .

Overview of the Writing Section

The writing section tests your ability to create written responses based on two different types of prompts. For the first prompt, you will read a short passage, listen to an academic lecture on the same topic, then write an essay which combines information from both sources. For the second prompt, the question differs depending on whether you are taking the computer-based version of the TOEFL iBT test or the Paper Edition.

The second question in the computer-based version of the Writing section requires you to state and support an opinion in an online classroom discussion (Writing for an Academic Discussion).

In the second question in the Paper Edition of the Writing section, you will read a short question about a familiar topic and write an essay in response to that question (Personal Experience Essay).

QUICK GUIDE: TOEFL iBT® Computer Test

Definition	The writing section tests your ability to understand written and spoken English and respond to prompts in writing. For each question, you will be required to understand the task, know how to write a well-organized response, and incorporate main ideas and details to answer the question.
Targeted Skills	In order to do well on the writing section you must be able to: • understand prompts that appear in writing. • take notes on material you hear and/or read, then combine them to create a well-organized response. • summarize and paraphrase ideas from a listening and/or reading passage. • express your ideas or the ideas of other people about a subject. • create a well-organized response in a limited time.
The Questions	The writing section comprises two questions. The first is an integrated writing task and the second is an academic discussion writing task (for more information about question types, see page 241).
Timing	The time that you have to prepare and respond to each question varies by question type.

Question 1: Integrated Task		Question 2: Academic Discussion Task	
Reading*	3 minutes	n / a	
Listening	3–5 minutes	n / a	
Writing Time	20 minutes	Writing Time	10 minutes

You will have **29 minutes** to complete the entire section.

*Remember, in Question 1 you will be able to see the reading on the screen while you write your essay but you will not be able to replay the listening passage. The reading passage will disappear from the screen while you listen to the lecture that follows but it will reappear when you begin writing so that you can refer to it as you work.

PAPER EDITION: Please note that, in the Paper Edition of the TOEFL iBT test, Question 2 is an independent task, where test-takers have 30 minutes to answer. The total test time is 50 minutes.

For information on the Paper Edition of the test, please see page 241.

Writing Section: Task Types

In the writing section, there are two types of tasks: integrated questions and independent questions. The main difference between the types of tasks is the skills involved in answering them.

Question 1: Integrated Task	Question 2 COMPUTER TEST: Academic Discussion Task	Question 2 PAPER TEST: Personal Experience Essay
The first task in the writing section (Reading / Lecture Synthesis Essay) is an integrated task. This task requires you to use a combination of reading, listening, and writing skills.	The second question on the COMPUTER TEST requires you to state and support an opinion in an online classroom discussion.	The second question (Personal Experience Essay) on the PAPER TEST is an independent task. For this question, you will write an essay about a general topic.

Writing Section: Scoring

The answers that you type for the writing section are sent to the ETS® Online Scoring Network. The TOEFL iBT test uses AI scoring to complement human scoring for the two tasks in the Writing section. Your responses will be reviewed and given a rating of 1–5. The scores are then added and converted to a score that falls on the 0–30 score range.

When scoring your responses, the raters will read the entire answer and assign you a rating based on your overall skill. This means that it's possible to make a few mistakes and still receive a top score as long as your overall response fulfills the general scoring criteria described below:

Scoring Category	What Raters Will Be Looking For in the Responses to Question 1	What Raters Will Be Looking For in the Responses to Question 2 COMPUTER TEST	What Raters Will Be Looking For in the Responses to Question 2 PAPER TEST
Topic Development	• You connected information from the reading passage and the lecture. • You explained the professor's position by providing specific details from the lecture. • You wrote between 125 and 225 words.	• A clearly stated opinion, whether you agree or disagree with the question or to what extent you agree. • You added to the ideas from the other contributors and did not simply repeat their points. Make sure your points are relevant and contain enough detail. • You supported your key point or points by using examples and details. • You wrote a minimum of 100 words.	• Your introduction clearly stated whether you agreed or disagreed with the statement. • You explained each of your key points by using specific personal examples and details. • You wrote at least 300 words.
Organization and Clarity	• You wrote a five-paragraph essay that included an introduction, three body paragraphs, and a conclusion. • Each body paragraph addresses a key point from the reading as well as the professor's position on that point. • You used transition words throughout your essay.	• You were aware of the task context: if it is a post to a discussion group it is not as formal as an academic essay but not as informal as a text message. • You used transitions to improve the flow of your answer.	• You wrote a five-paragraph essay that included an introduction, three body paragraphs and a conclusion. • Each body paragraph introduced a distinct key point which you supported with personal details and examples. • You used transitions to improve the flow of your essay.
Language Usage	• You used correct grammar and punctuation. • You made few, if any, spelling errors. • You used a variety of sentence structures and displayed a broad vocabulary.		

Challenges and Solutions

» **CHALLENGE 1: "I don't have time to write a complete essay."**

SOLUTION: Know the template for fully answering each question. That way you know what information you must include in your essay in order to get a high score. Then you can spend the majority of your time organizing your essay and thinking of good supporting details.

Template for Task 1	Template for Task 2: COMPUTER TEST	Template for Task 2: PAPER
Paragraph 1: Main topic from reading; Main topic from the lecture	**First sentences:** Recap the subject and state and support your opinion.	**Paragraph 1:** Topic sentence; Summary of Key Points
Paragraph 2: Key Point 1 from reading; Key Point 1 from lecture; Support from lecture	**Next sentences:** Provide some background to the issue – set the scene before you give your reasons.	**Paragraph 2:** Key Point 1; ersonal details
Paragraph 3: Key Point 2 from reading; Key Point 2 from lecture; Support from lecture	**Next sentences:** Give your own opinion or perspective about the discussion. Don't repeat ideas in the text. Make sure your point contributes to the discussion. You can make an additional point to those in the text or an opposite point or partially agree or disagree and say why.	**Paragraph 3:** Key Point 2; Personal details
Paragraph 4: Key Point 3 from reading; Key Point 3 from lecture; Support from lecture	**Next sentences:** Include appropriate examples, reasons, and details that clearly support your own viewpoint.	**Paragraph 4:** Key Point 3; Personal details
Paragraph 5: Conclusion	**Final sentence:** Sum up or conclude your position.	**Paragraph 5:** Conclusion

SOLUTION: Be aware of how much time you have. On the day of the test, you will see how much time is remaining on the on-screen clock that appears on the upper right side of the screen. While you work, be sure to check the clock. Use the following timing guide while you write:

Timing for Task 1 Total time: 20 minutes		Timing for Task 2: COMPUTER Total time: 10 minutes		Timing for Task 2: PAPER Total time: 30 minutes	
Time on the Clock	What you should be doing	Time on the Clock	What you should be doing	Time on the Clock	What you should be doing
20:00–18:00	Review notes and write a quick outline. Just write a few words to help you remember what you will write down.	10:00–9:00	Read the prompts carefully and brainstorm the topic. Try to come up with as many points as you can. Choose how you want to answer based on your points.	30:00–25:00	Read the prompt carefully and brainstorm the topic. Try to come up with as many points as you can for each side. Choose the side with the most supporting points.
18:00–4:00	Write your essay. Be sure that your essay has five paragraphs and that you include specific details from the professor's lecture in your essay.	9:00–1:00	Write your answer. Be sure to include relevant examples and explanations that refer to the points in the prompts.	25:00–4:00	Write your essay. Be sure that your essay has five paragraphs and that you include personal details to support your key points.
4:00–0:00	Review and edit your essay. Be sure to look for misspelled words and ungrammatical sentences.	1:00–0:00	Review and edit your answer. Be sure to look for misspelled words and ungrammatical sentences.	4:00–0:00	Review and edit your essay. Be sure to look for misspelled words and ungrammatical sentences.

SOLUTION: Practice typing as much as possible before the test. On the day of the test, you will have to type your essay on the computer. If you do not type fast, you will not be able to write your essay within the given time. So you should make sure to practice typing before the test in order to improve your typing speed.

» **CHALLENGE 2: "I'm afraid that the raters will not understand the ideas in my essay."**

SOLUTION: Use transition words. Transition words are expressions that connect two sentences together by indicating a shift in focus, continuing in the same line of thinking, drawing a conclusion, clarifying a point, indicating sequence, etc. If you use transition words throughout your essay, you will be able to improve the flow of your response and make it easier to understand. Use the following table as a reference of transition language and their uses:

Function	Transition Language	
Shift in focus	but	nonetheless
	conversely	on the contrary
	despite	on the other hand
	however	still
	in contrast	though
	nevertheless	yet
Continuing in the same line of thinking	additionally	furthermore
	also	in addition
	and	likewise
	besides that	moreover
Drawing a conclusion	accordingly	hence
	as a result	indeed
	consequently	therefore
	for that reason	thus
Clarifying a point	in other words	that is to say
	specifically	namely
Indicating Sequence	after	later
	as soon as	meanwhile
	before	next
	finally	soon
	in the first place	then
Giving Examples	For example,…	
	Take X, for instance.	
	One example of X is…	

SOLUTION: Work on improving your spelling. Remember, during the test there won't be an automatic spell-checker for you to rely on. While a few misspelled words won't affect your score, if you spell a lot of words incorrectly, it may keep the raters from understanding your meaning. One way to improve your spelling is to read a lot. This is because the more you see words in English, the more you will understand how common words are spelled. Another way to help your spelling is to practice writing. When you check your writing, circle all the misspelled words and make sure you learn how to spell them correctly.

SOLUTION: Don't use an idiomatic expression unless you are <u>sure</u> you know what it means. When the raters score your essay, they will look at how well you can use idiomatic expressions. However, if you use an idiomatic expression incorrectly, it will only harm your score.

» **CHALLENGE 3: "I have trouble talking about opinions."**

SOLUTION: Know when you will be required to express opinions. Question 1 asks you to describe the opinions of the professor while Question 2 requires you to give your opinion. Knowing this information will help you prepare before you take the test. Use the table below to help you know when and how to use opinion language.

Question	Whose Opinion Will You Give?	Expressions You Can Use in Your Response
Question 1: Academic Reading / Listening Synthesis Task	State the opinion of professor. The professor will clearly express agreement or disagreement with the main topic and provide three reasons to support this position. Do not give your own opinion for this task!	• The professor feels that . . . • In the lecture, the professor says that X is a good / bad idea. • The professor says she supports / opposes . . . • In the professor's opinion, X is good / bad . . . • The professor's view is that X is positive / negative . . . • The professor agrees / disagrees with the claim that . . .
Question 2: Personal Experience Task	Give your own opinion about whether you agree or disagree with the statement.	• While some people think that X, I personally believe that . . . • I know that some people feel differently, but it's my opinion that . . . • It's my opinion that . . . • I agree/disagree with the idea that . . . • Other people might disagree, but my view is that . . .

SOLUTION: Learn basic citation skills. On the **academic reading / lecture synthesis task**, you have to talk about attitudes that come from either a reading passage or an audio passage. Use the following citation expressions to indicate whether the information came from the reading or the lecture.

Expressions for Citing the Source
The author / professor thinks / feels that . . . The author / professor agrees / disagrees / opposes / supports . . . According to the passage / professor, . . . In the conversation, the professor says / argues / points out / makes the point that . . . In the reading / lecture, the author / professor says . . . . The author / professor supports X by saying / pointing out / arguing / giving an example of . . .

» CHALLENGE 4: "For the academic reading / lecture synthesis task, I'm supposed to reword the information from the passage and the lecture, but this is very difficult for me."

SOLUTION: Make sure you completely understand the meaning of what you are trying to paraphrase. When you paraphrase, you put the information from a source in your own words. But you can't do this effectively if you don't fully understand the meaning. Remember, the reading will appear on the screen, so you will be able to refer to the passage and review parts that you want to paraphrase to make sure you understand them. For the lecture, you should review your notes to make sure that you fully understand the main points made by the professor.

SOLUTION: Learn synonyms for common words that appear on the test. After all, part of paraphrasing involves using synonyms of key terms and phrases. So, by learning synonyms of words that commonly appear on the test, you will be able to paraphrase with ease. To practice, reread one of the reading passages for the integrated writing task in this book. Choose 10–15 key words that appear in the passage. Then look in a thesaurus for synonyms of these words and make a list to study and learn. You can then use these synonyms in your paraphrased sentence. See below for examples of how to use synonyms in your paraphrases.

Original Wording	Paraphrased Version Using Synonyms
A Lazarus taxon is a *species*[1] that was once *believed*[2] to have been extinct, but is later found to be *alive*[3].	*Types of organisms*[1] that were *thought*[2] to be extinct and are later found to still *exist*[3] are called a Lazarus taxon.
One advantage of using *surveys*[1] for *data collection*[2] is that it *allows*[3] *researchers*[4] to *ask*[5] *consumers*[6] questions about their attitudes and shopping behavior.	*Conducting surveys*[1] in order *to collect data*[2] is advantageous because it gives *scientists*[4] *the opportunity*[3] to *question*[5] *customers*[6] about their attitudes and shopping behavior.

SOLUTION: Don't copy the words and ideas exactly as they appear in a source. Paraphrasing is putting the ideas from a source into your own words. If you simply copy words and sentences from the reading passage, you will receive a zero for your essay. To avoid copying, check the original source after you create a paraphrase. Is the sentence structure and vocabulary different? If your paraphrase is too similar to the original, be sure to change it by using different types of sentence structures and synonyms of key words. Also, if you write down exactly what the professor says in your notes, be sure to put those words in quotation marks. That way, you will remember to paraphrase in your essay and not pass those words off as your own.

SOLUTION: Practice paraphrasing. The best way to improve your paraphrasing skills is to practice. Find a reading passage from the reading section of this book. Then choose a paragraph to paraphrase. Put the passage away and try paraphrasing. When you are done, compare your paraphrase with the source. Did you change key words by using synonyms? Also, did you change the sentence structures? Practice paraphrasing one paragraph a day until you feel confident about your paraphrasing skills.

» **CHALLENGE 5: "There's too much information to remember on the academic reading / lecture synthesis task."**

SOLUTION: During the integrated task, you will read a passage, then listen to the lecture about the same topic. You don't have to worry about taking notes on the reading passage because you will see it on your screen while you write your essay. However, you will need to take notes on the lecture. The lectures may include a lot of information, but remember that you are allowed to take notes during this portion of the test. Because of this, it's important to develop your note-taking skills. Use the following note-taking strategies to help you write down the most important information:

- Use abbreviations. You won't have enough time to write everything out, so be sure to use shorter forms whenever possible. Also, use abbreviations that make sense to you—it won't matter if you write something down if you don't remember what it means. See the table below for tips for abbreviations. Then, practice writing down things you hear using abbreviations, but remember to be sure you understand what they mean!

Abbreviation Tip	Examples	
Use numerals instead of writing out numbers	one, two, three, etc.→1, 2, 3, etc.	
Shorten words by leaving out letters	conversation, experiment → convo, expt	
Use symbols instead of words	Jane and Jack → Jane+Jack Jane or Jack → Jane / Jack Everyone except Jack → Everyone -Jack The numbers increased → The #s ↑ eight hundred dollars → $800 fifty percent → 50% at → @	
Other common abbreviations	without → w/o within → w/in approximately → approx. et cetera → etc.	because → b/c before → b4 example → ex regarding → re

- Study the table below for the basic information you should be writing down during the academic lecture:

What you should write down
• *Whether the professor agrees or disagrees with the main topic from the reading* • *Three reasons that the professor gives for either agreeing or disagreeing* • *Details such as studies or discoveries that support each of the professor's key points*

- Organize your notes as you write. It can be very helpful to write headings for all of the information you need to write down (Main Idea, Key Point 1, Support, etc.) Then, if you leave room beneath each of the above points, you can write down supporting details under them later.

» **CHALLENGE 6: "I have a hard time choosing what to write about on the Academic Discussion or Personal Experience Task."**

SOLUTION: Practice brainstorming techniques. Brainstorming involves thinking about the topic and trying to come up with major supporting details quickly. One technique you might find useful is to spend a minute or two writing down all of the points you can think of for both sides of the argument. Don't worry about whether the points you're writing down are good or not—sometimes, writing down a weak point will help you think of a better one. Try this technique for the topics in this book. When you are done, review your notes from brainstorming. Can you think of a way to adjust the technique so it works better for you?

SOLUTION: Don't waste time considering which point to support. When you are writing your answer, you should choose the position that is easiest for you to support. You can determine this by looking at the notes you've created when you brainstormed. Which side has more points? Also, remember that there are no right or wrong opinions on the TOEFL iBT test. In other words, you are <u>not</u> being graded based on your opinions themselves. What's really important is how well you support your opinion in your answer.

SOLUTION: Don't be afraid of making up personal examples to include in your answer. For the personal experience task, you are required to support all key points with relevant personal examples. However, nobody is going to check whether your personal examples are true or not. If you have to change the details of one of your examples so that it supports your key point better, go ahead and do it. It will make your essay even stronger.

SOLUTION: Make a list of familiar topics and practice coming up with key points for them. Give yourself about two to three minutes to think of key points for each topic. That way, you'll get used to thinking of supporting points in timed conditions like you'll have to on the day of the test. Use the topics from the list below or try to come up with your own topics:

- Some people think it is important to get a degree from a top school in order to get a good job. Others feel that real-world experience is more helpful for getting a good job. Which do you think is more important and why?
- Do you agree or disagree with the following statement?
    Teachers are the most influential people in a child's life.
- Some people think that having a good diet is the most important factor for physical health. Others think that exercise plays a larger role in health. Which do you think is true and why?
- Do you agree or disagree with the following statement?
    It is best to travel before starting a career.

Mini-Dictionary

Tests 1 and 2

abstract /ˈæbstrækt/

ADJECTIVE An **abstract** idea or way of thinking is based on general ideas rather than on real things and events. ○ *abstract principles such as justice* ○ *Fractional dimension is an abstract concept that enables mathematicians to measure the complexity of an object.* ○ *the faculty of abstract reasoning*

adhere /ædˈhɪər/ (**adheres, adhering, adhered**)

VERB If you **adhere to** a rule or agreement, you act in the way that it says you should. ○ *All members of the association adhere to a strict code of practice.*

affect /əˈfɛkt/ (**affects, affecting, affected**)

VERB If something **affects** a person or thing, it influences them or causes them to change in some way. ○ *Price changes must not adversely affect the living standards of the people.* ○ *More than seven million people have been affected by drought.* ○ *The new law will directly affect thousands of people.* ○ *Noise in factories can seriously affect workers' health.*

affordable /əˈfɔːrdəbəl/

ADJECTIVE If something is **affordable**, most people have enough money to buy it. ○ *The company makes wearable clothes at affordable prices.*

annually /ˈænyuəli/

ADVERB If an event takes place **annually**, it happens once every year. ○ *Production costs are reviewed annually to ensure the company is not wasting money.*

apprentice /əˈprɛntɪs/ **apprentices**

NOUN An **apprentice** is a young person who works for someone in order to learn their skill. ○ *I started off as an apprentice and worked my way up.*

approach /əˈproʊtʃ/ **approaches**

NOUN Your **approach** to a task, problem, or situation is the way you deal with it or think about it. ○ *We will be exploring different approaches to gathering information.*

area /ˈɛəriə/ **areas**

NOUN An **area** is a particular part of a town, a country, a region, or the world. ○ *She works in a rural area off the beaten track.*

assert /əˈsɜrt/ (**asserts, asserting, asserted**)

VERB If someone **asserts** a fact or belief, they state it firmly. [FORMAL] ○ *Mr. Helm plans to assert that the bill violates the First Amendment.* ○ *The defendants, who continue to assert their innocence, are expected to appeal.* ○ *"Kids today are too dependent on their devices," Jones asserted.* ○ *The American sugar industry has repeatedly asserted that quotas ensure a reliable supply of sugar.*

assume /əˈsum/ (**assumes, assuming, assumed**)

VERB If you **assume that** something is true, you imagine that it is true, sometimes wrongly. ○ *It is a misconception to assume that the two continents are similar.* ○ *If mistakes occurred, they were assumed to be the fault of the commander on the spot.*

astounding /əˈstaʊndɪŋ/

ADJECTIVE If something is **astounding**, you are shocked or amazed that it could exist or happen. ○ *The results are quite astounding.*

astute /əˈstut/

ADJECTIVE If you describe someone as **astute**, you think they show an understanding of behavior and situations, and are skillful at using this knowledge to their own advantage. ○ *She was politically astute.*

background /ˈbækgraʊnd/ (**backgrounds**)

NOUN The **background to** an event or situation consists of the facts that explain what caused it. ○ *The meeting takes place against a background of continuing political violence.* ○ *The background to the experience is important.*

basis /ˈbeɪsɪs/ (**bases**)

NOUN The **basis** of something is its starting point or an important part of it from which it can be further developed. ○ *Both factions have broadly agreed that the U.N. plan is a possible basis for negotiation.*

building block /ˈbɪldɪŋ blɒk/ (**building blocks**)

NOUN If you describe something as a **building block** of something, you mean it is one of the separate parts that combine to make that thing. ○ *molecules that are the building blocks of all life on earth*

characteristic /ˌkærɪktəˈrɪstɪk/ (**characteristics**)

NOUN The **characteristics** of a person or thing are the qualities or features that belong to them and make them recognizable. ○ *Genes determine the characteristics of every living thing.* ○ *their physical characteristics*

circulate /ˈsɜrkyəleɪt/ (**circulates, circulating, circulated**)

VERB When something **circulates**, it moves easily and freely within a closed place or system. ○ *a virus which circulates via the bloodstream* ○ *the sound of water circulating through pipes*

clarify /ˈklærɪfaɪ/ (**clarifies, clarifying, clarified**)

VERB To **clarify** something means to make it easier to understand, usually by explaining it in more detail. [FORMAL] ○ *It is important to clarify the distinction between the relativity of values and the relativity of truth.* ○ *A bank spokesperson was unable to clarify the situation.* ○ *You will want to clarify what your objectives are.*

classical studies /klæsɪkəl stʌdiz/

NONCOUNT NOUN **Classical studies** is the study of ancient Greek or Roman civilizations, especially their languages, literature, and philosophy. ○ *a classical studies degree* ○ *He was a classical studies major, and he could read Latin as if it were English.*

clinical /klɪnɪkəl/

ADJECTIVE **Clinical** means involving or relating to the direct medical treatment or testing of patients. ○ *The first clinical trials were expected to begin next year.* ○ *a clinical psychologist* ○ *the clinical aftereffects of the accident*

colonist /kɒlənɪst/ (**colonists**)

NOUN **Colonists** are the people who start a colony or the people who are among the first to live in a particular colony. ○ *The apple was brought over here by the colonists when they came.*

combustible /kəmbʌstɪbəl/

ADJECTIVE A **combustible** material or gas catches fire and burns easily. [FORMAL] ○ *The ability of coal to release a combustible gas has long been known.*

come up with (**comes, coming, came**)

PHRASAL VERB If you **come up with** an idea or solution, you find it or propose it. ○ *Several of the members have come up with suggestions of their own.*

component /kəmpoʊnənt/ (**components**)

NOUN The **components** of something are the parts that it is made of. ○ *Hydrogen is a key component of water.* ○ *The management plan has four main components.* ○ *The companies concerned were automotive component suppliers to the car manufacturers.*

comprise /kəmpraɪz/ (**comprises, comprising, comprised**)

VERB If you say that something **comprises** or **is comprised of** a number of things or people, you mean it has them as its parts or members. [FORMAL] ○ *The exhibition comprises 50 oils and watercolors.* ○ *The Coordinating Group is currently comprised of representatives from 73 financial institutions.*

consequence /kɒnsɪkwəns/ (**consequences**)

NOUN The **consequences** of something are the results or effects of it. ○ *Her lawyer said she understood the consequences of her actions.*

constantly /kɒnstəntli/

ADVERB If something happens **constantly**, or if you do something **constantly**, it happens all the time. ○ *The direction of the wind is constantly changing.*

consumer /kənsjuːməʳ/ (**consumers**)

NOUN A **consumer** is a person who buys things or uses services. ○ *The colder weather kept consumers from the shops.*

consumption /kənsʌmpʃən/

NOUN The **consumption** of food or drink is the act of eating or drinking something, or the amount that is eaten or drunk. [FORMAL] ○ *The average daily consumption of fruit and vegetables is around 200 grams.*

contemplate /kɒntəmpleɪt/ (**contemplates, contemplating, contemplated**)

VERB If you **contemplate** an action, you think about whether to do it or not. ○ *For a time, he contemplated a career as a medical doctor in the army.*

contribution /kɒntrɪbyuʃən/ (**contributions**)

NOUN If you make a **contribution to** something, you do something to help make it successful or to produce it. ○ *American economists have made important contributions to the field of financial and corporate economics.* ○ *He was awarded a prize for his contribution to world peace.*

counter argument /kɒuntəʳ ɑːʳgjʊmənt/ (**counter arguments**)

NOUN A **counter argument** is an argument that makes an opposing point to another argument. ○ *This was an attempt to develop a counter argument to the theory.*

course /kɔrs/ (**courses**)

NOUN A **course** is a series of lessons or lectures on a particular subject. ○ *universities that offer courses in business administration* ○ *a course on the modern novel*

criterion /kraɪtɪəriən/ (**criteria**)

NOUN A **criterion** is a factor on which you judge or decide something. ○ *The most important criterion for entry is that applicants must design and make their own work.* ○ *Our application had to meet three criteria if it was to succeed.*

crop /krɒp/ (**crops**)

NOUN **Crops** are plants such as wheat and potatoes that are grown in large quantities, usually for food. ○ *Rice farmers here still plant and harvest their crops by hand.* ○ *The main crop is wheat, and this is grown even on the very steep slopes.*

cubbyhole /kʌbi hoʊl/ (**cubbyholes**)

NOUN A **cubbyhole** is a very small room or space for storing things. ○ *It's in the cubbyhole under the stairs.*

cultivated /kʌltɪveɪtɪd/

ADJECTIVE If you describe someone as **cultivated**, you mean they are well educated and have good manners. [FORMAL] ○ *His mother was an elegant, cultivated woman.*

debunk /dibʌŋk/ (**debunks, debunking, debunked**)

VERB If you **debunk** a widely held belief, you show that it is false. If you **debunk** something that is widely admired, you show that it is not as good as people think it is. ○ *Historian Michael Beschloss debunks a few myths.*

decimate /dɛsɪmeɪt/ (decimates, decimating, decimated)

VERB To **decimate** something such as a group of people or animals means to destroy a very large number of them. ○ *The pollution could decimate the river's thriving population of kingfishers.*

declare /dɪklɛər/ (declares, declaring, declared)

VERB If you **declare** something, you state officially and formally that it exists or is the case. ○ *The government is ready to declare a permanent ceasefire.* ○ *His lawyers are confident that the judges will declare Mr. Stevens innocent.* ○ *Inspectors declared the grounds unsafe for public use.*

decline /dɪklaɪn/ (declines)

NOUN If there is a **decline in** something, it becomes less in quantity, importance, or quality. ○ *The reasons for the apparent decline in fertility are unclear.* ○ *Rome's decline in the fifth century* ○ *The first signs of economic decline became visible.*

detect /dɪtɛkt/ (detects, detecting, detected)

VERB To **detect** something means to find it or discover that it is present somewhere by using equipment or making an investigation. ○ *a sensitive piece of equipment used to detect radiation* ○ *Most skin cancers can be cured if detected and treated early.*

determine /dɪtɜrmɪn/ (determines, determining, determined)

VERB To **determine** a fact means to discover it as a result of investigation. [FORMAL] ○ *The investigation will determine what actually happened.* ○ *Testing needs to be done to determine the long-term effects on humans.* ○ *Science has determined that the risk is very small.*

device /dɪvaɪs/ (devices)

NOUN A **device** is an object that has been invented for a particular purpose, for example, for recording or measuring something. ○ *an electronic device that protects your vehicle 24 hours a day* ○ *An explosive device had been left inside a container.*

digit /dɪdʒɪt/ (digits)

NOUN A **digit** is a written symbol for any of the ten numbers from 0 to 9. ○ *Her cell phone number differs from mine by one digit.* ○ *Inflation is still in double digits.*

dilemma (dɪlɛmə) (dilemmas)

NOUN A **dilemma** is a difficult situation in which you have to choose between two or more alternatives. ○ *He was faced with the dilemma of whether or not to return to his country.* ○ *The issue raises a moral dilemma.*

display /dɪspleɪ/ (displays, displaying, displayed)

VERB When a computer **displays** information, it shows it on a screen. ○ *Your computer will detect the application and display the images onto the external screen.*

disposal /dɪspoʊzəl/

NONCOUNT NOUN **Disposal** is the act of getting rid of something that is no longer wanted or needed. ○ *methods for the permanent disposal of radioactive waste*

distinguished /dɪstɪŋgwɪʃt/

ADJECTIVE If you describe a person, an organization, or their work as **distinguished**, you mean that they have been very successful and have a good reputation. ○ *a distinguished academic family*

diverse /dɪvɜrs/

ADJECTIVE **Diverse** people or things are very different from each other. ○ *Albert Jones's new style will put him in touch with a much more diverse and perhaps younger audience.*

doggedly /dɔgɪdli/

ADVERB If you say that someone does something **doggedly**, you mean that they are determined to continue with it even if it becomes difficult or dangerous. ○ *She would fight doggedly for her rights as the children's mother.*

domestic /dəmɛstɪk/

ADJECTIVE **Domestic** means relating to or concerned with the home and family. ○ *a plan for sharing domestic chores* ○ *the sale of furniture and domestic appliances* ○ *victims of domestic violence*

dominant /dɒmɪnənt/

ADJECTIVE Someone or something that is **dominant** is more powerful, successful, influential, or noticeable than other people or things. ○ *a change that would maintain his party's dominant position in Texas* ○ *She was a dominant figure in the French film industry.*

drawback /drɔːbæk/ (drawbacks)

NOUN A **drawback** is an aspect of something or someone that makes them less acceptable than they would otherwise be. ○ *He felt the apartment's only drawback was that it was too small*

durability /dʊərəbɪlɪti/

NONCOUNT NOUN **Durability** is the quality of being strong and being able to last a long time without breaking or becoming weaker. ○ *Airlines recommend hard-sided cases for durability.*

earth-shattering /ɜrθʃætərɪŋ/

ADJECTIVE Something that is **earth-shattering** is very surprising or shocking. ○ *a truly earth-shattering discovery*

effect /ɪfɛkt/ (effects)

NOUN The **effect of** one thing **on** another is the change that the first thing causes in the second thing. ○ *Fine-particle pollution has a significant effect on human health.* ○ *The housing market is feeling the effects of the increase in interest rates.* ○ *Even minor head injuries can cause long-lasting psychological effects.*

element /ɛlɪmənt/ (elements)

NOUN The different **elements** of a situation, activity, or process are the different parts of it. ○ *Two key elements of the plan are sustainability and affordability.* ○ *The plot has all the elements not only of romance but of high drama.*

emit /ɪmɪt/ (emits, emitting, emitted)
VERB If something **emits** heat, light, gas, or a smell, it produces it and sends it out by means of a physical or chemical process. [FORMAL] ○ *The new device emits a powerful circular column of light.* ○ *the amount of carbon dioxide emitted*

enact /ɪnækt/ (enacts, enacting, enacted)
VERB If a particular event or situation **is enacted**, it happens; used especially to talk about something that has happened before. ○ *We could sense something of the tragedy that was being enacted in Europe.*

enactment /ɪnæktmənt/ (enactments)
NOUN The **enactment of** a law is the process in a legislature by which the law is agreed upon and made official. ○ *We support the call for the enactment of a Bill of Rights.*

encompass /ɪnkʌmpəs/ (encompasses, encompassing, encompassed)
VERB If something **encompasses** particular things, it includes them. ○ *His repertoire encompassed everything from Bach to Schoenberg.*

endow /ɪndaʊ/ (endows, endowing, endowed)
VERB If someone **endows** an institution, scholarship, or project, they provide a large amount of money that will produce the income needed to pay for it. ○ *The ambassador has endowed a $1 million public-service fellowships program.*

endure /ɪndʊər/ (endures, enduring, endured)
VERB If something or someone **endures** a force or action, they survive it or do not give in to it. ○ *He did not have to endure the numbing effect of an English February.* ○ *He endured a lot of suffering during his life.*

ensure /ɪnʃʊər/ (ensures, ensuring, ensured)
VERB To **ensure** something, or to **ensure that** something happens, means to make certain that it happens. [FORMAL] ○ *The United States' negotiators had ensured that the treaty was a significant change in direction.* ○ *Ensure that it is written into your contract.*

era /ɪərə/ (eras)
NOUN You can refer to a period of history or a long period of time as an **era** when you want to draw attention to a particular feature or quality that it has. ○ *the nuclear era* ○ *It was an era of austerity.*

evidence /ɛvɪdəns/
NONCOUNT NOUN **Evidence** is anything that you see, experience, read, or are told that causes you to believe that something is true or has really happened. ○ *The results gave clear statistical evidence of these phenomena.* ○ *Ganley said he'd seen no evidence of widespread fraud.*

exclude /ɪksklud/ (excludes, excluding, excluded)
VERB If you **exclude** something that has some connection with what you are doing, you deliberately do not use it or consider it. ○ *They eat only plant-based food and take care to exclude animal products from other areas of their lives.*

exclusive /ɪksklusɪv/
ADJECTIVE If you describe something as **exclusive**, you mean that it is limited to certain people, for example those who have a lot of money, and is therefore not available to everyone. ○ *The club was criticised for being too exclusive.*

exhibit /ɪgzɪbɪt/ (exhibits)
NOUN An **exhibit** is a painting, sculpture, or object of interest that is displayed to the public in a museum or art gallery. ○ *Shona showed me around the exhibits.*

expenditure /ɪkspɛndɪtʃər/
NONCOUNT NOUN **Expenditure** is the spending of money on something, or the money that is spent on something. [FORMAL] ○ *Policies of tax reduction must lead to reduced public expenditure.* ○ *They should cut their expenditure on defense.*

expertise /ɛkspɜrtiz/
NONCOUNT NOUN **Expertise** is special skill or knowledge that is acquired by training, study, or practice. ○ *Most local authorities lack the expertise to deal sensibly in this market.* ○ *students with expertise in forensics* ○ *a pooling and sharing of knowledge and expertise*

field /fild/ (fields)
NOUN A **field** is a particular subject of study or type of activity. ○ *Exciting artistic breakthroughs have recently occurred in the fields of painting, sculpture, and architecture.* ○ *Each of the authors is an expert in their field.*

finally /faɪnəli/
ADVERB You use **finally** in speech or writing to introduce a final point, question, or topic. ○ *And finally, a word about the winner and runner-up.*

financially /faɪnænʃəli/
ADVERB **Financially** means relating to or involving money. ○ *She's been struggling financially for years.*

found /faʊnd/ (founds, founding, founded)
VERB When an institution, company, or organization **is founded** by someone or by a group of people, they get it started, often by providing the necessary money. ○ *He founded the Missouri School of Journalism at University of Missouri.*

fragment /frægmənt/ (fragments)
NOUN A **fragment of** something is a small piece or part of it. ○ *There were fragments of metal in my shoulder.* ○ *She read everything, digesting every fragment of news.* ○ *glass fragments*

function /fˈʌŋkʃən/ (functions)

NOUN The **function** of something or someone is the useful thing that they do or are intended to do. ○ *This enzyme serves various functions.* ○ *The main function of the merchant banks is to raise capital for industry.*

fund /fˈʌnd/ (funds, funding, funded)

VERB When a person or organization **funds** something, they provide money for it. ○ *The Bush Foundation has funded a variety of faculty development programs.* ○ *The airport is being privately funded by a construction group.* ○ *a new, privately funded program*

grant /ɡrˈænt/ (grants, granting, granted)

NOUN A **grant** is an amount of money that a government or other institution gives to an individual or to an organization for a particular purpose. ○ *They received a special grant to encourage research.* ○ *Unfortunately, my application for a grant was rejected.*

hereditary /hɪrˈɛdɪtɛri/

ADJECTIVE A **hereditary** characteristic or illness is passed on to a child from an earlier generation before it is born. ○ *Cystic fibrosis a common fatal hereditary disease.* ○ *In men, hair loss is hereditary.*

home furnishing /hˈoʊm fɜrnɪʃɪŋ/ (home furnishings)

NOUN **Home furnishings** are the furniture, curtains, carpets, and decorations, such as pictures, in a room or house. ○ *To enable rental increases, you have to have luxurious home furnishings.*

hygiene /hˈaɪdʒin/

NONCOUNT NOUN **Hygiene** is the practice of keeping yourself and your surroundings clean, especially in order to prevent illness or the spread of diseases. ○ *It was difficult to ensure hygiene when doctors were conducting numerous operations in quick succession.* ○ *a strict regime of cleanliness and personal hygiene*

hypothesis /haɪpˈɒθɪsɪs/ (hypotheses)

NOUN A **hypothesis** is an idea which is suggested as a possible explanation for a particular situation or condition, but which has not yet been proved to be correct. [FORMAL] ○ *Work will now begin to test the hypothesis in rats.* ○ *Different hypotheses have been put forward to explain why these foods are more likely to cause problems.*

implement /ˈɪmplɪmɛnt, -mənt/ (implements, implementing, implemented)

VERB If you **implement** something such as a plan, you ensure that what has been planned is done. ○ *The government promised to implement a new system to control financial loan institutions.* ○ *The report sets out strict inspection procedures to ensure that the recommendations are properly implemented.*

implication /ɪmplɪkˈeɪʃən/ (implications)

NOUN The **implications** of something are the things that are likely to happen as a result. ○ *the political implications of his decision* ○ *The low level of investment has serious implications for future economic growth.*

imply /ɪmplˈaɪ/ (implies, implying, implied)

VERB If you **imply that** something is the case, you say something that indicates that it is the case in an indirect way. ○ *"What exactly are you implying?" I demanded.* ○ *The government is implying the problem is not serious.*

indistinguishable /ɪndɪstˈɪŋɡwɪʃəbəl/

ADJECTIVE If one thing is **indistinguishable from** another, the two things are so similar that it is difficult to know which is which. ○ *Replica weapons are indistinguishable from the real thing.*

industrial /ɪndˈʌstriəl/

ADJECTIVE You use **industrial** to describe things which relate to or are used in industry. ○ *industrial machinery and equipment* ○ *a link between industrial chemicals and cancer*

inevitable /ɪnˈɛvɪtəbəl/

ADJECTIVE If something is **inevitable**, it is certain to happen and cannot be prevented or avoided. ○ *If the case succeeds, it is inevitable that other trials will follow.* ○ *The defeat had inevitable consequences for foreign policy.*

infancy /ˈɪnfənsi/

NONCOUNT NOUN **Infancy** is the period of your life when you are a very young child. ○ *the development of the mind from infancy onward* ○ *Only 50 percent of babies survive infancy in this region.*

infant /ˈɪnfənt/ (infants)

NOUN An **infant** is a baby or very young child. [FORMAL] ○ *vaccination of newborn infants* ○ *the infant mortality rate*

inherit /ɪnhˈɛrɪt/ (inherits, inheriting, inherited)

VERB If you **inherit** a characteristic or quality, you are born with it, because your parents or ancestors also had it. ○ *We inherit many of our physical characteristics from our parents.* ○ *All people with asthma have inherited a gene that makes them susceptible to the disease.* ○ *Asthma can be an inherited condition.*

inspire /ɪnspˈaɪər/ (inspires, inspiring, inspired)

VERB If someone or something **inspires** you, they give you new ideas and a strong feeling of enthusiasm. ○ *In the 1960s, the electric guitar virtuosity of Jimi Hendrix inspired a generation.*

integrate /ˈɪntɪɡreɪt/ (integrates, integrating, integrated)

VERB If you **integrate** one thing **with** another, or one thing **integrates with** another, the two things become closely linked or form part of a whole idea or system. You can also say that two things **integrate**. ○ *The national plan involves integrating health and social care services.* ○ *Little attempt was made to integrate the parts into a coherent whole.*

interfere /ɪntərfˈɪər/ (interferes, interfering, interfered)

VERB Something that **interferes with** a situation, activity, or process has a damaging effect on it. ○ *Phytates interfere with your body's ability to absorb calcium.*

issue /ɪsjuː, ɪʃuː/ (issues)
NOUN An **issue** is an important subject that people are concerned about or discussing. ○ *Is it right for them to express a view on political issues?*

justify /dʒʌstɪfaɪ/ (justifies, justifying, justified)
VERB To **justify** a decision, action, or idea means to show or prove that it is reasonable or necessary. ○ *Ministers agreed that this decision was fully justified by economic conditions.*

key /kiː/
ADJECTIVE The **key** person or thing in a group is the most important one. ○ *He is expected to be the key witness at the trial.*

lack /læk/
NONCOUNT NOUN If there is a **lack of** something, there is not enough of it or it does not exist at all. ○ *Despite his lack of experience, he got the job.* ○ *The charges were dropped for lack of evidence.*

layer /leɪər/ (layers)
NOUN A **layer** of a material or substance is a quantity or piece of it that covers a surface or that is between two other things. ○ *The eyelids are protective layers of skin.* ○ *holes appearing in the ozone layer over the polar regions*

legislate /lɛdʒɪsleɪt/ (legislates, legislating, legislated)
VERB When a government or state **legislates** something, it passes a new law to cause it to happen or exist. [FORMAL] ○ *attempts to legislate a national energy strategy*

legislation /lɛdʒɪsleɪʃən/
NONCOUNT NOUN **Legislation** consists of a law or laws passed by a government. [FORMAL] ○ *The government has introduced draft legislation to increase the maximum penalty for car theft.* ○ *European legislation on copyright* ○ *changes to employment legislation* ○ *The government introduced legislation restricting trade union rights.* ○ *a highly complex piece of legislation*

legislative /lɛdʒɪsleɪtɪv/
ADJECTIVE **Legislative** means involving or relating to the process of making and passing laws. [FORMAL] ○ *Today's hearing was just the first step in the legislative process.* ○ *the country's highest legislative body*

liberal arts /lɪbərəl ɑrts/
NOUN At a university or college, **liberal arts** courses are on subjects such as history or literature rather than science, law, medicine, or business. ○ *The journalist says, "When you come out of a liberal arts background, you want to know why something is the way it is."* ○ *Firms now favor liberal arts degrees over the once-hot business degree.*

logo /loʊgoʊ/ (logos)
NOUN The **logo** of a company or organization is the special design or way of writing its name that it puts on all its products, notepaper, or advertisements. ○ *Staff should wear uniforms, and vehicles should bear company logos.* ○ *a red T-shirt with a logo on the front*

magnetic /mægnɛtɪk/
ADJECTIVE You use **magnetic** to describe something that is caused by or relates to the force of magnetism, the natural power of some objects and substances, especially iron, to attract other objects toward them. ○ *The moon exerts a magnetic pull on the Earth's water levels.* ○ *The electrically charged gas particles are affected by magnetic forces.*

mandate /mændeɪt/ (mandates)
NOUN If someone is given a **mandate** to carry out a particular policy or task, they are given the official authority to do it. ○ *How much longer does the special prosecutor have a mandate to pursue this investigation?*

material /mətɪəriəl/ (materials)
NOUN A **material** is a solid substance. ○ *electrons in a conducting material such as a metal* ○ *the design of new absorbent materials* ○ *recycling of all materials*

moral /mɒrəl/ (materials)
ADJECTIVE **Moral** means relating to beliefs about what is right or wrong ○ *She describes her own moral dilemma in making the film.*

motivate /moʊtɪveɪt/ (motivates, motivating, motivated)
VERB If you are **motivated** by something, it causes you to behave in a particular way. ○ *They are motivated by a need to achieve.*

no matter
PHRASE You use **no matter** in expressions such as "no matter how" and "no matter what" to say that something is true or happens in all circumstances. ○ *No matter what your age, you can improve your fitness by following this program.*

notable /noʊtəbəl/
ADJECTIVE Someone or something that is **notable** is important or interesting. ○ *The proposed new structure is notable not only for its height, but for its shape.* ○ *With a few notable exceptions, the students were a pretty conscientious bunch.*

novice /nɒvɪs/ (novices)
NOUN A **novice** is someone who has been doing a job or other activity for only a short time and so is not experienced at it. ○ *For expert and novice alike, it's a foolproof system.* ○ *Business novices learn the entrepreneurial ropes fast.*

objective /əbdʒɛktɪv/ (objectives)
NOUN Your **objective** is what you are trying to achieve. ○ *Our main objective was the recovery of the child safe and well.* ○ *Our objective is to become the number one digital corporation.*

obstruct /əbstrʌkt/ (obstructs, obstructing, obstructed)
VERB If something **obstructs** a road or passage, it blocks it, preventing anything from passing. ○ *Drivers who park their cars illegally, particularly obstructing traffic flow, deserve to be punished.*

obtain /əbteɪn/ **(obtains, obtaining, obtained)**
VERB To **obtain** something means to get it or achieve it. [FORMAL] ○ *Evans was trying to obtain a fake passport.* ○ *This type of movie memorabilia is becoming increasingly difficult to obtain.*

oppose /əpoʊz/ **(opposes, opposing, opposed)**
VERB If you **oppose** someone or **oppose** their plans or ideas, you disagree with what they want to do and try to prevent them from doing it. ○ *Mr. Taylor was not bitter towards those who had opposed him.* ○ *Some of the parents opposed the idea of a bilingual education.*

option /ɒpʃən/ **(options)**
NOUN An **option** is something that you can choose to do in preference to one or more alternatives. ○ *She argues that the country is putting too much emphasis on the military option.* ○ *What other options do you have?*

organism /ɔrgənɪzəm/ **(organisms)**
NOUN An **organism** is an animal or plant, especially one that is so small that you cannot see it without using a microscope. ○ *Not all chemicals normally present in living organisms are harmless.* ○ *insect-borne organisms that cause sleeping sickness*

partially /pɑrʃəli/
ADVERB If something happens or exists **partially**, it happens or exists to some extent, but not completely. ○ *He was born with a rare genetic condition which has left him partially sighted.* ○ *partially hydrogenated oils*

perceive /pərsiv/ **(perceives, perceiving, perceived)**
VERB If you **perceive** someone or something **as** doing or being a particular thing, it is your opinion that they do this thing or that they are that thing. ○ *Stress is widely perceived as contributing to coronary heart disease.* ○ *Bioterrorism is perceived as a real threat in the United States.*

petition /pətɪʃən/ **(petitions)**
NOUN A **petition** is a document signed by a lot of people that asks a government or other official group to do a particular thing. ○ *a petition signed by 4,500 people*

policy /pɒlɪsi/ **(policies)**
NOUN A **policy** is a set of ideas or plans that is used as a basis for making decisions, especially in politics, economics, or business. ○ *The plans include changes in foreign policy and economic reforms.*

predatory /prɛdətɔri/
ADJECTIVE **Predatory** animals live by killing other animals for food. ○ *predatory birds like the eagle*

prestigious /prɛstɪdʒəs, -stɪdʒəs/
ADJECTIVE A **prestigious** institution, job, or activity is respected and admired by people. ○ *It's one of the best equipped and most prestigious schools in the country.*

prevail /prɪveɪl/ **(prevails, prevailing, prevailed)**
VERB If a situation, attitude, or custom **prevails** in a particular place at a particular time, it is normal or most common in that place at that time. ○ *A similar situation prevails in Canada.* ○ *Just how these ideas are expressed depends on the ideas prevailing in society at the time.*

prevent /prɪvɛnt/ **(prevents, preventing, prevented)**
VERB To **prevent** something means to ensure that it does not happen. ○ *Further treatment aims to prevent the cancer from spreading.* ○ *We recognized the possibility and took steps to prevent it from happening.*

proliferation /prəlɪfəreɪʃən/
NONCOUNT NOUN The **proliferation** of something is a fast increase in its quantity. [FORMAL] ○ *the proliferation of nuclear weapons*

prolonged /prəlɔŋd/
ADJECTIVE A **prolonged** event or situation continues for a long time, or for longer than expected. ○ *a prolonged period of low interest rates*

prominent /prɒmɪnənt/
ADJECTIVE Something that is **prominent** is very noticeable or is an important part of something else. ○ *Here the window plays a prominent part in the design.* ○ *Romania's most prominent independent newspaper*

pursuit /pərsut/
NONCOUNT NOUN The **pursuit of** something is the process of trying to understand and achieve it. ○ *a young woman whose relentless pursuit of excellence is conducted with single-minded determination*

random /rændəm/
ADJECTIVE A **random** sample or method is one in which all the people or things involved have an equal chance of being chosen. ○ *The survey used a random sample of two thousand people across the United States.* ○ *The competitors will be subject to random drug testing.*

range /reɪndʒ/ **(ranges)**
NOUN A **range** is the complete group that is included between two points on a scale of measurement or quality. ○ *The average age range is between 35 and 55.* ○ *products available in this price range*

rational /ræʃənəl/
ADJECTIVE **Rational** decisions and thoughts are based on reason rather than on emotion. ○ *They are asking you to look at both sides of the case and come to a rational decision.* ○ *It was the most rational explanation at the time.*

reduce /rɪdus/ **(reduces, reducing, reduced)**
VERB If you **reduce** something, you make it smaller in size or amount, or less in degree. ○ *It reduces the risks of heart disease.* ○ *Consumption is being reduced by 25 percent.* ○ *The reduced consumer demand is also affecting company profits.*

reduction /rɪdʌkʃən/ **(reductions)**

NOUN When there is a **reduction in** something, it is made smaller. ○ *This morning's inflation figures show a reduction of 0.2 percentage points from 5.8 percent to 5.6.* ○ *Many companies have announced dramatic reductions in staff.* ○ *the reduction of inflation and interest rates*

refining /rɪfaɪnɪŋ/

NONCOUNT NOUN **Refining** is the process of making a substance pure by having all other substances removed from it. ○ *oil refining*

reform /rɪfɔrm/ **(reforms, reforming, reformed)**

VERB If someone **reforms** something such as a law, social system, or institution, they change or improve it. ○ *his plans to reform the country's economy* ○ *A reformed party would have to win the approval of the people.* ○ *proposals to reform the tax system*

regard /rɪgɑrd/ **(regards, regarding, regarded)**

VERB If you **regard** someone or something **as** being a particular thing or as having a particular quality, you believe that they are that thing or have that quality. ○ *She was regarded as the most successful chancellor of modern times.* ○ *I regard creativity both as a gift and as a skill.* ○ *The vast majority of people would regard these proposals as unreasonable.*

regulate /rɛgyəleɪt/ **(regulates, regulating, regulated)**

VERB To **regulate** an activity or process means to control it, especially by means of rules. ○ *The powers of the Federal Trade Commission to regulate competition are increasing.* ○ *As we get older, the temperature-regulating mechanisms in the body tend to become a little less efficient.* ○ *regulating cholesterol levels*

relevance /rɛləvəns/

NONCOUNT NOUN Something's **relevance to** a situation or person is its importance or significance in that situation or to that person. ○ *My private life has no relevance to my public role.* ○ *There are additional publications of special relevance to new graduates.*

relevant /rɛləvənt/

ADJECTIVE Something that is **relevant to** a situation or person is important or significant in that situation or to that person. ○ *Is socialism still relevant to people's lives?* ○ *We have passed all relevant information on to the police.*

renowned /rɪnaʊnd/

ADJECTIVE A person or place that is **renowned** is well known, usually because they do or have done something good. ○ *The university has a renowned toxicology center.*

restrict /rɪstrɪkt/ **(restricts, restricting, restricted)**

VERB If you **restrict** something, you put a limit on it in order to reduce it or prevent it from becoming too great. ○ *There is talk of raising the admission requirements to restrict the number of students on campus.* ○ *The site restricts access to data through the use of passwords and encryption.*

restriction /rɪstrɪkʃən/ **(restrictions)**

NOUN A **restriction** is an official rule that limits what you can do or that limits the amount or size of something. ○ *Some restriction on funding was necessary.* ○ *the justification for this restriction of individual liberty* ○ *the lifting of restrictions on air travel*

retail apparel /riteɪl əpærəl/

NONCOUNT NOUN **Retail apparel** is clothing that is made to be sold in stores. ○ *a chain of 104 fashion retail apparel stores*

reverse /rɪvɜrs/ **(reverses, reversing, reversed)**

VERB When someone or something **reverses** a decision, policy, or trend, they change it to the opposite decision, policy, or trend. ○ *They have made it clear they will not reverse the decision to increase prices.* ○ *The rise, the first in ten months, reversed the downward trend in the country's jobless rate.*

sail through **(sails, sailing, sailed)**

PHRASAL VERB If someone or something **sails through** a difficult situation or experience, it is easy and successful for them. ○ *While she sailed through her exams, he struggled.*

scope /skoup/

NOUN The **scope of** an activity, topic, or piece of work is the whole area which it deals with or includes. ○ *Mr. Dobson promised to widen the organization's scope of activity.* ○ *the scope of a novel*

secondary /sɛkəndɛri/

ADJECTIVE If you describe something as **secondary**, you mean that it is less important than something else. ○ *The street erupted in a huge explosion, with secondary explosions in the adjoining buildings.* ○ *The actual damage to the brain cells is secondary to the damage caused to the blood supply.*

segment /sɛgmənt/ **(segments)**

NOUN A **segment of** something is one part of it, considered separately from the rest. ○ *the less privileged segments of society* ○ *the third segment of his journey*

set forth **(sets forth, setting forth, set forth)**

PHRASAL VERB If you **set forth** a number of facts, beliefs, or arguments, you explain them in writing or speech in a clear, organized way. ○ *Dr. Mesibov set forth the basis of his approach to teaching students.*

sin tax /sɪn tæks/ **(sin taxes)**

NOUN A **sin tax** is a tax on something that is considered morally or medically harmful, such as sugar. ○ *There are serious questions over whether sin taxes change behavior.*

site /saɪt/ **(sites)**

NOUN A **site** is a piece of ground that is used for a particular purpose or where a particular thing happens. ○ *When we arrived, we realised the hotel was little more than a building site.* ○ *a bat sanctuary with special nesting sites*

specimen /spɛsɪmɪn/ (specimens)

NOUN A **specimen of** something is an example of it which gives an idea of what the whole of it is like. ○ *The commissioning editor asked me for a specimen of my poetry.*

spectrum /spɛktrəm/ (spectra, spectrums)

NOUN A **spectrum** is a range of a particular type of thing. ○ *She'd seen his moods range across the emotional spectrum.* ○ *Public figures across the political spectrum have denounced the act.* ○ *DNA screening is available for a wide spectrum of conditions.*

speed reading /spid ridɪŋ/

NOUN **Speed reading** is reading something very fast. ○ *JFK, one of the first politicians to understand the benefits of speed reading, managed 1,000 words a minute.*

spur of the moment

PHRASE If you do something **on the spur of the moment**, you do it suddenly, without planning it beforehand. ○ *They admitted they had taken a vehicle on the spur of the moment.*

steep /stip/ (steeper, steepest)

ADJECTIVE A **steep** increase or decrease in something is a very big increase or decrease. ○ *Consumers are rebelling at steep price increases.* ○ *Many smaller economies are suffering their steepest economic declines for half a century.*

strain /streɪn/ (strains)

NOUN A **strain of** a germ, plant, or other organism is a particular type of it. ○ *Every year new strains of influenza develop.*

strategy /strætədʒi/ (strategies)

NOUN A **strategy** is a general plan or set of plans intended to achieve something, especially over a long period. ○ *Next week, health officials gather in Amsterdam to agree on a strategy for controlling malaria.* ○ *a customer-led marketing strategy*

suitable /sutəbəl/

ADJECTIVE Someone or something that is **suitable for** a particular purpose or occasion is right or acceptable for it. ○ *Please tell me why you think you are suitable for the job.* ○ *The organization must provide suitable accommodation for the family.*

survey /sɜrveɪ/ (surveys)

NOUN If you carry out a **survey**, you try to find out detailed information about a lot of different people or things, usually by asking people a series of questions. ○ *The council conducted a survey of the uses to which farm buildings are put.* ○ *According to the survey, overall world trade has also slackened.*

sustainable /səsteɪnəbəl/

ADJECTIVE You use **sustainable** to describe the use of natural resources when this use is kept at a steady level that is not likely to damage the environment. ○ *the management, conservation, and sustainable development of forests* ○ *Try to buy wood that you know has come from a sustainable source.*

switch /swɪtʃ/ (switches, switching, switched)

VERB If you **switch to** something different, for example to a different system, task, or subject of conversation, you change to it from what you were doing or saying before. ○ *We went organic and switched to a plant-based diet.* ○ *The law would encourage companies to switch from coal to cleaner fuels.*

symbol /sɪmbəl/ (symbols)

NOUN A **symbol of** something such as a number or a sound is a shape or design that is used to represent it. ○ *One wall was covered in pencil scribblings, all kinds of symbols and numbers which to me were unintelligible.* ○ *mathematical symbols and operations*

take for granted

PHRASE If you **take something for granted**, you believe that it is true or accept it as normal without thinking about it. ○ *Respiration controls our life and yet it is something we take for granted.*

technique /tɛknik/ (techniques)

NOUN A **technique** is a particular method of doing an activity, usually a method that involves practical skills. ○ *tests performed using a new technique* ○ *developments in the surgical techniques employed* ○ *traditional bread-making techniques*

term /tɜrm/ (terms)

NOUN A **term** is a word or expression with a specific meaning, especially one which is used in relation to a particular subject. ○ *Myocardial infarction is the medical term for a heart attack.*

territory /tɛrətɔri/ (territories)

NOUN **Territory** is land that is controlled by a particular country or ruler. ○ *None of the former Spanish territories enjoyed long periods of independence.*

testify /tɛstɪfaɪ/ (testifies, testifying, testified)

VERB When someone **testifies** in a court of law, they give a statement of what they saw someone do or what they know of a situation, after having promised to tell the truth. ○ *Several eyewitnesses testified that they saw someone leaving the building just before midnight.* ○ *Eva testified to having seen Herndon with his gun on the stairs.* ○ *He refused to testify against his former coworkers.*

theory /θɪəri/ (theories)

NOUN A **theory** is a formal idea or set of ideas that is intended to explain something. ○ *Einstein formulated the Theory of Relativity in 1905.*

therefore /ðɛərfɔr/

ADVERB You use **therefore** to introduce a logical result or conclusion. ○ *Muscle cells burn lots of calories and therefore need lots of fuel.* ○ *We expect to continue to gain new customers and therefore also market shares.*

trait /treɪt/ (traits)

NOUN A **trait** is a particular characteristic, quality, or tendency that someone or something has. ○ *Several studies looked at the personality traits of successful entrepreneurs.* ○ *Do we inherit traits such as agility and sporting excellence, and musical or artistic ability?*

trigger /trɪgər/ (triggers, triggering, triggered)

VERB If something **triggers** an event or situation, it causes it to begin to happen or exist. ○ *The interview triggered a wave of complaints from listeners* ○ *The current recession was triggered by a slump in consumer spending.*

tuition /tuɪʃən/

NONCOUNT NOUN **Tuition** is the money paid by students to the school or college that they attend. ○ *You need to pay your tuition and support yourself financially.*

undergo /ʌndərgoʊ/ (undergoes, undergoing, underwent, undergone)

VERB If a person or thing **undergoes** something necessary or unpleasant, it happens to them. ○ *New recruits have been undergoing training in recent weeks.* ○ *When cement powder is mixed with water, it undergoes a chemical change and hardens.*

undertaking /ʌndərteɪkɪŋ/ (undertakings)

NOUN An **undertaking** is a task or job, especially a large or difficult one. ○ *Organizing the show has been a massive undertaking.*

undesirable /ʌndɪzaɪərəbəl/

ADJECTIVE If you describe something or someone as **undesirable**, you do not want them or you think they are harmful. ○ *We have come to view sweating as an undesirable and socially unacceptable activity.*

unorthodox /ʌnɔrθədɒks/

ADJECTIVE If you describe someone's behavior, beliefs, or customs as **unorthodox**, you mean that they are different from what is generally accepted. ○ *The reality-based show followed the unorthodox lives of the celebrity family.*

utilize /yutɪlaɪz/ (utilizes, utilizing, utilized)

VERB If you **utilize** something, you use it. [FORMAL] ○ *Sound engineers utilize a range of techniques to enhance the quality of the recordings.* ○ *Minerals can be absorbed and utilized by the body in a variety of different forms.*

vary /vɛəri/ (varies, varying, varied)

VERB If things **vary**, they are different from each other in size, amount, or degree. ○ *Assessment practices vary in different schools or colleges.* ○ *The text varies from the earlier versions.* ○ *Different writers will prepare to varying degrees.*

venture /vɛntʃər/ (ventures)

NOUN A **venture** is a project or activity that is new. ○ *The project is a joint venture between the Museum and the Research Institute.*

verify /vɛrɪfaɪ/ (verifies, verifying, verified)

VERB If you **verify** something, you check that it is true by careful examination or investigation. ○ *continued testing to verify the accuracy of the method* ○ *A clerk simply verifies that the payment and invoice amount match.*

versatile /vɜrsətaɪl/

ADJECTIVE A material that is **versatile** can be used for many different purposes or in many different ways. ○ *She was wearing a versatile blue denim skirt.*

vertical /vɜrtɪkəl/

ADJECTIVE Something that is **vertical** stands or points straight up. ○ *The price variable is shown on the vertical axis, with quantity demanded on the horizontal axis.* ○ *The gadget can be attached to any vertical or near-vertical surface.*

via /vaɪə, viə/

PREPOSITION If you do something **via** a particular means or person, you do it by making use of that means or person. ○ *The relief workers contact their colleagues back home via satellite technology.*

volume /vɒlyum/ (volumes)

NOUN A **volume** is one book or journal in a series of books or journals. The abbreviation vol. is used in written notes and bibliographies. ○ *the first volume of his autobiography* ○ *The article appeared in volume 41 of the journal Communication Education.*

vulnerable /vʌlnərəbəl/

ADJECTIVE If someone or something is **vulnerable to** something, they have some weakness or disadvantage which makes them more likely to be harmed or affected by that thing. ○ *People with high blood pressure are especially vulnerable to diabetes.*

wane /weɪn/ (wanes, waning, waned)

VERB If something **wanes**, it becomes gradually weaker or less, often so that it eventually disappears. ○ *While his interest in these sports began to wane, a passion for lacrosse developed.*

whereas /wɛəræz/

CONJUCTION You use **whereas** to introduce a comment which contrasts with what is said in the main clause. ○ *Pensions are linked to inflation, whereas they should be linked to the cost of living.* ○ *Whereas the population of working age increased by 1 million between 1981 and 1986, today it is barely growing.*

Tests 3 and 4

accuracy /ˈækjʊrəsi/

NONCOUNT NOUN The **accuracy** of measurements is their quality of being true or correct. ○ *We cannot guarantee the accuracy of these figures.*

achievement /əˈtʃiːvmənt/ **(achievements)**

NOUN An **achievement** is something which someone has succeeded in doing, especially after a lot of effort. ○ *Reaching this agreement so quickly was a great achievement.*

acknowledge /ækˈnɒlɪdʒ/ **(acknowledges, acknowledging, acknowledged)**

VERB If you **acknowledge** a fact or a situation, you accept or admit that it is true or that it exists. [FORMAL] ○ *We have to acknowledge that something is wrong with the system.*

adaptation /ˌædæpˈteɪʃən/

NONCOUNT NOUN **Adaptation** is the act of changing something such as your behaviour to make it suitable for a new purpose or situation. ○ *Most living creatures are capable of adaptation when compelled to do so.*

administration /ædˌmɪnɪˈstreɪʃən/ **(administrations)**

NOUN The **administration** of a company or institution is the group of people who organize and supervise it. ○ *They accused the administration of bias.*

administrative assistant /ædˌmɪnɪstrətɪv əˈsɪstənt/ **(administrative assistants)**

NOUN An **administrative assistant** is a person employed to help an executive in the organization of a department. ○ *His brother was an administrative assistant at a cleaning supplies firm.*

advocate /ˈædvəkət/ **(advocates)**

NOUN An **advocate** of a particular person, action, or plan is someone who recommends them publicly. [FORMAL] ○ *He was a strong advocate of free-market policies.*

allege /əˈlɛdʒ/ **(alleges, alleging, alleged)**

VERB If you **allege** that something bad is true, you say it but do not prove it. [FORMAL] ○ *The writer alleges that her husband and the assistant had been plying her with tainted food.*

allegedly /əˈlɛdʒɪdli/

ADVERB If something is **allegedly** true, it has been stated but has not been proved to be true. [FORMAL] ○ *He allegedly crashed into the front of the restaurant while trying to park.*

all expenses paid /ˌɒl ɪkˈspɛnsiːz ˈpeɪd/

PHRASE A holiday or a trip that is **all expenses paid** is free, with everything already paid for. ○ *He was flown out to Bangkok for five days, all expenses paid.*

all the rage /ˌɒl ðə ˈreɪdʒ/

PHRASE When something is popular and fashionable, you can say that it is **all the rage**. [INFORMAL] ○ *It was all the rage a few years ago.*

ancestor /ˈænsɛstər/ **(ancestors)**

NOUN Your **ancestors** are the people from whom you are descended. ○ *He could trace his ancestors back seven hundred years.*

apathy /ˈæpəθi/

NONCOUNT NOUN You can use **apathy** to talk about someone's state of mind if you are criticizing them because they do not seem to be interested in or enthusiastic about anything. ○ *They listed some of the symptoms of depression, including low energy, reduced motivation, and apathy.*

architecture /ˈɑːrkɪtɛktʃər/

NONCOUNT NOUN **Architecture** is the art of planning, designing, and constructing buildings. ○ *He studied classical architecture and design in Rome.*

area /ˈɛəriə/ **(areas)**

NOUN You can use **area** to refer to a particular subject or topic, or to a particular part of a larger, more general situation or activity. ○ *She wants to be involved in every area of your life.*

artificial /ˌɑːrˈtɪfɪʃəl/

ADJECTIVE **Artificial** objects, materials, or processes do not occur naturally and are created by human beings, for example using science or technology. ○ *The city is dotted with small lakes, natural and artificial.*

assembly /əˈsɛmbli/ **(assemblies)**

NOUN An **assembly** is a group of people gathered together for a particular purpose. ○ *He waited until complete quiet settled on the assembly.*

associate /əˈsoʊsieɪt/ **(associates, associating, associated)**

VERB If you **associate** someone or something **with** another thing, the two are connected in your mind. ○ *Through science we've got the idea of associating progress with the future.*

assume /əˈsjuːm/ **(assumes, assuming, assumed)**

VERB If you **assume** that something is true, you imagine that it is true, sometimes wrongly. ○ *If the package is wrapped well, we assume the contents are also wonderful.*

attribute /əˈtrɪbjuːt/ **(attributes, attributing, attributed)**

VERB If you **attribute** something to an event or situation, you think that it was caused by that event or situation. ○ *The striker attributes the team's success to a positive ethos at the club.*

authentic /ɔːˈθɛntɪk/

ADJECTIVE An **authentic** object is genuine. ○ *We had an exclusive tasting of the finest authentic prosecco from a nearby vineyard.*

automatically /ˌɔːtəˈmætɪkli/

ADVERB If something happens **automatically**, it happens without people needing to think about it. ○ *As an account customer, you are automatically entitled to a variety of benefits.*

ballot /bælət/ (ballots)
NOUN A **ballot** is a piece of paper on which you indicate your choice or opinion in a secret vote. ○ *Election boards will count the ballots by hand.*

behalf /bɪhɑːf/
PHRASE If you do something **on someone's behalf**, you do it for that person as their representative. ○ *She made an emotional public appeal on her son's behalf.*

Bermuda Triangle /bəˈmjuːdə traɪæŋɡᵊl/
NOUN The **Bermuda Triangle** is an area in the Atlantic Ocean where it is said that ships and aeroplanes have disappeared mysteriously. ○ *A group of aircraft disappeared in the Bermuda Triangle in 1945.*

blank /blæŋk/ (blanker, blankest)
ADJECTIVE Something that is **blank** has nothing on it. ○ *He tore a blank page from his notebook.*

brainstorming /breɪnstɔːmɪŋ/
NOUN **Brainstorming** is intensive discussion to solve problems or generate ideas. ○ *Anna brought curiosity and creativity to their brainstorming sessions.*

bubble /bʌbᵊl/ (bubbles)
NOUN A **bubble** is an imaginary space that some people form around themselves to keep a comfortable distance away from other people or objects. ○ *The majority of residents are couples in their personal bubbles.*

bulky /bʌlki/ (bulkier, bulkiest)
ADJECTIVE Something that is **bulky** is large and heavy. Bulky things are often difficult to move or deal with. ○ *They bought bulky items like lawn mowers.*

candidate /kændɪdeɪt/ (candidates)
NOUN A **candidate** is someone who is being considered for a position, for example someone who is running in an election or applying for a job. ○ *We all spoke to them and John emerged as the best candidate.*

cast /kɑːst, kæst/ (casts, casting, cast)
VERB When you **cast** your vote in an election, you vote. ○ *About ninety-five per cent of those who cast their votes approve the new law.*

chord /kɔːʳd/ (chords)
NOUN A **chord** is a number of musical notes played or sung at the same time with a pleasing effect. ○ *Everyone knows the opening chords of "Stairway to Heaven."*

claim /kleɪm/ (claims)
NOUN A **claim** is something which someone says which they cannot prove and which may be false. ○ *He repeated his claim that the people backed his action.*

claim (claims, claiming, claimed)
VERB If you say that someone **claims** that something is true, you mean they say that it is true but you are not sure whether or not they are telling the truth. ○ *He claimed that it was all a conspiracy against him.*

clarify /klærɪfaɪ/ (clarifies, clarifying, clarified)
VERB To **clarify** something means to make it easier to understand, usually by explaining it in more detail. [FORMAL] ○ *A bank spokesperson was unable to clarify the situation.*

collectibles /kəlɛktəbᵊlz/
PLURAL NOUN **Collectibles** are objects which are valued very highly by collectors because they are rare or beautiful. ○ *Many of these cushions have survived and are now collectibles.*

colony /kɒləni/ (colonies)
NOUN You can refer to a place where a particular group of people lives as a particular kind of **colony**. ○ *The pretty town of Cranbrook became a thriving artists' colony.*

commemorative /kəmɛmərətɪv/
ADJECTIVE A **commemorative** object or event is intended to make people remember a particular event or person. ○ *The king unveiled a commemorative plaque.*

commission /kəmɪʃᵊn/ (commissions)
NOUN A **commission** is a piece of work that someone is asked to do and is paid for. ○ *Just a few days ago, I finished a commission.*

commodity /kəmɒdɪti/ (commodities)
NOUN A **commodity** is something that is sold for money. [BUSINESS] ○ *The government increased prices on several basic commodities like bread and meat.*

commonly /kɒmənli/
ADVERB If something is **commonly** used, it is used often. ○ *Parsley is probably the most commonly used of all herbs.*

community /kəmjuːnɪti/ (communities)
NOUN A particular **community** is a group of people who are similar in some way. ○ *There is plenty of support in the business community for improving the process.*

community service /kəmjuːnɪti sɜːʳvɪs/
NONCOUNT NOUN **Community service** is unpaid work that criminals sometimes do as a punishment instead of being sent to prison. ○ *He was sentenced to 140 hours' community service.*

compensate /kɒmpənseɪt/ (compensates, compensating, compensated)
VERB To **compensate** someone for money or things that they have lost means to pay them money or give them something to replace that money or those things. ○ *To ease financial difficulties, farmers could be compensated for their loss of subsidies.*

competent /kɒmpɪtənt/

ADJECTIVE Someone who is **competent** is efficient and effective. ○ *He was a loyal, distinguished and very competent civil servant.*

compulsory /kəmpʌlsəri/

ADJECTIVE If something is **compulsory**, you must do it or accept it, because it is the law or because someone in a position of authority says you must. ○ *In East Germany, learning Russian was compulsory.*

confined /kənfaɪnd/

ADJECTIVE If something is **confined to** a particular place, it exists only in that place. If it is **confined to** a particular group, only members of that group have it. ○ *The problem is not confined to Germany.*

conflicting /kənflɪktɪŋ/

ADJECTIVE **Conflicting** ideas, beliefs, or accounts are very different from each other and it seems impossible for them to exist together or to each be true. ○ *There were conflicting reports over when he finally decided to quit.*

consistent /kənsɪstənt/

ADJECTIVE If one fact or idea is **consistent with** another, they do not contradict each other. ○ *New goals are not always consistent with the existing policies.*

Constitution /kɒnstɪtjuːʃən/

NOUN The **Constitution** of the United States is the system of laws which formally states people's rights and duties. ○ *It is a fundamental right under the American Constitution.*

consultation /kɒnsəlteɪʃən/ (consultations)

NOUN A **consultation** is a meeting which is held to discuss something. ○ *Next week he'll be in Florida for consultations with the President.*

contradict /kɒntrədɪkt/ (contradicts, contradicting, contradicted)

VERB If one statement or piece of evidence **contradicts** another, the first one makes the second one appear to be wrong. ○ *The images on screen contradict his claims.*

contribute /kəntrɪbjuːt/ (contributes, contributing, contributed)

VERB If you **contribute** to something, you say or do things to help to make it successful. ○ *He believes he has something to contribute to the discussion.*

controversial /kɒntrəvɜːʃəl/

ADJECTIVE If you describe something or someone as **controversial**, you mean that they are the subject of intense public argument, disagreement, or disapproval. ○ *The changes are bound to be controversial.*

crack down on /kræk daʊn ɒn/ (cracks down on, cracking down on, cracked down on)

PHRASAL VERB If people in authority **crack down on** a group of people, they become stricter in making the group obey rules or laws. ○ *The government has cracked down hard on those campaigning for greater democracy.*

cycle /saɪkəl/ (cycles)

NOUN A **cycle** is a series of events or processes that is repeated again and again, always in the same order. ○ *The figures marked the final low point of the present economic cycle.*

deafness /dɛfnəs/

NONCOUNT NOUN Someone's **deafness** is their inability to hear anything or hear very well. ○ *Because of her deafness she had had to become an expert lip reader.*

decline /dɪklaɪn/ (declines, declining, declined)

VERB If something **declines**, it becomes less in quantity, importance, or strength. ○ *The number of staff has declined from 217,000 to 114,000.*

demonstration /dɛmənstreɪʃən/ (demonstrations)

NOUN A **demonstration** of a fact or situation is a clear proof of it. ○ *This is a clear demonstration of how technology has changed.*

deny /dɪnaɪ/ (denies, denying, denied)

VERB When you **deny** something, you state that it is not true. ○ *They all denied ever having seen her.*

depression /dɪprɛʃən/

NOUN **Depression** is a mental state in which you are sad and feel that you cannot enjoy anything, because your situation is so difficult and unpleasant. ○ *Mr. Thomas was suffering from depression.*

descendant /dɪsɛndənt/ (descendants)

NOUN Something current which developed from an older thing can be called a **descendant** of it. ○ *They are the descendants of plants imported by the early settlers.*

determining factor /dɪtɜːrmɪnɪŋ fæktər/ (determining factors)

NOUN The **determining factor** is the factor that influences the final decision. ○ *The determining factor is the cost.*

dismiss /dɪsmɪs/ (dismisses, dismissing, dismissed)

VERB If you **dismiss** something, you decide or say that it is not important enough for you to think about or consider. ○ *Mr Wakeham dismissed the reports as speculation.*

display /dɪspleɪ/ (displays, displaying, displayed)

VERB If you **display** a characteristic, quality, or emotion, you behave in a way which shows that you have it. ○ *It was unlike Gordon to display his feelings.*

distinctive /dɪstɪŋktɪv/

ADJECTIVE Something that is **distinctive** has a special quality or feature which makes it easily recognizable and different from other things of the same type. ○ *His voice was very distinctive.*

distort /dɪstɔːᶳt/ **(distorts, distorting, distorted)**
VERB If you **distort** a statement, fact, or idea, you report or represent it in an untrue way. ○ *The senator has said his remarks at the weekend have been distorted.*

document /dɒkjəmɛnt/ **(documents, documenting, documented)**
VERB If you **document** something, you make a detailed record of it in writing or on film or tape. ○ *He wrote a book documenting his prison experiences.*

domestic /dəmɛstɪk/
ADJECTIVE¹ A **domestic** animal is one that is not wild and is kept either on a farm to produce food or in someone's home as a pet. ○ *Pine martens are a similar size to a domestic cat.*
ADJECTIVE² **Domestic** items and services are intended to be used in people's homes rather than in factories or offices. ○ *A lot of the vintage domestic objects came from her grandmother's home.*

edition /ɪdɪʃᵊn/ **(editions)**
NOUN An **edition** is a particular version of a book, stamp, magazine, or newspaper that is printed at a certain time. ○ *A paperback edition is now available in bookstores.*

eligible /ɛlɪdʒɪbᵊl/
ADJECTIVE Someone who is **eligible** to do something is qualified or able to do it, for example because they are old enough. ○ *Almost half the population are eligible to vote in today's election.*

endure /ɪndjʊəᶳ/ **(endures, enduring, endured)**
VERB If you **endure** a painful or difficult situation, you experience it and do not avoid it or give up, usually because you cannot. ○ *Her friendly nature is all the more remarkable for the immense suffering she endured.*

enforce /ɪnfɔːᶳs/ **(enforces, enforcing, enforced)**
VERB If people in authority **enforce** a law or a rule, they make sure that it is obeyed. ○ *One of the officer's duties was to help the council to enforce the ban.*

establish /ɪstæblɪʃ/ **(establishes, establishing, established)**
VERB If someone **establishes** something such as an organization, a type of activity, or a set of rules, they create it or introduce it in such a way that it is likely to last for a long time. ○ *The U.N. has established detailed criteria for who should be allowed to vote.*

establishment /ɪstæblɪʃmənt/
NOUN You refer to the people who have power and influence in the running of a country, society, or organization as the **establishment**. ○ *Shopkeepers would once have been pillars of the establishment.*

estimated /ɛstɪmeɪtɪd/
ADJECTIVE An **estimated** number has been roughly calculated. ○ *An estimated 60% of the electorate voted in the election.*

evident /ɛvɪdənt/
ADJECTIVE If something is **evident**, you notice it easily and clearly. ○ *His footprints were clearly evident in the heavy dust.*

expertise /ɛkspɜːᶳtiːz/
NONCOUNT NOUN **Expertise** is special skill or knowledge that is acquired by training, study, or practice. ○ *The problem is that most local authorities lack the expertise to deal with the problem.*

exponential /ɛkspənɛnʃᵊl/
ADJECTIVE **Exponential** means growing or increasing very rapidly. [FORMAL] ○ *The policy tried to check the exponential growth of public expenditure.*

export
VERB /ɪkspɔːᶳt/ **(exports, exporting, exported)** To **export** products or raw materials means to sell them to another country. ○ *The nation also exports rice.*
NOUN /ɛkspɔːᶳt/ **(exports)** **Export** is the act of selling goods to another country and sending them there. ○ *The company focuses on the production and export of cheap casual wear.*

feature /fiːtʃəᶳ/ **(features, featuring, featured)**
VERB When something such as a film or exhibition **features** a particular person or thing, they are an important part of it. ○ *This spectacular event, now in its 5th year, features a stunning catwalk show.*

federal /fɛdərəl/
ADJECTIVE **Federal** means belonging or relating to the national government of a federal country rather than to one of the states within it. ○ *The federal government controls just 6% of the education budget.*

fee /fiː/ **(fees)**
NOUN A **fee** is a sum of money that you pay to be allowed to do something. ○ *He hadn't paid his membership fee.*

fertility rate /fəᶳtɪliti reɪt/ **(fertility rates)**
NOUN The **fertility rate** of a woman or a female animal or bird is the average number of children or young that would be born to her over her lifetime. ○ *Around the world the fertility rate has fallen and continues to fall.*

fiber /faɪbəᶳ/ **(fibers)**
NOUN A **fiber** is a thin thread of a natural or artificial substance, especially one that is used to make things. ○ *If you look at the paper under a microscope you will see the fibers.*

format /fɔːᶳmæt/ **(formats)**
NOUN The **format** of something is the way or order in which it is arranged and presented. ○ *I had met with him to explain the format of the program.*

formation /fɔːᶳmeɪʃᵊn/
NONCOUNT NOUN The **formation** of something is the starting or creation of it. ○ *This is the first step in the formation of a new government.*

foundation /faʊndeɪʃᵊn/ (foundations)

NOUN The **foundation** of a building or other structure is the layer of bricks or concrete below the ground that it is built on. ○ *This will serve as the joint foundation of a new church and mosque.*

function /fʌŋkʃᵊn/ (functions, functioning, functioned)

VERB If you say that someone **is functioning**, you mean that they are living as normal. ○ *She is now 22 and has a job and friends, so I think she is functioning OK.*

fundamental /fʌndəmɛntᵊl/

ADJECTIVE You use **fundamental** to describe things, activities, and principles that are very important or essential. They affect the basic nature of other things or are the most important element upon which other things depend. ○ *Our constitution embodies all the fundamental principles of democracy.*

gender /dʒɛndər/ (genders)

NOUN **Gender** is the state of being male or female in relation to the social and cultural roles that are considered appropriate for men and women. ○ *Gender stereotyping can be as damaging for men as it can for women.*

generate /dʒɛnəreɪt/ (generates, generating, generated)

VERB To **generate** something means to cause it to begin and develop. ○ *The president said the reforms would generate new jobs.*

guarantee /gærəntiː/ (guarantees, guaranteeing, guaranteed)

VERB If you **guarantee** something, you promise that it will definitely happen, or that you will do or provide it for someone. ○ *All students are guaranteed campus accommodation for their first year.*

gyrate /dʒaɪreɪt/ (gyrates, gyrating, gyrated)

VERB If something **gyrates**, it changes in a rapid and uncontrolled way. ○ *Oil prices gyrated yesterday as some nations began to cut production.*

hazard /hæzərd/ (hazards)

NOUN A **hazard** is something which could be dangerous to you, your health or safety, or your plans or reputation. ○ *A new report suggests that chewing-gum may be a health hazard.*

hereditary /hɪrɛdɪtri/

ADJECTIVE A **hereditary** characteristic or illness is passed on to a child from its parents before it is born. ○ *In men, hair loss is hereditary.*

icebox /aɪs bɒks/ (iceboxes)

NOUN An **icebox** is a large metal container which is kept cool, usually by electricity, so that food that is put in it stays fresh. ○ *They would store it in specially designed iceboxes to keep it frozen.*

Impressionist painter /ɪmprɛʃənɪst peɪntər/ (Impressionist painters)

NOUN An **Impressionist painter** is an artist who paints in a style that concentrates on the effect of light rather than on detail. ○ *The Impressionist painter most readily associated with London is Claude Monet.*

incident /ɪndɪkeɪt/ (incidents)

NOUN An **incident** is something that happens, often something that is unpleasant. [FORMAL] ○ *These incidents were the latest in a series of disputes between the two companies.*

indicate /ɪndɪkeɪt/ (indicates, indicating, indicated)

VERB¹ If one thing **indicates** another, the first thing shows that the second is true or exists. ○ *A survey of retired people has indicated that most are independent and enjoying life.*

VERB² If you **indicate** an opinion, an intention, or a fact, you mention it in an indirect way. ○ *Mr. Rivers has indicated that he may resign.*

induce /ɪndjuːs/ (induces, inducing, induced)

VERB To **induce** a state or condition means to cause it. ○ *Doctors said surgery could induce a heart attack.*

inherent /ɪnhɛrənt, -hɪər-/

ADJECTIVE The **inherent** qualities of something are the necessary and natural parts of it. ○ *Stress is an inherent part of modern life.*

initially /ɪnɪʃəli/

ADVERB **Initially** means soon after the beginning of a process or situation, rather than in the middle or at the end of it. ○ *Initially, they were wary of Simon.*

innate /ɪneɪt/

ADJECTIVE An **innate** quality or ability is one which a person is born with. ○ *They have an innate sense of fairness.*

innocence /ɪnəsəns/

NONCOUNT NOUN If someone proves their **innocence**, they prove that they are not guilty of a crime. ○ *He claims he has evidence which could prove his innocence.*

innovation /ɪnəveɪʃᵊn/ (innovations)

NOUN An **innovation** is a new thing or a new method of doing something. ○ *The vegetarian burger was an innovation which was rapidly exported to Britain.*

insert /ɪnsɜːrt/ (inserts, inserting, inserted)

VERB If you **insert** a comment into a piece of writing or a speech, you include it. ○ *They wanted to insert a clause calling for a popular vote on the issue.*

integral /ɪntɪgrəl/

ADJECTIVE Something that is an **integral** part of something is an essential part of that thing. ○ *Rituals and festivals form an integral part of every human society.*

intense /ɪntɛns/
ADJECTIVE If you describe an activity as **intense**, you mean that it is very serious and concentrated, and often involves doing a great deal in a short time. ○ *The battle for third place was intense.*

inverted /ɪnvɜːʳtɪd/
ADJECTIVE Something that is **inverted** has been turned the other way up or back to front. [FORMAL] ○ *Oak furniture often has inverted hearts and mottos.*

investment /ɪnvɛstmənt/ (**investments**)
NOUN If you describe something you buy as an **investment**, you mean that it will be worth the money, because it will make you more money in the future. ○ *Art is an investment to be admired and appreciated on a daily basis.*

journal /dʒɜːʳnəl/ (**journals**)
NOUN A **journal** is a magazine, especially one that deals with a specialized subject. ○ *All our results are published in scientific journals.*

lava /lɑːvə/
NOUN **Lava** is the very hot liquid rock that comes out of a volcano. ○ *The volcano in the distance was spilling molten lava.*

legitimize /lɪdʒɪtɪmaɪz/ (**legitimizes, legitimizing, legitimized**)
VERB To **legitimize** something, especially something bad, means to officially allow it, approve it, or make it seem acceptable. [FORMAL] ○ *They will accept no agreement that legitimizes the division of the country.*

levy /lɛvi/ (**levies, levying, levied**)
VERB If a government or organization **levies** a sum of money, it demands it from people or organizations. ○ *Taxes should not be levied without the authority of the government.*

lie detector test /laɪ dɪtɛktəʳ tɛst/ (**lie detector tests**)
NOUN A **lie detector test** is a test that someone takes to discover whether they are telling the truth about something. ○ *Undercover agents were accepted into the gang only after lie detector tests.*

lobby /lɒbi/ (**lobbies, lobbying, lobbied**)
VERB If you **lobby** someone such as a member of a government or council, you try to persuade them that a particular law should be changed or that a particular thing should be done. ○ *Care workers from all over the UK lobbied Parliament last week to demand a better financial deal.*

maintenance /meɪntɪnəns/
NONCOUNT NOUN The **maintenance** of a building, vehicle, road, or area is the process of keeping it in good condition by regularly checking it and repairing it when necessary. ○ *The window had been replaced last week during routine maintenance.*

mandatory /mændətri/
ADJECTIVE If an action or procedure is **mandatory**, people have to do it, because it is a rule or a law. [FORMAL] ○ *Attendance is mandatory for the entire day.*

market value /mɑːʳkɪt væljuː/ (**market values**)
NOUN The **market value** of something is the amount of money you can get if you sell it to the public. [BUSINESS] ○ *Facebook had a market value of $104 billion when it launched in 2012.*

materials /mətɪəriəlz/
PLURAL NOUN **Materials** are the things that you need for a particular activity. ○ *The builders ran out of materials.*

mature /mətjʊəʳ/ (**matures, maturing, matured**)
VERB When a child **matures**, it becomes an adult. ○ *You will learn what to expect as your child matures physically.*

migratory /maɪgrətəri/
ADJECTIVE A **migratory** bird, fish, or animal is one that migrates every year. ○ *Once a year these migratory birds return to Tasmania to breed.*

monitor /mɒnɪtəʳ/ (**monitored, monitoring, monitored**)
VERB If you **monitor** something, you regularly check its development or progress, and sometimes comment on it. ○ *You need feedback to monitor progress.*

myth /mɪθ/ (**myths**)
NOUN If you describe a belief or explanation as a **myth**, you mean that many people believe it but it is actually untrue. ○ *It is a damaging and misleading myth that planning is a barrier to housebuilding.*

nestling /nɛstlɪŋ/ (**nestlings**)
NOUN A **nestling** is a young bird that has not yet learned to fly. ○ *The male shares the feeding of the nestlings with the female.*

nomination /nɒmɪneɪʃən/ (**nominations**)
NOUN A **nomination** is an official suggestion of someone as a candidate in an election or for a job. ○ *He announced his candidacy for the presidential nomination.*

obtain /ɒbteɪn/ (**obtains, obtaining, obtained**)
VERB To **obtain** something means to get it or achieve it. [FORMAL] ○ *Evans was trying to obtain a false passport and other documents.*

occupation /ɒkjʊpeɪʃən/ (**occupations**)
NOUN Your **occupation** is your job or profession. ○ *I suppose I was looking for an occupation which was going to be an adventure.*

occurrence /əkʌrəns/ (**occurrences**)
NOUN An **occurrence** is something that happens. [FORMAL] ○ *Complaints seemed to be an everyday occurrence.*

participate /pɑːʳtɪsɪpeɪt/ (**participates, participating, participated**)
VERB If you **participate** in an activity, you take part in it. ○ *They expected him to participate in the ceremony.*

penalty /pɛnəlti/ (penalties)

NOUN A **penalty** is a punishment that someone is given for doing something which is against a law or rule. ○ *The maximum penalty is up to 7 years' imprisonment.*

perception /pərsɛpʃən/ (perceptions)

NOUN Your **perception** of something is the way that you think about it or the impression you have of it. ○ *He is interested in how our perceptions of death affect the way we live.*

perforation /pɜːrfəreɪʃən/ (perforations)

NOUN **Perforations** are small holes that are made in something, especially in paper. ○ *Tear off the form along the perforations.*

persuasive speech /pərsweɪsɪv spiːtʃ/ (persuasive speeches)

NOUN A **persuasive speech** is a speech that is likely to persuade a person to believe or do a particular thing. ○ *Every student has to deliver a three-part persuasive speech to an audience.*

pesticide /pɛstɪsaɪd/ (pesticides)

NOUN **Pesticides** are chemicals which farmers put on their crops to kill harmful insects. ○ *The insects are in decline, endangered by disease, pesticides, and a changing climate.*

physiological /fɪziəlɒdʒɪkəl/

ADJECTIVE **Physiological** refers to the way that a human or animal's body or a plant functions. ○ *They will also collect physiological data, such as body temperature, weight, and heart rate.*

polling place /poʊlɪŋ pleɪs/ (polling places)

NOUN A **polling place** is a place where people go to vote at an election. ○ *I bumped into him and three colleagues outside a polling place.*

primitive /prɪmɪtɪv/

ADJECTIVE If you describe something as **primitive**, you mean that it is very simple in style or very old-fashioned. ○ *It's using some rather primitive technology.*

procedure /prəsiːdʒər/ (procedures)

NOUN A **procedure** is a way of doing something, especially the usual or correct way. ○ *Police insist that he did not follow the correct procedure in applying for a visa.*

process /proʊsɛs/ (processes)

A **process** is a series of actions which are carried out in order to achieve a particular result. ○ *They decided to spread the building process over three years.*

prospect /prɒspɛkt/ (prospects)

NOUN If there is some **prospect** of something happening, there is a possibility that it will happen. ○ *Unfortunately, there is little prospect of seeing these big questions answered.*

psychological /saɪkəlɒdʒɪkəl/

ADJECTIVE **Psychological** means concerned with a person's mind and thoughts. ○ *Robyn's loss of memory is a psychological problem, rather than a physical one.*

publicity stunt /pʌblɪsɪti stʌnt/ (publicity stunts)

NOUN A **publicity stunt** is something that is done to attract the public's attention to someone or something. ○ *It was all just a publicity stunt.*

publish /pʌblɪʃ/ (publishes, publishing, published)

VERB When a company **publishes** a book or magazine, it prints copies of it, which are sent to shops to be sold. ○ *They publish reference books.*

radical /rædɪkəl/

ADJECTIVE **Radical** changes and differences are very important and great in degree. ○ *The country needs a period of calm without radical change.*

radius /reɪdiəs/ (radii)

NOUN The **radius** around a particular point is the distance from it in any direction. ○ *Nigel has searched for work in a ten-mile radius around his home.*

rags /rægz/

PLURAL NOUN **Rags** are old torn clothes. ○ *They were walking along the dusty road in rags.*

rationalize /ræʃənəlaɪz/ (rationalizes, rationalizing, rationalized)

VERB If you try to **rationalize** attitudes or actions that are difficult to accept, you think of reasons to justify or explain them. ○ *I poured my thoughts out on paper in an attempt to rationalize my feelings.*

red herring /rɛd hɛrɪŋ/ (red herrings)

NOUN If you say that something is a **red herring**, you mean that it is not important and it takes your attention away from the main subject or problem you are considering. ○ *As Dr. Smith left he said that the inquiry was something of a red herring.*

reinforce /riːɪnfɔːrs/ (reinforces, reinforcing, reinforced)

VERB If something **reinforces** a feeling, situation, or process, it makes it stronger or more intense. ○ *The guidelines reinforce best practice in schools.*

reject /rɪdʒɛkt/ (rejects, rejecting, rejected)

VERB If you **reject** something such as a proposal, a request, or an offer, you do not accept it or you do not agree to it. ○ *Seventeen publishers rejected the manuscript before anyone saw its potential.*

rely on /rɪlaɪ ɒn/ (relies on, relying on, relied on)

PHRASAL VERB If you **rely on** someone or something, you need them and depend on them in order to live or work properly. ○ *They relied heavily on the advice of the professionals.*

resemble /rɪzɛmbəl/ **(resembles, resembling, resembled)**
VERB If one thing or person **resembles** another, they are similar to each other. ○ *The fish had white, firm flesh that resembled chicken.*

restriction /rɪstrɪkʃən/ **(restrictions)**
NOUN A **restriction** is an official rule that limits what you can do or that limits the amount or size of something. ○ *The relaxation of travel restrictions means they are free to travel and work.*

retain /rɪteɪn/ **(retains, retaining, retained)**
VERB To **retain** something means to continue to have that thing. [FORMAL] ○ *If left covered in a warm place, this rice will retain its heat for a good hour.*

secure /sɪkjʊər/ **(secures, securing, secured)**
VERB If you **secure** something that you want or need, you obtain it, often after a lot of effort. [FORMAL] ○ *Graham's achievements helped secure him the job.*

seek /siːk/ **(seeks, seeking, sought)**
VERB If you **seek** something such as a job or a position, you try to find or obtain one. [FORMAL] ○ *They have had to seek work as laborers.*

sign language /saɪn læŋgwɪdʒ/ **(sign languages)**
NOUN **Sign language** is movements of your hands and arms used to communicate. There are several official sign languages, used for example by deaf people. ○ *Her son used sign language to tell her what happened.*

signify /sɪgnɪfaɪ/ **(signifies, signifying, signified)**
VERB If an event, a sign, or a symbol **signifies** something, it is a sign of that thing or represents that thing. ○ *Fever accompanied by a runny nose usually signifies a cold.*

simultaneously /sɪməlteɪniəsli/
ADVERB Things which happen or exist **simultaneously** happen or exist at the same time. ○ *The two guns fired almost simultaneously.*

spouse /spaʊs/ **(spouses)**
NOUN Someone's **spouse** is the person they are married to. ○ *It was a long, three-hour lunch, just him, her and their spouses.*

stance /stæns/ **(stances)**
NOUN Your **stance** on a particular matter is your attitude to it. ○ *Congress had agreed to reconsider its stance on the proposal.*

statistic /stətɪstɪk/ **(statistics)**
NOUN **Statistics** are facts which are obtained from analyzing information expressed in numbers, for example information about the number of times that something happens. ○ *Official statistics show real wages declining by 24%.*

stereotype /stɛriətaɪp/ **(stereotypes)**
NOUN A **stereotype** is a fixed general image or set of characteristics that a lot of people believe represent a particular type of person or thing. ○ *There's always been a stereotype about successful businessmen.*

stocks and bonds /stɒks ənd bɒndz/
PLURAL NOUN **Stocks and bonds** are types of investment, either as ownership of a part of a company or as a loan to a company. ○ *Global investors plowed money back into stocks and bonds last week.*

submit /səbmɪt/ **(submits, submitting, submitted)**
VERB If you **submit** a piece of work to someone, you formally send it to them so that they can consider it or decide about it. ○ *They submitted their reports to the CEO yesterday.*

subtle /sʌtəl/ **(subtler, subtlest)**
ADJECTIVE Something that is **subtle** is not immediately obvious or noticeable. ○ *There are slow and subtle changes that take place in all living things.*

synthetic /sɪnθɛtɪk/
ADJECTIVE **Synthetic** products are made from chemicals or artificial substances rather than from natural ones. ○ *Boots made from synthetic materials can usually be washed in a machine.*

targeted /tɑːgɪtɪd/
ADJECTIVE A **targeted** group of people are a group of people who others try to appeal to and affect their decisions. ○ *For big brands sending samples to a targeted audience could prove more effective than traditional advertising.*

tension /tɛnʃən/
NONCOUNT NOUN **Tension** is a feeling of worry and anxiety which makes it difficult for you to relax. ○ *Smiling and laughing has actually been shown to relieve tension and stress.*

theoretical /θiːərɛtɪkəl/
ADJECTIVE If you describe a situation as a **theoretical** one, you mean that although it is supposed to be true or to exist in the way stated, it may not in fact be true or exist in that way. ○ *These fears are purely theoretical.*

trait /treɪt, treɪ/ **(traits)**
NOUN A **trait** is a particular characteristic, quality, or tendency that someone or something has. ○ *Many of our personality traits are developed during those early months.*

treaty /triːti/ **(treaties)**
NOUN A **treaty** is a written agreement between countries in which they agree to do a particular thing or to help each other. ○ *They proposed a global treaty on cutting emissions.*

undermine /ˌʌndəʳˈmaɪn/ (undermines, undermining, undermined)

VERB If you **undermine** something, you make it less strong or less secure than it was before, often by a gradual process or by repeated efforts. ○ *Some intelligence agencies are accused of trying to undermine the government.*

---

unique /juːˈniːk/

ADJECTIVE Something that is **unique** is the only one of its kind. ○ *The area has its own unique language, Catalan.*

---

upside down /ˌʌpsaɪd ˈdaʊn/

ADJECTIVE If something is **upside down**, it has been turned round so that the part that is usually lowest is above the part that is usually highest. ○ *The painting was hung upside down.*

---

valid /ˈvælɪd/

ADJECTIVE A **valid** argument, comment, or idea is based on sensible reasoning. ○ *They put forward many valid reasons for not exporting goods.*

---

validity /vəˈlɪdɪti/

NONCOUNT NOUN The **validity** of something such as a ticket or other document is the fact that it can be used and will be accepted by people in authority. ○ *Formal checks would take place on the validity of travel documents.*

---

visible /ˈvɪzɪbəl/

ADJECTIVE If something is **visible**, it can be seen. ○ *The warning lights were clearly visible.*

---

voluntary /ˈvɒləntri/

ADJECTIVE **Voluntary** actions or activities are done because someone chooses to do them and not because they have been forced to do them. ○ *The scheme, due to begin next month, will be voluntary.*

---

whiskers /ˈhwɪskəʳ/

PLURAL NOUN You say that someone has **whiskers** when they have a beard or that part of it growing on the sides of their face. ○ *The hair on his head was dark, but the whiskers on his face were white.*

Audio Script

Listening 1

Questions 1 through 5

Track 1 [page 18]

Listen as a student consults with a university employee.

Student: Is this the bursar's office?

Employee: Yes, it is. Can I help you?

Student: I need to register for next semester's classes, but my advisor told me I have a hold on my account and can't register.

Employee: Well, then it must be a financial hold if your advisor told you to come to the bursar's office. If it had been an academic hold, you would have to go to the dean's office. Let me check. Can you spell your last name for me, or do you know your ID number?

Student: It's probably easier if I give you my ID number. It's 66011406.

Employee: Ah, here you are. That's right. You owe $32.00 for parking tickets. Your license number is 76841, correct?

Student: Oh no! I paid that last week. I have the receipt somewhere in my backpack. Here it is.

Employee: Let me see the receipt. You're right. My apologies. Sometimes the interoffice emails take a few days to get updated into our system. While you're here, Mr. Hatayadom, did I pronounce your name correctly?

Student: Close enough. I'm used to it by now. The stress is on the *DOM*, HatayaDOM. It's equally hard to spell and pronounce!

Employee: I see you're not on the monthly tuition payment plan. Many students pay this way, so they don't have to come up with so much money all at once.

Student: Can international students pay this way?

Employee: Of course. There's a ninety dollar annual service fee to the company—we use College Payment Services, a local company—and then you pay them monthly. You then won't be billed from us any longer. They pay us, and you work out a monthly payment plan with them. But, it's totally up to you. I have their brochure if you want to take it with you. It explains how it works and how to contact the company.

Student: Sure. I'll read it over and discuss it with my parents. Umm, are you sure the hold has been removed from my account?

Employee: Take a look. If you had a hold, there would be an X in the hold column. It's empty.

Student: OK. Thanks. Now I have to hope my advisor is still in her office to approve my course choices.

Employee: Good luck Mr. Hatayadom, and feel free to stop by any time.

Student: Thanks, but let's hope I won't have to.

Track 2 [page 19]

Listen again to part of the passage. Then answer the question.

Employee: Can you spell your last name for me, or do you know your ID number?

Student: It's probably easier if I give you my ID number.

Why does the student say this?

Student: It's probably easier if I give you my ID number.

Questions 6 through 11

Track 3 [page 20]

Listen to a lecture in a genetics class.

Professor: Welcome to Genetics 101. I'm sure most of you have had some class work in your high school biology class with genetics: why some people have blue eyes, why some have curly hair, and so on. This course will examine the relationship between genetics and biochemistry and the impact on medicine, disease, and agriculture today. I know that some of you are taking this course to fulfill your science elective and have no intention of majoring in one of the natural sciences, whereas this course is required for biology majors. I hope to make this course interesting to all of you nevertheless. I predict that you will find many of the lectures and case studies extremely interesting and relevant to your lives.

I hope you've all read chapter one in our textbook. We begin, of course, with the father of genetics, Gregor Johann Mendel, the Austrian botanist and monk. I'm sure you recall how his experiments with the breeding of garden peas led to the development of this field of study. In case you're a little rusty, let me remind you of his experiments. He studied the inheritance of seven distinct traits in garden pea plants. These traits included seed shape, were they smooth or wrinkled, and plant height, were they tall or short plants?

He then—remember he was a monk, so he was a very patient man—bred and crossbred hundreds of plants and observed the characteristics of each successive generation. Like all organisms that reproduce, pea plants produce their offspring through the union of special cells called gametes. In pea plants, a male gamete, or pollen grain, combines with a female gamete, or egg cell, to form a seed.

Mendel concluded that plant traits are handed down through hereditary elements in the gametes. These elements we now call genes. Each gene can have slightly different information related to one trait. We call these variants alleles. He reasoned that each plant receives a pair of alleles for each trait, one allele from each of its parents. Based on his experiments, he concluded that if a plant inherits two different alleles for one trait, one allele will be dominant and the other will be recessive. The trait of the dominant allele will be visible in the plant. For example, the allele for smooth seeds is dominant, and the allele for wrinkled seeds is recessive. A plant that inherits a different copy of each allele will have round seeds.

Now, most of Mendel's theories have been proved although some exceptions have been found. I'm going to get off track for a couple of minutes to discuss the difficulties of predicting red hair. Since I'm a carrot-top myself, I find the issue near and dear to my heart. The myth that redheads might die off in the near future has drawn considerable attention. Due to the recessive and not dominant nature of red hair, it takes two carriers to have a red-headed child. You can have brown hair but still be carrying the recessive allele for red hair. Let's look at some charts. If both parents are carriers but not redheads, there is a 25% chance of producing redheads. If one parent had red hair and the other is a carrier, there's a 50-50 chance. If both parents have red hair, then all offspring will be red headed. I'll share with you that I have two children, and one has brown hair. Can you tell me what color hair my wife has? It's actually a tricky question, and I'll explain why in Wednesday's class.

Track 4 [page 21]

Listen again to part of the passage. Then answer the question.

Professor: I'm sure you recall how his experiments with the breeding of garden peas led to the development of this field of study. In case you're a little rusty, let me remind you of his experiments. He studied the inheritance of seven distinct traits in garden pea plants. These traits included seed shape, were they smooth or wrinkled and plant height, were they tall or short plants?

What does the professor mean when he says this?

Professor: In case you're a little rusty…

Questions 12 through 17

Track 5 [page 22]

Listen to a discussion from a philosophy class.

Professor: Remember we're leaving for Brook Farm this Saturday at 8:30 A.M. It should take us about four hours to get there.

Student 1: But professor? I know I read it burned down.

Professor: Yes, that's partially correct. The central building burned down in 1846, and all that remains of the community who lived there from 1841 to 1846 are cellar holes.

Student 2: So if that's all that's left, why are we going?

Professor: Good question. Today there is a new push to sow the seeds for a New Brook Farm, one that will support sustainable farming and community education. I've been asked, since I'm a Transcendentalist scholar, if my students and I would be interested in taking the lead on this new venture.

Student 3: With everything we've been studying about Transcendentalists, I think the founding fathers would delight in this rebirth.

Professor: Agreed. And there will be a connection with children from area schools as well. So those of you who are getting a teaching certificate can perhaps help us out here.

Student 4: Didn't I read that the land though wasn't suitable for farming, and since they embraced physical labor, the lack of farming led to the downfall of Brook Farm?

Professor: That's partially correct. One of the biggest issues back in the 1840s for them was a lack of water power. Today that won't be an issue. The site is on the city water line, and there will be plenty of water for limited farming. Remember it will be farming with an emphasis on school-aged children, so no large machinery.

Student 2: Will it be organic?

Professor: I'm afraid that would be too expensive. It will be crops that you would find at a local farmer's market such as herbs and whatever the public seems to want.

Student 1: How many people actually lived at Brook Farm?

Professor: They began with 15. Each member worked several hours a day on the farm so they could be close to nature. They believed that the physical world is secondary to the spiritual world, but they wanted to be financially self-sufficient. Some wealthy authors of the day, including Nathaniel Hawthorne, lived there briefly, but the idea was that the community would live off what it produced. It lasted only six years and never had more than 120 members at one time.

Student 2: Were they all philosophers?

Professor: Yes, in the sense that they all believed in Transcendentalism as a philosophy for life, encompassing literature, religion, and social issues. Don't forget, it wasn't all work. After work and dinner, they had plenty of time for music, dancing, card playing, dramatic readings, costume parties, sledding, and skating.

Student 3: I think the young students would enjoy seeing us dressed in costumes, such as typical clothing of the 1840s.

Student 4: And we should probably come up with a list of herbs or other small plants and vegetables that wouldn't be hard to grow quickly.

Professor: I'm glad to see you're getting excited about the project. Remember to read chapter 3 before Saturday, and bring with you a notebook…

Track 6 [page 23]

Listen again to part of the passage. Then answer the question.

Professor: And there will be a connection with children from area schools as well. So those of you who are getting a teaching certificate can perhaps help us out here.

Why does the professor say this?

Professor: Those of you who are getting a teaching certificate can perhaps help us out here.

Questions 18 through 22

Track 7 [page 24]

Listen to a conversation between a student and a professor.

Student: I was wondering if you had the time to go over some ideas I have for my persuasive speech. My presentation is a week from Thursday.

Professor: Sure. This is a good time. It's my office hour. Come in and have a seat. What ideas have you come up with?

Student: I know you told us to stay away from the usual topics, like why everyone should vote, but I'm afraid the two ideas I have aren't so original.

Professor: Perhaps you misunderstood me. I didn't say the idea had to be original. What I did say is if you

choose a topic that most students already have an opinion about, it's hard to get them to be open-minded about your speech. Do you remember I suggested you can do a quick paper survey to see where the class stands? If you were doing why everyone should vote, for example, you could just message your classmates asking "Are you planning to vote in the next election?" If you find that most of the class is planning NOT to vote, it will affect what you present. So what have you come up with?

Student: One idea is that we should stop buying shampoo in single-use plastic bottles and the second is that the shuttle bus from the subway to campus should run later on the weekends.

Professor: Two good topics. Let me hear your research on both.

Student: With shampoo, I thought I'd begin with a rhetorical question—like you suggest. How many of you have bought a bottle of shampoo in the past month? I'm sure many hands will go up. I then will discuss the research about the amount of plastic from water bottles in landfills and in the ocean and how that plastic will remain for the next couple of hundred years.

Professor: Remember those facts and statistics need to be recent and reliable and you need to tell us where you got the information from. What will you discuss after you give the facts and statistics? You'll need to have expert testimony. Since it's a persuasive speech, you'll need to be clear on what it is you want the students to do. How can they change their lives without making the expectation too difficult to enact?

Student: I'm good with the research part. I'm still grappling with the enactment part. I know it's easy to buy shampoo in bottles. I don't want to ask them to do something they're not going to do. I think I might have a good idea. I've been talking with the campus store about ordering bars of shampoo that don't have any packaging and have our school's logo imprinted on them. I might be able to get some at a steep discount since it was my idea, and then I could hand them out. I'm hoping the student government activities fund will give me the money to buy them.

Professor: Freebies are always good. That topic is sounding better and better. Tell me about the second one.

Student: I don't know if you know that the shuttle bus stops running at 11 p.m. on weekends. That means we have to leave downtown no later than 10:30 to make sure we're at the shuttle stop by 11. That's ridiculously early.

Professor: Do you have any idea approximately how many students would like to take a later shuttle? This topic is less academic, but it certainly is relevant to our class. You could find out what time other colleges and universities in our area stop running their shuttles, and you could have the class sign a petition. That's an easy expectation.

Student: Now I'm even more confused because I feel I have two good topics! Thanks for your advice and for listening.

Professor: My pleasure.

Track 8 [page 25]

Listen again to part of the passage. Then answer the question.

Professor: Tell me about the second one.

Student: I don't know if you know that the shuttle bus stops running at 11 p.m. on weekends. That means we have to leave downtown no later than 10:30 to make sure we're at the shuttle stop by 11.

Why does the student say this?

Questions 23 through 28

Track 9 [page 26]

Listen to a lecture in an economics class.

Professor: Today we're going to begin our study of game theory. It's probably one of the most seemingly simple yet complex economic theories. This so-called branch of economics uses math to study strategy. In game theory, any situation, such as a board game, sports, a game of luck, or military decisions, are called games. What I'm saying is that game theory is used to study any situation in which more than one person makes choices.

The players are not always even people. Players can be people, companies, or even armies. Each player wants something. For example, a company wants to make as much money as it can or a country wants to win a war. Sometimes the players work cooperatively, but oftentimes they compete against one another.

One well-known game is called the prisoner's dilemma. It's an imaginary situation that explains why people do not cooperate in real life. Here's how the dilemma works. Imagine this situation. The police catch two criminals after they have committed a crime. The police do not know which person committed the crime and which one just helped. They question the two in separate cells. Each prisoner can either stay silent or blame the crime on the other person. If both stay silent, they go to jail for only six months. If one betrays, and the other stays silent, the one that stays silent goes to jail for 10 years, and the other one does not go to jail at all. If they both betray each other, they each go jail for 2 years. No matter what happens, the prisoners will never see each other again.

If you're a prisoner in this situation, and you care only about yourself, the way to get the smallest sentence is to betray the other prisoner. No matter what, you get a shorter sentence when you betray than when you don't. If the other prisoner stays silent and doesn't betray, then betraying means you do not go to jail at all instead of going for 6 months. If the other prisoner betrays, then betraying lets you go to jail for 2 years instead of 10 years. In other words, it's always best for you to betray even though the two of you would be better off if you both remained silent. But can you take a chance that the other prisoner will stay silent? We use the term "dominant strategy" to mean that strategy that is always the best thing for you to do. In this case, it's betraying the other prisoner no matter what the other prisoner does.

This situation is like many other situations in the real world. For example, if two countries are trying to decide whether to make new weapons, they are better off if neither country does. But sometimes the countries are in the same situation as the prisoners; each country cares only about itself, and it's better off if it "betrays" the other country by making weapons.

The prisoner's dilemma does not have the same result if some of the details are different. If the prisoners—or countries—can talk with each other and plan for the future, they might both decide to cooperate and not betray each other because they hope that decision will make the other country help them in the future. In game theory, this is called a "repeated game." If the players are altruistic, that is they care about each other, they might be OK with going to jail, so they can help the other person. We will continue this topic next class with some other dilemmas and some other mathematical models. Answer the problem set that's assigned on the syllabus.

Track 10 [page 28]

Listen again to part of the passage. Then answer the question.

Professor: But sometimes the countries are in the same situation as the prisoners; each country cares only about itself, and it's better off if it "betrays" the other country by making weapons.

What does the professor mean when she says this?

Professor: … and it's better off if it betrays the other country …

Speaking 1

Track 11 [page 30]

1. You will be asked your opinion about a familiar topic. Listen to the question, and then prepare your response. You will have 15 seconds to prepare a response and 45 seconds to speak. You can take notes on the main points of a response.

   Some students choose to attend a large university with thousands of students. Others choose to attend a small one. Would you prefer to attend a large university or a small one? Use reasons and details to support your response.

Track 12 [page 31]

2. You will read a short passage and then listen to a conversation about the same topic. You will then answer a question about about them. You will have 45 seconds to read the passage. You can take notes on the main points of the reading passage.

Listen to two students discuss the announcement.

Man: Did you get the announcement? It went out via email a few minutes ago.

Woman: Yeah. I got a text also. How long do you think we're going to be stuck at the hotel?

Man: I wouldn't say "stuck." It's air conditioned and there's an indoor pool. Housekeeping even cleans the rooms every day!

Woman: I know it's much nicer in the hotel than in Shaw, but I'd still rather be in the dorm. It's way too inconvenient to go back to the hotel between classes, and we had to leave so quickly I don't have most of my clothes or books. I've worn the same sweater for three days in a row, and I'm afraid my grades will slip this semester. The worst part is I don't have my notes to study for this week's chemistry test.

Man: All of my teachers have been so nice about it. One put books on reserve in the library, another handed out notes from all earlier lectures, and my economics professor has invited those of us in the hotel to his house for dinner.

Woman: Aren't you the lucky one. No wonder you're not complaining! I'm hoping that we can back in the dorm today or tomorrow to get some stuff out.

Now answer the following question:

How do these students feel about staying in the hotel? Explain the reasons they give.

Track 13 [page 33]

3. You will read a short passage and then listen to a conversation about the same topic. You will then answer a question about about them. You will have 45 seconds to read the passage. You can take notes on the main points of the reading passage.

Listen to the passage.

Professor: So we've been discussing whether or not parents should sleep with their children in the same bed. Those of you from cultures where this practice is common may find the American obsession with this question—should parents sleep with their children or shouldn't they—somewhat amusing.

Pressure on parents not to sleep with babies in the United States comes from many sources, such as relatives and other parents. Even some pediatricians discourage the practice, for they fear the parents will roll over and suffocate the child. A commonly held American belief has been that children, beginning in infancy, need to learn to take care of their own needs; therefore, sleeping with a parent interferes with this ability.

However, there is a small but growing movement in the U.S. that encourages co-sleeping arrangements. These parents turn to Japan as an example of successful co-sleeping for hundreds of years. Dr. Harkness of the University of Connecticut conducted cross-cultural studies and found no correlation between having babies sleep alone and developing a sense of autonomy.

Now answer the following question:

Using examples from different cultures, explain the thinking behind different sleeping arrangements.

Track 14 [page 35]

4. You will listen to part of a lecture. You can take notes on the main points of the listening passage.

Professor: And now we move onto the next machine. Today we're all familiar with this one in front of us. This machine produces a CT scan, which stands for Computed Tomography scan. It is a medical imaging method that employs tomography. Tomography is the process of generating a two-dimensional image of a slice or section through a three-dimensional object, a tomogram. Undergoing a CT scan is a painless procedure. The CT scan uses digital geometry processing to generate a three-dimensional image of the inside of an object. Many pictures of the same area are taken from many angles and then placed together to produce a 3-D image. The Greek word *tomos* means to slice and the Greek word *graphein* means to write. Inside a CT scanner there is an X-ray detector that can see hundreds of levels of density. It can see tissues inside a solid organ. The data are transmitted to a computer, which builds up a 3-D cross-sectional picture of the part of the body and displays it on the screen. CT scans are very useful in getting a very detailed 3-D image of certain parts of the body, such as soft tissues, the pelvis, blood vessels, the lungs, the brain, the abdomen, and bones.

The first patient brain scan using X-ray computed tomography—the CT scan—was done on October 1, 1971 in England. Since its introduction in the 1970s, the CT scan has become an important tool in place of traditional X-rays due to its production of superior images that often detect disease at an earlier stage than the traditional X-ray can. The usage of these scans has increased dramatically since 1980, due to improved technology, speed, and a greater number of machines, thereby lowering the cost. An estimated 84 million scans were performed last year in the U.S.

What is not commonly known is that the Beatles, perhaps the most famous musical band in history, funded the research to build the CT scan prototype. The CT scan invention earned the 1979 Nobel Prize in Medicine.

Now answer the following question:

How does the professor explain what a CT scan is and how it was funded?

Writing 1

Track 15 [page 39]

Listen to the passage.

Professor: Although kids everywhere may delight in the fact that bees are no longer stinging them on playgrounds and in their backyards as frequently as they used to, the decline in the honeybee populations in the U.S. and around the globe signals a major environmental imbalance that can have far-reaching implications for our agricultural food supply.

The world first took notice in 2006 as beekeepers and scientists began reporting an alarming decline in the bee populations on a number of continents. You might ask why were so many of us caught off guard? Was it a sudden disappearance, or had bee populations been slowly decreasing? Actually the answer is that the numbers dramatically fell suddenly in the middle of the decade. At that time some rather weird and peculiar explanations began circulating. What was causing the bee deaths?

A recent gathering of leading bee biologists yielded no agreement as to the single cause, but most agree that a combination of factors, with one major culprit, is causing the decline. The effects of global warming causing more viruses, as well as radiation from the rapid growth of cell phones, contribute to the bee demise. Most scientists place most of the blame squarely on pesticides that affect the central nervous system of the insect, causing death. Although there are laws in place that restrict the dose of these pesticides, evidence suggests that even low doses can produce severe problems, impacting bees' memory and ability to return home to the hive.

Now answer the following question:

How does the information in the listening passage cast doubt on the information presented in the reading passage?

Listening 2

Questions 1 through 5

Track 16 [page 68]

Listen as a student consults with a professor.

Student:	Hi, Professor Brown. I'm Lauren Klee. You've been assigned to me as an advisor since Professor Jenkinson left. Do you have a few minutes to discuss some questions I have about my major?
Professor:	Hello Lauren. Come in and have a seat. Please tell me more about your situation, and we'll try to sort it out. What is your major right now?
Student:	Well, currently I'm a first semester junior majoring in biology. I do want to apply to medical school, but I've been finding some of the advanced science courses a grind. I thought maybe I should switch to history or business, since those majors might be easier for me.
Professor:	If you switched now, when would you take all the science prerequisites for med school?
Student:	I've already taken a lot of them. I thought if I switched, I could bring up my GPA and have a better shot at med school.
Professor:	Oh, you believe the nonscience courses are easier. Perhaps you're right. What is your GPA?
Student:	A 3.0.
Professor:	Hmm. I'm sure you know it's very competitive to get into med school. Since you've already taken a lot of the prereqs, why not remain a biology major? If you switched now, would you be able to graduate in four years? Don't medical schools prefer their applicants to be science majors?
Student:	Not necessarily. What they look at is one, your GPA, two, how you do on the entrance exams and three, that you've taken all the prereqs. Some students do that after they graduate. And I did check out exactly how many courses I'd need if I switched majors. You know since the college started using its new advising program, I can use the "What If" link on the college website and see exactly how many and which courses I would need if I switched my major, to say history or business.
Professor:	And how many required courses would you have left for each of those?
Student:	Seven for history and eight for business.
Professor:	Then it shouldn't be a problem since you have a year and a half left. I do suggest you make sure

to take all the required premed courses however. Some of them are not offered every semester.

Student:	For sure. Thanks so much.

Questions 6 through 11

Track 17 [page 70]

Listen to a lecture in a legal studies class.

Professor:	Remember last class we were discussing how important expert witnesses can be when presenting your case in the courtroom. Today I want to review with you the qualities lawyers look for in hiring an expert witness to take the stand. Although there are no specific requirements that all experts must meet, depending on the case and the subjects involved, lawyers selecting an expert look for the following criteria. First, it may seem obvious, but a lawyer needs to determine that he or she gets along with the expert. Second, the lawyer needs to verify that this witness is someone that the judge and, more importantly, the jury will understand, respect, like, and trust. If a jury of ordinary people cannot understand or believe the witness, this testimony is worthless.

Next, different fields of expertise have different educational requirements. In some cases, advanced degrees are mandatory. If you're trying to prove someone's medical condition, your witness must be a licensed medical doctor who is currently practicing. The more impressive the credentials, such as published articles, the more likely the jury will believe the testimony. On the other hand, if you are attempting to prove that a building was set on fire, a firefighter with many years of experience would suffice. If the expert works in a field for which state or federal licensing is required, obviously the expert should have the required license. Of course, if the witness has written something that is inconsistent with his or her expected testimony, there would be a lot of explaining to do, as you can assume that the other side will find out about it. In such cases, the lawyer would possibly be better off using an expert who had never written anything.

Some lawyers look for those witnesses who have a history as expert witnesses. Lawyers are understandably nervous about using a witness who may not understand the pressure involved in a cross-examination. Others prefer a fresh face who has rarely testified and is not likely to be regarded as a professional witness, one who testifies often. Juries may perceive this kind of witness as someone who testifies just for the money.

Speaking of money, experts can be expensive to hire. With that said, you can figure that an expert will charge slightly more than the typical amount he or she normally earns. You can be sure that this amount will be raised in the cross-examination. So, for example, if you have a dentist testifying who normally earns a hundred dollars an hour, and it is revealed that you are paying the dentist five hundred dollars an hour, how would you react if you were sitting on the jury? Would you probably conclude that this expert was being paid an extra four hundred dollars an hour in an effort to buy the testimony?

As I told you last class, experts play critically important roles in the courtroom. The more important or complex the matter, the more likely it is that one or more experts will be involved for each side.

Track 18 [page 71]

15. Listen again to part of the passage. Then answer the question.

Professor: So, for example, if you have a dentist testifying who normally earns a hundred dollars an hour, and it is revealed that you are paying the dentist five hundred dollars an hour, how would you react if you were sitting on the jury?

What does the professor mean when he says this?

Professor: How would you react if you were sitting on the jury?

Questions 12 through 17

Track 19 [page 72]

Listen to a discussion in a chemistry class.

Professor: Welcome to Organic Chemistry. Today we'll be talking about some of the basics of molecules. We'll see how molecules govern every aspect of our lives. For example, how do chemicals—of course made up of molecules—regulate our bodies? Why did your muscles ache after the Zumba class you took this morning? What is in the pill you took to get rid of the headache you had after studying all night for a final exam? Since I've asked you all to have your cards folded with your first names facing me, I'll be calling on you to answer some of my questions. Can you think of any other questions that examining molecules can answer? I see a hand up. Yes, Samantha.

Student 1: Of course. What happens to gasoline after I fill up my car?

Professor: Good question. Anyone else? Brandon?

Student2: Why does garlic smell the way it does?

Professor: Yup. Another? What about you, Ashley?

Student 3: I'm not sure, but, aren't there different molecular compositions to the clothes we wear? Like how is silk different from polyester?

Professor: Exactly. We'll find the answers to these questions and many many others that you have probably asked yourself as we study organic chemistry together this semester. Does anyone know the definition of organic chemistry, say in contrast to other chemical disciplines, such as inorganic or physical chemistry?

Student 1: I remember, hopefully correctly from high school, that organic chemistry studies carbon and its compounds. Aren't these compounds called organic molecules?

Professor: That's correct. These organic molecules constitute the building blocks of life. Fats, sugars, proteins, and the nucleic acids are compounds in which the principal component is carbon. So are countless substances that we take for granted in everyday life. Back to your answer, Ashley. All the clothes that we wear are made up of organic materials, some of natural fibers, like what?

Student 2: Silk, as Ashley said, and cotton.

Professor: And artificial ones, like the polyester she also mentioned. Every day we use and are surrounded by products made of organic compounds, such as toothbrushes and shampoo as well as furniture, food, and cooking utensils. Consequently, organic chemical industries are among some of the largest in the world, such as…?

Student 1: Plastics and pharmaceuticals. You mentioned pills and furniture.

Student 3: Yeah, Someone mentioned gasoline, so petroleum refining, right?

Student 2: And you mentioned fats and sugars, so I'm guessing all the food producers.

Professor: You're all exactly right. Organic substances such as gasoline, medicines, and even pesticides have improved the quality of our lives. However, the uncontrolled disposal of organic chemicals has polluted the environment, causing deterioration of animal and plant life as well as injury and disease to humans. If we are to create useful molecules and learn to control their effects, we need knowledge of their properties and understanding of their behavior. We need to apply the principles of organic chemistry. Our first chapter, that I hope you've all read for today, will explain how the basic ideas of chemical structure and bonding apply to organic molecules. Most of it I'm sure was a review of the topics you covered in your general chemistry courses.

Track 20 [page 73]

Professor: Every day we use and are surrounded by products made of organic compounds such as toothbrushes and shampoo as well as furniture, food, and cooking utensils. Consequently, organic chemical industries are among some of the largest in the world, such as…?

What does the professor mean when he says this?

Professor: Organic chemical industries are among some of the largest in the world, such as…?

Questions 18 through 23

Track 21 [page 74]

Listen to a lecture in a dental hygiene class.

Professor: When I was going to school, I would be sent down to the principal's office for chewing gum in school. We were told that chewing gum was bad, that it caused cavities. And of course, no one liked to clean up gum that had been stuck under desks. Like chocolate and coffee, gum is now being rehabilitated. It turns out that sugar-free gum can actually prevent cavities in children. Instead of banning it, we should require children to chew it in school to promote their oral health.

The human mouth is host to many bacteria. The one that is primarily responsible for cavities is called streptococcus mutans. When the bacteria encounter sugar, acids are produced. Saliva, the fluids in your mouth, neutralizes acid, so teeth can handle some exposure. But large amounts of sugar, such as the amount found in a candy bar or a soda, overwhelm saliva. Prolonged exposure to that acid will damage the protective enamel on teeth. This process is called demineralization and eventually causes cavities.

Chewing gum of any kind increases saliva production, thereby helping to neutralize more acid. However, many gums are sweetened with sugar, which of course increases the acid level, canceling out the positive benefits. Replacing sugar in gum with xylitol, a naturally occurring sweetener found in fruits and vegetables that has fewer calories than regular sugar, fixes this problem.

More saliva and less acid seem to cause the teeth to remineralize, that means it actually reverses some cavities. But most important, chewing xylitol gum inhibits the growth of the strep bacteria, which are not able to metabolize the sweetener. Less infectious strains of bacteria slip off the teeth, and this positive xylitol effect lasts years. The gum seems to work best when it's chewed routinely just before children's adult teeth come in, at about ages 5 and 6.

We have known about this for a surprisingly long time. High quality randomized studies in Finland and Belize showed the benefits of chewing xylitol-sweetened gum. In Belize, ten-year-old children who chewed this type of gum decreased the risk of cavities by up to 70 percent, and a follow-up study showed that the benefit lasted up to five years. Studies in day care centers in Finland showed that xylitol chewing gum may also reduce ear infections in children by up to 40 percent.

So why haven't school systems or the government acted on this information? Perhaps school administrators do not know about the international data. Certainly, after a century of bubbles blown in class, it must be difficult for them to see chewing gum as a virtue instead of a vice. But they do need to come around.

In the United States alone more than 50 million hours of school are missed every year because of dental problems, not to mention those lost because of ear infections. There is an easy, cost-effective solution: having children chew gum with significant amounts of xylitol, which can usually be found in any corner store. The best way to ensure that all children take advantage of xylitol gum is to have them chew it in school, in kindergarten, and beyond. Ideally, they would chew three to five times a day for five minutes each time. Not only will it improve their health and school attendance but they might actually enjoy it.

Track 22 [page 75]

Listen again to part of the passage. Then answer the question.

Professor: When I was going to school, I would be sent down to the principal's office for chewing gum in school. We were told that chewing gum was bad, that it caused cavities. And of course, no one liked to clean up gum that had been stuck under desks.

Why does the professor say this?

Professor: And of course, no one liked to clean up gum that had been stuck under desks.

Questions 24 through 28

Track 23 [page 76]

Listen to a discussion between a professor and a student.

Professor: Ali, can you stay for a few minutes after class?

Student: Of course. Is there a problem?

Professor: No, I just want to have a quick word with you before lunch. You have in your hand that first paper I just returned today. I know you haven't had a chance to look it over. After you do, I suggest you go to the writing center with it.

Student: Oh, the one in Ricker Hall?

Professor: Have you ever been?

Student: No, I thought it was for students who really couldn't write well, but I guess maybe I'm in that category.

Professor: It's for everyone, and everyone's writing can improve. I'd like you to take the paper with you and have one of the tutors there go over it with you.

Student: Is it my grammar or spelling or what?

Professor: That's part of it, but the writing center does not do line editing for those kinds of errors. What they do is take a look at my comments in those areas and recognize the patterns of errors. For example, I recall I wrote on your paper that you made several errors with dangling modifiers. They'll be able to give you some exercises for that.

Student: Yeah, I know I have some grammar problems. What else?

Professor: What I'd really like them to help you with has to do with organization. Your thesis statement needs to be more precise because that affects the whole paper. Once that is better crafted, you'll be better able to find evidence and make sure each paragraph is related to the thesis. You'll see also that the introduction needs to have more background.

Student: Ouch.

Professor: It's not a bad introduction but the opening statement needs more context. You need to say why it's important for us to read about the topic and explain what was happening at the time. It's difficult for the reader to get an insight into the topic unless you give them these things.

Student: Yes, I see.

Professor: Hey, it's just the first paper, and on a positive note, many of your ideas are very interesting, and the evidence you use from the readings supports your claims very nicely. I can see you spent a lot of time in the library researching and it's obvious that you're really interested in the subject. You looked at the key academics in the field and put together some good summaries of their ideas.

Student: Thanks. I was starting to feel totally depressed.

Professor: That's certainly not my intention. I see lots of potential but you need to order and present your argument better. We're really lucky to have such an exceptional writing center on campus. Once you go, I'd like you to rewrite the paper, by next week if possible. You should rewrite it before we start the next one.

Student: I'll go right now and make an appointment. Do I just show up?

Professor: You can make an appointment in person, on the phone, or by email. I'm confident that you'll be able to raise your grades with a bit of additional help.

Track 24 [page 77]

Listen again to part of the passage. Then answer the question.

Professor: Hey, it's just the first paper, and on a positive note, many of your ideas are very interesting, and the evidence you use from the readings supports your claims very nicely.

Why does the professor say this?

Professor: and on a positive note

Speaking 2

Track 25 [page 80]

1. You will be asked your opinion about a familiar topic. Listen to the question, and then prepare your response. You will have 15 seconds to prepare a response and 45 seconds to speak. You can take notes on the main points of a response.

   Company A and Company B are both going to launch a new product. Company A decides to launch it with a low price initially, and then raise the price later on. Company B decides to launch it for a higher price and advertise it a lot.

   Which strategy is better? Use reasons and details to support your response.

Track 26 [page 81]

2. You will read a short passage and then listen to a conversation about the same topic. You will then answer a question about about them. You will have 45 seconds to read the passage. You can take notes on the main points of the reading passage.

Listen to two students talking.

Man: Did you know we can have free dental checkups done at the campus dental clinic?

Woman: No. I hadn't heard that. How did you find out?

Man: There was a notice that just went up, and one of the dental hygiene students in my math class made an announcement about it. They're looking for volunteers. Seems they need to find a certain number of patients to practice on in order to pass their clinic class.

Woman: Would you want a student working on your teeth?

Man: Someone made a joke about it when she asked, so she explained that a registered dentist is always in the clinic and walks around checking every student and patient.

Woman: Well, I guess the students are just cleaning your teeth, right? They're not doing procedures like filling cavities or pulling teeth, are they?

Now answer the following question:

The students express their opinions about going to the campus dental clinic. State their opinions and explain the resaons they give for holding those opinions.

Track 27 [page 83]

3. You will read a short passage and then listen to part of a lecture about the same topic. You will then answer a question about them. You will have 45 seconds to read the passage. You can take notes on the main points of the reading passage.

Listen to the passage. You can take notes on the main points of the listening passage.

Professor: Taxes on products that are known to cause health issues are generally known as 'sin taxes'. For example, let's take the tax on sugary beverages and drinks like sodas which contain added sugar. We know that consuming too much sugar can have severe health consequences, such as an increased risk of Type 2 diabetes, heart disease, stroke. It makes sense financially for the consumer too—according to one study, if people reduced their intake of sugary sodas by about one-fifth then it would save them between $100 and $300 per year. Furthermore, these products are price

sensitive. A study at Harvard in 2013 showed that if you increase the price of soda by 20 cents, consumption dropped by 16%. Furthermore, it's an easy sell—making things that are bad for your health more expensive is bound to be good for society. So policy makers consider that taxes on these products are a good idea. But let's take a moment to think about this too.

Not everyone can afford to pay increased taxes. When these taxes hit people, we often find that it produces a black or hidden market that avoids the usual means of sale. But also we need to look at what choices people actually have. In urban areas, sugary drinks may be the only option, particularly if the price of bottled water is also expensive.

There's also the moral question of whether people should have the freedom to choose for themselves what they do, even if it will result in health problems. Do governments really have the right to influence consumer behavior?

Now answer the following question:

Using examples from different perspectives on tax, explain the thinking behind 'sin taxes'.

Track 28 [page 85]

4. Listen to part of a lecture. You can take notes on the main points of the listening passage.

Professor: Textile fragment analysis from the excavation of a fifth-century Mayan tomb, in the Central American country of Honduras, has recently revealed high quality fabrics, which strongly suggests that the Mayans were highly skilled spinners and weavers. Also inside the tomb the remains of a woman of high status who was buried during the fifth century were found. Tiny fragments of 49 textile samples were brought back to a U.S. laboratory for analysis. Special microscopes examined each specimen for yarn structure, fabric structure, and the finish. Due to the climate of the warm and humid tropics, the discovery of these specimens is remarkable.

The analysis found different threads made from cotton, various grass forms, and all kinds of plant fibers. In the ancient Mayan tomb, there were as many as 25 layers of fabrics on a platform covering pottery. All of them had a different fabric structure, color, and yarn size. It is likely that the tomb was reopened several times, and additional layers of textiles were laid there years after the woman's death. One of the fabrics had an especially high thread count of

100 yards per inch, which is considered high for textiles even nowadays. In order to fashion such exceptional textiles, the Mayans used many different kinds of sophisticated weaving tools. No evidence of such tools in the same period have been found anywhere else. The discovery from the tomb speaks to the technology the Mayans had at the time for spinning and weaving very fine fabrics.

Now answer the following question:

How does the professor explain the skill level of ancient Mayans?

Writing 2

Track 29 [page 89]

Listen to part of a lecture in a hospitality class.

Professor: While cruise companies advertise extensively on television and online, as future travel agents, you should carefully consider whether or not to recommend a cruise to a client. Due to some well-publicized problems at sea, prices for cruises are at an all-time low. But before you let the price be the deciding factor, consider some of the negatives of cruising.

First of all, the all-inclusive price pays for usually a small interior room. A balcony room is an expensive upgrade. Also, land tours are not part of the deal, nor are expensive on-board spa treatments.

Because there are so many people on board in a confined, albeit large space, travelers may have to put up with noisy neighbors who disregard the no-smoking signs or party all night long. The constant waiting in line for meals and being part of a big group may not be everyone's cup of tea. Loudspeaker announcements seem never ending.

More importantly, viruses, such as norovirus and the virus that causes COVID-19, spread easily between people in close quarters. If viruses are spreading on board a cruise ship, both passengers and crew members may become infected.

Although travelers on cruises visit many places, there's no option to stay longer at any port that seems exciting, nor is there a chance to meet locals, or sample the cuisine.

Sometimes rough seas make even hardy travelers seasick, so these cruisers cannot enjoy all the onboard activities, meals, and entertainment.

Now answer the following question:

How does the information in the listening passage cast doubt on the information presented in the reading passage?

Listening 3

Questions 1 through 6

Track 30 [page 118]

Listen to a lecture in a linguistics class.

Professor: I'm sure many of you have heard of the small but famous island off the coast of Massachusetts, Martha's Vineyard. In recent years many famous celebrities and politicians have visited and also bought homes on the island.

There are some interesting demographic facts that I will touch on briefly today, but the island is the focus of our linguistics class due to the high rate of hereditary deafness, the fact that it was home to one of the earliest known deaf communities in the United States, and the unique sign language that developed on the island.

Known primarily as a summer colony, it is accessible only by boat and air. The island was originally inhabited by the Wampanoag Native Americans and was known in their language as Noepe or land amid the streams. In 1642 the Wampanoag numbered around 3,000, but by 1764 their number had dropped to 313. A British explorer, Bartholomew Gosnold, sailed to the island in 1602 and renamed it. As such it is the eighth-oldest surviving English place name in the United States. No one knows who Martha was, but Gosnold's mother-in-law and second child were both named Martha. In the late nineteenth century, a US Board on Geographic Names worked to standardize place-name spellings and forced Martha's Vineyard to become Martha Vineyard. The board reversed its decision and today only five locations in the US have a place name with a possessive apostrophe.

Back to our topic for today. A high rate of hereditary deafness was documented in Martha's Vineyard for almost two centuries. The island's deaf heritage cannot be traced to one common ancestor and is thought to have originated in the Weald, a region in the English county of Kent, prior to immigration. Researcher Nora Groce estimates that by the late 19th century, one in 155 people on the Vineyard was born deaf, almost 20 times the estimate for the nation at large.

Mixed marriages between deaf and hearing spouses comprised 65% of all deaf marriages on the island in the late nineteenth century, dramatically higher than the mainland average of 20 percent, where most frequently deaf individuals married other deaf ones. A sign language known as Martha's Vineyard Sign Language, or MVSL, evolved. MVSL was commonly used by hearing residents as well as deaf ones until the middle of the twentieth century. This practice allowed deaf residents to smoothly integrate into society.

In the twentieth century, tourism became a mainstay in the island economy. However, jobs in tourism were not as deaf-friendly as fishing and farming had been. Consequently, as intermarriage and further migration joined the people of Martha's Vineyard to the mainland, the island community more and more resembled the nation. The last person born into the island's sign language tradition died in 1952, but a few elderly residents were able to recall MVSL as recently as the 1980s when research into the language began.

Track 31 [page 120]

Questions 7 through 12

Listen to a lecture in an art history class.

Professor: Mary Cassatt is one of the best-loved American Impressionists. On the screen is a portrait of Mary Cassatt, painted by another Impressionist painter and friend, Edgar Degas. Mary Cassatt was the daughter of a well-to-do real estate and investment broker, and her upbringing reflected her family's high social standing. Her schooling prepared her to be a wife and mother and included such classes as homemaking, embroidery, music, sketching, and painting. During the 1850s, the Cassatts took their children abroad to live in Europe for several years. Though women of her day were discouraged from pursuing a career, Mary had decided to become an artist when she was just a child. At 16 she enrolled in Philadelphia's Pennsylvania Academy of the Fine Arts. However, she found the male faculty and her fellow students to be patronizing and resentful of her attendance. She decided to leave the program and move to Europe, where she could study the works of the Old Masters on her own, first-hand. Despite her family's strong objections (her father declared he would rather see his daughter dead than living abroad as a "bohemian"), Mary Cassatt left for Paris in 1866. She began her study with private art lessons in the Louvre, where she copied masterpieces. Tiring of the copying, she found an environment in France where she could work and learn from other artists. She had grown tired of the traditional style that she had studied, and the new movement of Impressionism appealed to her. The qualities of her work that were typically Impressionist were her use of light colors, her visible brushstrokes, and her choice of day-to-day subject matter. She continued to study and paint in relative obscurity until 1868 when one of her portraits was selected at the prestigious Paris Salon, an annual exhibition run by the French government.

With her father's disapproving words echoing in her ears, Cassatt submitted the well-received painting under the name Mary Stevenson. In 1870, soon after the outbreak of the Franco-Prussian War, Mary Cassatt reluctantly returned home to live with her parents. The artistic freedom she enjoyed while living abroad was missing upon her return to Philadelphia. Not only did she have trouble finding proper supplies, but her father refused to pay for anything connected with her art. To raise funds, she tried unsuccessfully to sell some of her paintings in New York. When she tried again to sell them through a dealer in Chicago, the paintings were tragically destroyed in a fire in 1871. In the midst of these obstacles, Cassatt was contacted by the Archbishop of Pittsburgh. He wanted her to paint copies of two works by the Italian master Correggio. Cassatt accepted and left immediately for Europe, where the originals were on display in Parma, Italy. With the money she earned from the commission, she was able to resume her career in Europe. The Paris Salon accepted her paintings for exhibitions in 1872, 1873, and 1874, which helped secure her artist status. Though she felt indebted to the Salon, Mary Cassatt began to feel constrained by its rigid guidelines. No longer concerned with what was fashionable or commercial, she began to experiment artistically. Her new work drew criticism for its bright colors and unflattering accuracy of its subjects.

Let's look at a painting Cassatt did during this period.

Notice the subject matter. It's of people doing something very ordinary, two women sitting having tea together. It's entitled appropriately Afternoon Tea Party. She also painted women quietly reading or writing letters. She became particularly well known for her paintings of peaceful, loving moments shared by mothers and their young children.

Track 32 [page 122]

Questions 13 through 17

Listen as a student consults with a professor.

Student: Professor Chase, I was hoping I could review my notes with you before the exam. I want to make sure I'm not confused about Frank Lloyd Wright's architecture styles.

Professor: Sure Caitlyn. Come in and have a seat. I did say today from three to four I'd be available for review. It looks as though you're the only one taking me up on the offer. What seems to be confusing you?

Student: I wanted to start with Wright's own home in Oak Park, Illinois. I know from the photographs that it's surfaced with wood shingles. I thought his preferred materials were cement and stucco.

Professor: Yes, the home is made of shingles and brick. Remember it was built in 1889, and he had just begun to work. By 1896, his first distinctive style, known as Prairie Style, evolved.

Student: Wasn't that the Willit's House—the first one of its kind?

Professor: Yes, let me find the picture I showed in class. See how the spaces inside the home expand into the outdoors through porches and terraces? Because of their low, horizontal form, the homes seem to grow out of the ground. The effect was emphasized by his use of wood and other materials as they appear in nature. The home was built in 1901.

Student: Can you go over the textile-block houses again?

Professor: Of course. Let me pull up some pictures. Look at these pictures of several houses Wright designed in southern California in the 1920s. They're noted for their precast concrete blocks.

Student: But don't they all look different?

Professor: Yes, he used a different pattern for each house.

Student: He really was amazing. Especially how he adapted local materials for different projects. I know a big part of the test will be on the Japanese hotel. Can you tell me again about the materials he used?

Professor: Yes, you do have the notes don't you? Why don't you tell me what you know.

Student: I'm sorry to be asking you all these questions. I'm the only non-architecture major in the class, and I know everyone else knows so much more about Wright than I do. OK, let me see my notes. The Imperial Hotel was Wright's major work in Japan. He made liberal use of soft lava, or what the Japanese call Oya stone. The hotel's floating foundation, among other design elements, helped to minimize damage when earthquakes struck.

Professor: Our time is almost up. Pay attention to the local elements Wright used in his other major works. I know you'll do fine on the test.

Track 33 [page 123]

Listen again to part of the passage. Then answer the question.

Professor: Sure Caitlyn. Come in and have a seat. I did say today from three to four I'd be available for review. It looks as though you're the only one taking me up on the offer.

Why does the professor say this?

Professor: It looks as though you're the only one taking me up on the offer.

Track 34 [page 124]

Questions 18 through 23

Listen to a lecture in a merchandising class.

Professor: A vintage motorcycle. An 18-carat gold watch. An autograph of a famous rock star. Are these better purchases than, say, stocks? Commodities? Real Estate? With stocks and bonds prone to big price swings lately, many investors are devoting a piece of their portfolio to art, antiques, and other rare items. For these buyers, such items aren't just an escape from the head-spinning complexities and unpredictability of the market, they're the purest form of supply and demand economics. Granted, collecting things, be they Japanese tin toys from the 1950s or German dolls from the late 1800s, is not new. Now, though, more people are buying with one eye on possible returns, not just to put the collection away in the attic. In a study of collectors in 2008, 74 percent said investment potential was driving their buying decisions. And let's not forget that collectibles can be a lot of fun.

Of course, collecting poses risks and challenges. To begin with, what the market may be for your ceramic vase may be hard to track. In addition, some items need to be insured and others require special storage.

The *Wall Street Journal* has compiled a suggested list of items for collecting. Item number one: motorcycles. They're easier to store than cars, another beloved collectible.

They're also easier to repair. Are you buying the motorcycle for an investment or do you actually want to ride it? If you do ride it, the value obviously decreases. If there's an accident, the investment can literally be totally wiped out. Some brands are more desirable, as are older models, say from the 1940s and 50s. A 1929 Brough Superior Model originally cost $275. It sold in 2010 for $458,000. Obviously, those items are out of your price range, but as future merchandisers, I want you to have your eye on collectibles, even less expensive ones such as used jeans and athletic footwear. The *Wall Street Journal*'s comments apply to these items as well. Are you buying those used jeans because you want to wear them, or are you putting them away as an investment?

The next collectible the *Journal* mentions is watches. Although most of you just look at your phones to tell time, watches aren't just for keeping time. They're increasingly about showcasing status. They are almost an international currency unto themselves. The biggest problem with watches is fakes—either the whole watch or parts of them. If a watch has the original box and paperwork it will be worth more.

The last item I want to mention is autographs. In an era where everyone is famous for at least fifteen minutes, autograph collecting has become our way of capturing our obsession with all things related to celebrities. Once a celebrity dies and can no longer sign an autograph, the price instantly rises. The most famous autographs are from iconic figures of the twentieth century: Marilyn Monroe, John F. Kennedy, Mohammed Ali. Just as with watches, fakes are rampant. I thought I had made a great find a few years ago. A dealer told me it was an autographed photo of three of the stars from the 1980 champion Boston Celtics. Afterward, I found it was a poster and there were thousands sold.

Track 35 [page 125]

Listen again to part of the passage. Then answer the question.

Professor: Obviously those items are out of your price range, but as future merchandisers, I want you to have your eye on collectibles.

Professor: I want you to have your eye on collectibles.

Track 36 [page 126]

Questions 24 through 28

Narrator: Listen to a conversation between a professor and two students.

Professor: Hi Vinnie! Hi Fatima! Are you going to submit your thesis posters for the conference in San Diego?

Student 1: Hi Professor Lin. We were just talking about that! We weren't going to until you told us on Monday that there would be funding to go there. How many students can go?

Professor: There'll be funding for three students from your class.

Student 2: Three students? That's good! What funding are you offering?

Professor: Well, if you're successful the department will give you the cost for a ticket to the conference, plus 50% of your living expenses.

Student 2: Hey, that's pretty good!

Professor: Well, it doesn't cover your travel costs, so you'd have to plan your journey carefully.

Student 2: Yeah, it's in San Diego, isn't it? I've always wanted to go there.

Student 1: It's a long way. We could catch a Greyhound bus or take an overnight train rather than flying. But we're getting ahead of ourselves, do you really think we've got a chance?

Student 2: The odds aren't bad. There are only 12 students in the seminar.

Professor: Well, think about it and let me know. I need the posters by next Friday so that I can submit them to the conference committee. Then if they get accepted, I can finalize the funding.

Student 2: My problem is the deadline. Because the seminar deadline is a month after that, I haven't even started it.

Student 1: Me neither. When you told us earlier in the semester about the conference and the student poster part, I knew I didn't have money to go to San Diego. But I'm very interested!

Professor: It's a great opportunity, you should go for it.

Student 2: Well, we finished the research last semester. And we've spent several classes on poster design, and you've given us the template to use. You know, the one with the college logo at the top and a space at the bottom left for our biodata.

Professor: I think if you spent some focused time on this you could make the deadline and have a good chance of getting the poster presentations accepted.

Student 1: Yeah, thanks Professor Lin. Fatima, do you want to go over to the design lab with me at about 4? The lab assistant is there then, and he can help us.

Student 2: What time is it now? Noon. Ok. I'll be in the library making a rough sketch for my thesis. I want it to look really visual, you know – have an impact as soon as people see it. And besides, we can't go to the lab empty handed. The lab assistant always says he can work up your ideas but can't do it for you.

Student 1: Fatima, if you apply, it'll inspire me. It would be so much fun to go.

Professor: Let alone how good it will look on your résumé that you presented at a national conference!

Student 1: There's not much time to finish. It's going to be tight.

Professor: Good luck!

Track 37 [page 127]

Listen again to part of the passage.

Student 1: There's not much time to finish. It's going to be tight.

Why does the student say this?

Student 1: It's going to be tight.

Speaking 3

Track 38 [page 130]

1. You will be asked your opinion about a familiar topic. Listen to the question, and then prepare your response. You will have 15 seconds to prepare a response and 45 seconds to speak. You can take notes on the main points of a response.

    Some people like to plan things. Others prefer not to plan and spontaneously react to events. Which is the best approach? Use reason and details to support your response.

Track 39 [page 131]

2. You will read a short passage and then listen to a conversation about the same topic. You will then answer a question about them. You will have 45 seconds to read the passage. You can take notes on the main points of the reading passage.

    Listen to two students discuss the announcement.

Female:	Did you hear that President Brown is retiring after 15 years?
Male:	Wow. He's really going to be missed.
Female:	Yeah, he came to just about every activity, like football games and even the junior formal. He danced all night!
Male:	And he's done so much for the university. He was instrumental in getting the donation for the naming of the business school. Under his watch we first started granting PhD degrees, and now we have that highly ranked Physician Assistant program, the only one in the state.
Female:	I can understand why he would want to retire. He's probably going to write a book or maybe teach a course somewhere.
Male:	Or maybe just travel. He probably hasn't had a real vacation in 15 years.
Female:	Did you see the announcement about the Search Committee for the new president? They're looking for two students to serve on it. Would you be interested?
Male:	I'm sure it would be a unique opportunity as a student, participating in interviews and evaluating candidates, but I bet it would be a very big time commitment. What about you?
Female:	I'm not sure. Like you, I know it would be a once-in-a-lifetime experience, and especially since we'll be interviewing ourselves for jobs in a few short months, we could pick up a lot of pointers. On the other hand, it will be hours and hours of meetings, some all day I heard.
Male:	I'd like to be able to influence the committee to find another president like Dr. Brown. Someone who would be really involved with the students. Let me know what you decide. Maybe we'll both put our hats into the ring.

Now answer the following question:

The students express their opinions about serving on the search committee. State their opinions and the reasons they give for holding those opinions.

Track 40 [page 133]

3. You will read a short passage and then listen to a part of a lecture about the same topic. You will then answer a question about them. You will have 45 seconds to read the passage. You can take notes on the main points of the reading passage.

Now listen to the passage.

Professor:	As you should understand from the reading, books hundreds of years old are oftentimes in

much better shape than those written only 50 years ago. Unfortunately, bookbinders were not aware 50 years ago that using paper made of only tree fibers will produce a substance that turns the pages brown. How fortunate for us that the pages Johann Sebastian Bach wrote his musical compositions on was paper made in the 18th century which contained rags and weren't made up of only tree fiber. Only last month a notebook of Bach's with some chords on it was discovered. Because the notebook was legible, musicians were able to produce a new musical composition using these chords written almost 300 years ago.

Now answer the following question:

Explain why Bach's notebook, which was discovered only last month, was still legible.

Track 41 [page 135]

4. You will listen to part of a lecture. You can take notes on the main points of the listening passage.

Professor:	Apart from the wheel, perhaps one of humanity's most important inventions is the shoe. Indirect evidence points to humans wearing protective foot coverings from as early as 50,000 years ago—we know this from the way our toes developed to become less broad and narrower. But the earliest direct evidence dates back 9,000 years when a pair of ancient sandals were found in California. Flip-flops, as we know them, originated with the ancient Egyptians in 4000 BCE.

The need to protect our feet is almost universal, with different cultures across the world developing a form of open-toed footwear, or sandals. Archeologists have seen pictures of them in ancient murals. Another pair found in Europe was made of papyrus leaves and dated back approximately 1,500 years. Around the fifteenth century, the Masai of Africa made them out of rawhide. In India, they've been made from wood for hundreds of years. In China and Japan, rice straw was used.

It was really in the 1940s that flip-flops caught on in the US, when they became part of American popular culture. They began to be made from plastic and sport the bright colors that were so popular in the 1950s. Since 2010, more than 150 million pairs have been made every year. Why are they called "flip-flops"? It's probably due to the sound they make when walking. And they have come to dominate the casual footwear of women and men.

Listening 4

Questions 1 through 5

Track 43 [page 168]

Listen as a student consults with the Dean.

Student: Hi, Dean True. I'm David Brooks. I was told to speak to you about wanting to start a drama club.

Dean: Come in, David. Tell me what you'd like to happen on campus.

Student: Well, I was talking with Professor Roberto. He teaches the drama class, and several of us were saying we wish we had a drama club on campus that could put on plays and bring performances to campus. He told us that about ten years ago there was a group, and he was the advisor.

Dean: I wasn't here then. All campus clubs get chartered and funding through my office, so let's talk for a while, and I'll see what we can come up with.

Student: First, I realize that finding a dedicated space on campus will probably be impossible. I've been looking into every nook and cranny, and I think I've come up with something.

Dean: Let me hear.

Student: You know the old gym, the one attached to Holbrook Hall? It really has no official function anymore. I know sometimes it's used for temporary storage or for informational gatherings, but if we could have even half of it.

Dean: Oh, the far end, with the stage on it. Is that what you mean?

Student: Exactly. And it wouldn't cost much to put up a dividing wall and then half of it could still be used for whatever.

Dean: And what were you thinking about a budget?

Student: I asked Professor Roberto what he thought. This is what we came up with. We'd need a small amount for advertising to get it going. Then we'd need seed money for the first play. We thought we could charge a small admission fee. That way we could recoup some of the money. But we'd need money for the play permissions.

Dean: Excuse me, do you mean if you put on an established play you have to pay a royalty fee? I bet that's expensive.

Student: Professor Roberto says it really varies, and he knows a lot of ones that are really cheap. We

wouldn't put on something really famous, like West Side Story.

Dean: But wouldn't lots of other items be very expensive, like lighting and seating.

Student: Yeah. Those are the two big ones. We were hoping maybe there's some way we could get a community grant from the town or maybe one of our trustees would donate the money.

Dean: Those solutions won't help us immediately. I'll tell you what you can do. There is money available in the student activities fund. We get a small yearly allowance. Since there are no other new clubs that have petitioned this year, yours will be at the top of the list. But here's what you need to submit. It's spelled out on this sheet here.

1. Name of club.

2. Faculty Advisor.

3. List of members. You could probably find enough from your drama class. It needs to be at least ten. And it's a good idea if they are from a mix of classes. You wouldn't want all seniors who will graduate this year.

4. Proposed space for meetings, and in your case, performances.

5. Time and place of weekly or biweekly meetings.

6. Amount of seed money. Make sure you're very specific here. These proposals get looked at by a group that wants to make sure everything is well thought out.

Student: I'm on it. You'll have it by next week. Thanks so much.

Questions 6 through 11

Track 44 [page 170]

Listen to a discussion from a sports management class.

Professor: I know that some of you are planning to be high school athletic coaches. It's important to have a sense of history for the sports you are coaching. Today we're focusing on football.

Student 1: You mean soccer or American football?

Professor: Football. But it's easy to see where the confusion arose between soccer and football. The first game of what we call football resembled soccer. It was played in the eastern United States around 1850. Instead of kicking a ball into a net as is done in today's soccer games, players kicked the ball across the opposing team's goal line. Interesting to note, there were 30 or more players on the field at one time. As you know, today both soccer and football teams compete with only 11 players.

Student 2: While rugby has 15.

Professor: We'll get to rugby in a minute. OK. As this soccer-like game became more and more popular, stricter rules were instituted, and colleges established teams. Back to the first intercollegiate game. It was played on November 6, 1869, in New Brunswick, New Jersey. Rutgers beat Princeton 6 to 4. Back to rugby, at this game each team had 25 men, playing with rugby-like rules, but like modern football it was strategy, surprise, and physicality.

Student 1: I always thought the first football game was played at Harvard.

Professor: That's technically right. The first game most closely resembling modern-day football took place at Harvard in 1875 between Harvard and a visiting team from McGill University from Montreal, Canada. The Canadians preferred to play rugby.

Student 2: That's why I mentioned rugby. I think our football resembles British rugby more than soccer.

Professor: You're right. Rugby is an English game that allows running while holding the ball and tackling opposing players. The Harvard team wanted to play its game of soccer, advancing the ball primarily by kicking. The teams reached a compromise. They played two games, the first using Harvard's rules and the next one following McGill's rules. Harvard enjoyed McGill's game so much that the university presented it to other Eastern schools.

Student 1: Why didn't they just call it rugby?

Professor: Because it was a hybrid of soccer and rugby, they gave it a new name: football. This new game quickly gained followers. Running while holding the ball and tackling became as integral to the game as kicking had been to soccer. The Eastern colleges soon began to alter and improve this modified soccer game. One of the first football players, Walter Camp, became a pivotal force in updating the game. He's widely considered to be the most important figure in the development of American football.

Student 2: He played at Yale, didn't he?

Professor: Correct. In the 1880s he helped establish official rules that were intended to increase the action and competitive nature of the game. He also reduced the size of the playing field and lowered the number of players from 15 to 11.

Student 1: When did the expansion further west take place?

Professor: Good question. In 1880 there were only eight university teams. By 1900 there were 43. In 1879 the University of Michigan became the first school west of Pennsylvania to establish a team. Other Midwestern schools followed suit. The numbers of players increased even more when towns formed their own teams of young men who didn't attend high school or college.

Student 2: And we all know about those rivalries today!

Track 45 [page 171]

Listen again to part of the passage. Then answer the question.

Professor: Back to rugby, at this game each team had 25 men, playing with rugby-like rules, but like modern football it was strategy, surprise, and physicality.

Prompter: Why does the professor say this?

Professor: But like modern football it was strategy, surprise, and physicality.

Questions 12 through 17

Track 46 [page 172]

Listen to a lecture in an American history class.

Professor: Using ice to preserve food led to the nineteenth-century development of the icebox. I recall my grandparents would say "icebox" instead of refrigerator. OK, but I'm sure none of you know who first came up with the idea of a refrigerator. Anyone know? Well, the entrepreneur was a Boston businessman named Frederic Tudor, who became known as the "Ice King." A passing remark at a party in 1805 gave him the idea of exploiting one of New England's few natural resources—the ice on its ponds.

By 1825 Tudor and his partner Nathaniel Wyeth had perfected an ice-cutting machine that mechanized the process of cutting slabs of ice. Through trial and error they worked out the best methods for building and insulating ships to transport the ice, as well as icehouses to store it. The earlier underground icehouses suffered a minimum 60 percent seasonal loss due to melting. Inside Tudor's heavy, double wood walls with sawdust insulation, loss from melting was only eight percent. In 1833, Tudor sent one of his ships with 180 tons of ice from Boston to Calcutta, crossing the equator twice in a voyage of four months and arriving with the ice still frozen. Although the main export markets were the American South and Caribbean islands, Tudor shipped his product all over the world and found plenty of customers locally in Boston as well. In the 1850s, Tudor's company exported up to 150,000 tons of ice a year while at the same time developing an American market.

Tudor's accomplishments helped make possible the icebox—an American word—which by 1860 had become a domestic must-have in American homes all across the country. These large wooden boxes on legs were lined with tin and zinc and interlined with charcoal, cork, sawdust, or straw. Many were handsome pieces of furniture. A large block of ice was held in a tray or compartment near the top of the box. Cold air circulated down and around storage compartments in the lower section. More expensive models had spigots for draining ice water from a catch pan or holding tank. Cheaper models used a drip pan that was placed under the box and had to be emptied at least daily. The users had to replace the melted ice, normally by obtaining new ice from an iceman.

Back to my grandparents. They regaled me with stories of their iceman, who delivered blocks of ice to their home by horse and buggy. We're talking about the early 1900s until refrigeration became prevalent in the 1930s, when refrigerators began using electricity instead of ice to keep their contents cold.

Iceboxes helped to improve the American diet and lengthened the season for fruits and vegetables. Meat could be preserved longer without salting, pickling, spicing, sun drying, or smoking. Ice cream became a popular at home treat rather than a rare luxury. Americans began putting ice in their drinks even though European visitors were appalled. Even iced tea, to the dismay of the hot-tea-loving British, appeared before the Civil War.

Track 47 [page 173]

Listen again to part of the passage. Then answer the question.

Professor: The users had to replace the melted ice, normally by obtaining new ice from an iceman. Back to my grandparents. They regaled me with stories of their iceman, who delivered blocks of ice to their home by horse and buggy.

How does the professor feel about the stories?

Questions 18 through 22

Track 48 [page 174]

Listen as a student consults with a professor.

Student: Professor Stein. Do you have a few minutes?

Professor: Sure Michael. Come on in and have a seat. Let me just finish this email. There. What's up?

Student: I was hoping to go over the different fallacies of persuasive speaking.

Professor: What's confusing you?

Student: Well, there's so many. I almost don't know where to start.

Professor: OK. I have an idea. I'll name the fallacy or defective proof and let's see if you can give me an example or explain it. How does that sound?

Student: Um, good I hope.

Professor: Let's start with the Red Herring Fallacy.

Student: I remember you said that herring is a kind of fish, and something about how hunters would use it to throw the dogs off track, right?

Professor: Go on.

Student: And it means that while speaking you would distract the listener with sensational or irrelevant material.

Professor: Right. Good job. Next, Myth of the Mean Fallacy.

Student: I get that. It's using an average to hide a problem. Let's say I want to show that my company pays really good wages, so I say the average salary is 80,000. But that's only because the vice presidents are making great salaries and the administrative assistants are making one quarter of that, but I just give you an average. The one that gets me mixed up is Post Hoc. I know it's a defective argument. I'm mixed up with that one and non sequitur.

Professor: I like explaining Post Hoc. Post means after. You assume that because one event followed the other, the first caused the second. We see this behavior all the time with athletes. They'll say I need to wear certain socks or a certain headband in order to win the game because when I wore it last, I won. Is that one clear?

Student: Now I understand it. I remember now you said something about athletes, but there were so many that we covered I was getting mixed up. And non sequitur?

Professor: That one is from the Latin, meaning it doesn't follow. I like giving the example of a five-year-old child. When a child is asked, "How many legs does a spider have?" She might reply, "My brother has a snake." To her, the ideas follow, but as adults, we know the response doesn't respond to the question. For example, we make a conclusion not from what's been proven. Can you give me an example of a non-sequitur?

Student: I'll try. I'm not sure, but back to the child example. If you were to ask me, "What will be on the exam?" and I answer, "Is it time to leave?" the answer doesn't follow the question.

Professor: And why is that so important in writing and speaking?

Student: When we're trying to make or prove a point, our evidence has to logically follow. Am I right?

Professor: Absolutely. You're going to be fine.

Student: Thanks so much. Just talking them out really helped.

Track 49 [page 175]

Listen again to part of the passage. Then answer the question.

Professor: OK. I have an idea. I'll name the fallacy or defective proof and let's see if you can give me an example or explain it. How does that sound?

What does the professor mean when she says this?

Professor: How does that sound?

Questions 23 through 28

Track 50 [page 176]

Listen to a lecture in a psychology class.

Professor: We have seen that groups do not perform as well as a number of individuals working alone, although groups do usually outperform a single person. Why do people love the idea of working in groups? Why do companies around the world want everyone to be a team player? Why do they form teams?

The chapter you read on brainstorming suggested a partial answer. Remember, brainstorming is an idea that was developed by advertising executives in the 1950s to increase the creativity of their groups, and only after it had made its mark in ad groups did psychologists begin to conduct research on it. Brainstorming is a form of creative thinking in groups, using a procedure in which all group members are encouraged to generate as many ideas as possible without holding back or worrying about being wrong. They are also encouraged to build on each other's ideas. The core assumption is that creative people can feed off each other's thinking processes and create energy, thereby coming up with more and better ideas than could the same number of people working alone. When researchers actually check the quality and quantity of ideas, the performance of brainstorming groups is quite disappointing. Groups can be smarter than individuals, but brainstorming groups don't perform as well as independent individuals. Group members don't work independently and contribute their separate ideas. Rather, they interact, which raises the likelihood that some will feel left out, will defer to the opinions of others, will be too shy to criticize the group, or in other ways will be held back from contributing what they can. The chapter noted that people believe teams will outperform the same number of people working individually, even though that belief usually turns out to be wrong. Maybe people are just stuck in a mistaken view of reality and make their decisions based on that mistake.

A more complex and reasonable answer was given by Allen and Hecht in 2004. They reviewed a great many published studies and observed a consistent pattern. Many people, business managers included, believe that teams are highly effective for improving performance, but in reality the majority of teams don't live up to their reputation, both in the lab and in real business organizations. If performance were the only measure, then most corporations and other organizations should forget about teamwork and promote individual excellence. But performance is not the only measure, and working in teams has many side benefits.

People enjoy their work more. Working in teams satisfies their need to belong. It enables them to feel confident, effective, and superior, if only because many members of teams think they are the star, or at least a crucial team member who deserves a large share of the credit for the team's success—if there is any. The enjoyment and other psychological benefits of teams may explain why people are so eager to form and join them, even if they really do not improve performance most of the time.

Speaking 4

Track 51 [page 180]

1. You will be asked your opinion about a familiar topic. Listen to the question, and then prepare your response. You will have 15 seconds to prepare a response and 45 seconds to speak. You can take notes on the main points of a response.

   Do you prefer to work in a group or do a project by yourself? Use reasons and details to support your response.

Track 52 [page 181]

2. You will read a short passage and then listen to a conversation about the same topic. You will then answer a question about them. You will have 45 seconds to read the passage. You can take notes on the main points of the reading passage.

Listen to two students discuss the announcement.

Student 1: Are you going back home this summer?

Student 2: Yeah, my parents really want me to. I stayed on campus last summer, and I haven't been home for almost two years. It's such a hassle though.

Student 1: You mean what to do with all your stuff? Did you see the posting around campus about storing your stuff in Green Hall?

Student 2: No, what did it say?

Student 1: I can't remember all the details since I live close to campus and take everything home, but it's something about one charge for a medium box and another for a larger box, and the boxes will be securely guarded in Green Hall basement.

Student 2: That would be a life saver. I didn't know what I was going to do. I thought about asking you, ha ha. Didn't you keep all your roommates' stuff last summer?

Student 1: Right, and my parents weren't too happy about it. We don't have such a large place, and all summer my parents complained about my friends' junk that was supposed to be in my room but took up half of the garage.

Student 2: Not to worry. I won't ask you, but tell me again where you saw the notice.

Student 1: Are you free now? We can walk over to Green Hall, and you can see the different box sizes and sign up I think.

Student 2: What would I do without you?

Now answer the following question:

How do the students react to the announcement? State their opinions about using the service and explain the reasons they give for holding those opinions.

Track 53 [page 183]

3. You will read a short passage and then listen to part of a lecture about the same topic. You will then answer a question about them. You will have 45 seconds to read the passage. You can take notes on the main points of the reading passage.

Professor: Every so often news of another mysterious disappearance in the Bermuda Triangle hits the airwaves. We, in the scientific world, examine these events carefully to determine their authenticity. We begin with Christopher Columbus, who recorded in his diary seeing bright lights, including a great flame of fire, in the area. The great flame was most probably a meteor and the lights in the sky were reflections of lights on land. For many years the disappearance in 1892 of a famous lost ship, the *Mary Celeste*, was blamed on forces in the Triangle. Ship remains were found many years later off the coast of Portugal, thousands of miles from the Triangle. The third intriguing tale surrounded the disappearance of six US military aircraft on a routine mission in 1945. For several years the Triangle area was thought to be to blame. The squad commander was unfit to fly and led the squad of inexperienced pilots off course. Instead of south and west, the pilots flew north and east, running out of fuel in the Atlantic Ocean, where the planes sank to a depth of 30,000 feet below the surface of the sea and were not discovered for many years.

Now answer the following question:

Explain the facts behind the mysteries of the Bermuda Triangle.

Track 54 [page 185]

4. You will listen to part of a lecture. You can take notes on the main points of the listening passage.

Professor: In reality, the probability of being attacked in an elevator is virtually zero. Yet, the way people act toward others when they ride together in an elevator suggests that they have serious concerns about their safety. If the elevator is crowded, everyone stands still and stares at the ceiling, the floor, their cell phones or the button panel as if they've never seen any of these items before. When two strangers ride together, they stand as far apart as possible, and avoid facing each other directly, making eye contact, speaking to one another, or making any sudden movements or noises.

Much of our elevator behavior is not the result of rational thinking. It's an automatic, instinctive response to the situation. The threat of aggression is not real, yet our minds respond as if it were and produce behaviors that are meant to protect us. Elevators are relatively recent inventions, but the social challenges they pose are nothing new. The scenario of being in close proximity to others in a restricted space has been repeated innumerable times in the history of humankind. In 1966 an anthropologist named Edward T. Hall wrote a book entitled *The Hidden Dimension*, in which he argues that when a person invades someone else's space, all kinds of trouble ensue. According to Hall, personal space is like an invisible bubble that people always carry around themselves. The radius of the bubble can be short or long, depending on the individual or the cultural norms of the society in which they live. Noting that human personal space is the equivalent of an animal's territory, Hall suggested that aggressive responses to violations of personal space represent attempts to defend one's territory. I'm sure you've all noticed that when people from some cultures talk to each other, they stand much more closely than those from other cultures.

Now answer the following question:

How does the professor explain elevator behavior?

Track 55 [page 189]

Listen to the passage.

Professor: We've had a lot of discussion on campus lately about whether or not to convert our playing field to an artificial turf one. It's definitely the way to go. The only downside reported is the temperature on very, very hot days. As long as practices in the hottest days of the summer are held early in the morning, the fields do not present problems to the athletes.

The older fields of the 1950s did contain lead and some other chemicals. Tests of artificial turf fields manufactured in the last decade show that these fields contain very low levels of lead or any other chemicals.

The initial cost may seem high, but afterwards the cost benefits become apparent. The turf does not grow, so it does not need constant mowing, reseeding, or fertilizing and, in some cases, pesticides. Water costs are negligible, whereas grass water costs are exorbitant. These fields can be permanently marked for multiple sports, so they are not a one-sport field as claimed. Snow can easily be removed with special equipment. The fields' ability to heat up in the sun also helps melt snow, allowing the fields to be playable before grass ones.

In heavy rains, grass fields can flood and become muddy, necessitating cancelation and rescheduling of games. Grass fields need resting time between heavy uses in order to allow the grass to recover. When grass fields are overused, the areas with bare grass, holes, and slippery mud lead to accidents. There is no data to support the claim that playing on artificial turf causes more accidents.

Now answer the following question:

How does the information in the listening passage challenge the information presented in the reading passage?

Answer Key

Practice Test 1

Reading 1

1.	C	4.	B	7.	D	10.	2, 3, 6
2.	B	5.	A	8.	A		
3.	D	6.	C	9.	A		

Reading 2

11.	A	14.	B	17.	C	20.	1, 3, 6
12.	C	15.	D	18.	A		
13.	A	16.	C	19.	C		

Reading 3   This Answer key is for the Paper Edition only.

21.	D	24.	B	27.	A	30.	1, 5, 6
22.	A	25.	C	28.	D		
23.	A	26.	C	29.	B		

Practice Test 1

Listening

1.	D	7.	A, C	13.	C	19.	C, D, E
2.	A, C	8.	C	14.	A, B	20.	C
3.	A	9.	D	15.	C	21.	B
4.	B	10.	D	16.	A	22.	C
5.	C	11.	B	17.	D	23.	C
6.	C	12.	D	18.	B	24.	A

25.   B, C

26.   1. YES;   2. NO;   3. YES;   4. NO

27.   A

28.   C

Practice Test 2

Reading 1

1.	A	4.	A	7.	A	10.	2, 4, 6
2.	C	5.	C	8.	A		
3.	B	6.	C	9.	B		

Reading 2

11.	A	14.	C	17.	C	20.	1, 3, 6
12.	B	15.	D	18.	D		
13.	A	16.	D	19.	A		

Reading 3 This Answer key is for the Paper Edition only.

21.	A	23.	B	25.	C	27.	C
22.	D	24.	D	26.	A	28.	C

29. Organic fertilizer: Meal from cotton kernels; Mulch: By-product from cotton ginning; Housing insulation: Recycled old jeans

30. 2, 3, 5

Practice Test 2

Listening

1.	D	9.	B	17.	C	25.	A, C
2.	A, D	10.	A	18.	B	26.	A, D
3.	B	11.	B, D	19.	C	27.	C
4.	A, B, D	12.	C	20.	4, 3, 2, 1	28.	B
5.	B	13.	A, B	21.	A, B, C		
6.	D	14.	C	22.	C		
7.	B	15.	C	23.	C		
8.	D	16.	C	24.	D		

Practice Test 3

Reading 1

1.	D	4.	B	7.	A	10.	2, 4, 5
2.	D	5.	D	8.	D		
3.	A	6.	C	9.	B		

Reading 2

11.	B	14.	B	17.	D	20.	1, 2, 3
12.	B	15.	A	18.	B		
13.	D	16.	C	19.	C		

Reading 3 | This Answer key is for the Paper Edition only.

21.	D	24.	D	27.	B	30.	1, 3, 5
22.	D	25.	C	28.	C		
23.	A	26.	D	29.	B		

Practice Test 3

Listening

1. D
2. C

3. A
4. B

5. B, C

6. 4. Celebrities and politicians visit and live on the island.
   1. The tribe of Wampanoag dropped to 313.
   2. Marriages between deaf and hearing spouses comprised 65% of all deaf marriages.
   3. The last person born into the sign language community died.

7. B
8. A

9. C
10. B

11. D

12. 2. She begins private art lessons in the Louvre.
    3. The Archbishop of Pittsburgh commissions her work.
    4. The Paris Salon accepts her paintings three years in a row.
    1. Cassatt enrolls in Philadelphia's Pennsylvania Academy of Fine Arts.

13. B

14. D

15. C

16. California houses: Precast concrete blocks
    Imperial Hotel: Soft lava
    Willit's House: Wood and other materials as they appear in nature

17. A, C, D
18. B
19. A
20. C

21. C, D
22. D
23. B, C
24. D

25. B
26. C
27. B
28. B

Practice Test 4

Reading 1

1.	B	4.	C	7.	B	10.	2, 4, 5
2.	A	5.	C	8.	D		
3.	B	6.	C	9.	C		

Reading 2

11.	D	14.	C	17.	C	20.	3, 5, 6
12.	D	15.	C	18.	A		
13.	A	16.	B	19.	C		

Reading 3

This Answer key is for the Paper Edition only.

21.	D	24.	D	27.	A	30.	3, 4, 5
22.	B	25.	B	28.	A		
23.	B	26.	C	29.	D		

Practice Test 4

Listening

1.	D	5.	C	9.	A, D	13.	B
2.	C	6.	C	10.	B, C	14.	B, C
3.	A	7.	D	11.	D		
4.	B	8.	B	12.	B		

15. Cheaper models: Used a drip pan that was placed under the box
More expensive models: Used spigots for draining ice water from a catch pan
Refrigeration models: Used electricity instead of ice

16.	A	20.	C	24.	B	28.	D
17.	2, 4, 1, 3	21.	B	25.	C, D		
18.	A	22.	D	26.	A		
19.	A, D	23.	A	27.	B, C		

Sample Answers

Practice Test 1

Speaking

Question 1

There are some good reasons to attend a large university just as there are some good reasons to attend a small one. Personally, I would rather attend a large one although I know there are many people who don't feel that way. First of all, I like the idea of having many students around me. If I were at a small school, I think I would feel that very quickly I would know everyone and would want to meet new people. I'm not saying I need tons of friends, just that I would enjoy meeting many people. I went to a small high school and wished I had gone to a larger one. Second, at a large university there would be a wide variety of courses I could take. By having the ability to take many different courses my first year, I would be able to decide what I then want to major in. At a smaller school I wouldn't have such a variety.

Question 2

The man and the woman feel very differently about staying in the hotel. The man, on the one hand, expresses many advantages. The hotel has air conditioning and a pool. Obviously the dorm has none of those things. Instead of having to change and launder his own sheets, the hotel does it for him. His teachers have been really considerate about the fact that he and others are not on campus. One put books on reserve in the library. Another gave out lecture notes from previous classes, and another invited those staying in the hotel to his house for dinner.

On the other hand, the woman feels really stuck staying in the hotel. She admits the hotel is nicer than the dorm, but she lists many disadvantages in staying here. She can't go back to her room between classes like she could when she's in the dorm. Because of the fire, they all had to leave quickly, so she doesn't have most of her books or clothes. She's had to wear the same sweater for three days in a row. She's worried about her grades, especially because she has a big chemistry test this week and doesn't have her notes. She's really hoping she can get back into the dorm soon so that she can get some of her stuff.

Question 3

The reading passage discusses parent/child sleeping arrangements. They vary around the world. Should young children sleep with their parents or in a separate room? The passage then mentions that in the United States usually children do not sleep with their parents, whereas in Japan it's different. In Japan usually no one, including children, ever sleeps alone. About half of Japanese children sleep in the same bed as their mother or father, and others sleep with brothers or sisters.

The listening passage points out that Americans seem to be obsessed with whether or not children should sleep with parents and that those from other cultures where this practice is commonplace may find humor in the debate. He explains that the American pressure NOT to sleep with children has many sources, such as relatives, other parents, and even the children's doctors who fear that if a child is in bed with a parent, the parent may roll over, killing the baby. In America, many believe that children need to learn, even as infants, how to be self-sufficient. Sleeping with a parent would somehow prevent children from being independent.

However, the listening passage adds that there is now a small but growing movement in the United States that favors parents and children co-sleeping, pointing to Japan where parents and children have slept together for hundreds of years. A university doctor conducted some cross-cultural studies and found no connection between sleeping alone as babies and being able to develop a sense of independence.

Question 4

It's really interesting that the well-known CT scan machine was funded by the Beatles, the famous rock-and-roll band. Most people don't know that even though most people are familiar with this machine. The first time the machine was used was in England in 1971 when it took a brain scan. It uses computer-processed X-rays that produce slices of specific body areas.

The CT scan images are far superior to traditional X-rays that had been commonly used until 1971, and it can detect disease much earlier. The number of CT scan procedures has increased dramatically since 1980 because of improvements in technology and the speed of the scan. Initially the machines cost more, but since more have been produced, the cost has decreased. This machine earned the Nobel Prize in Medicine.

Writing

Question 1

The reading passage asserts that the main reason for the decrease in the number of bees around the world is the increase in using cell phones. When cell phones are used near hives, radiation is generated, and as a result, the bees do not return to the hives. These results were proven in two different European university studies. The conclusion of the studies suggests that the microwaves emitted from cell phones are what affect the navigational skills of the bees, causing their inability to return to their hives. Although initially the rapid bee decrease was inexplicable, the cell phone magnetism explains the occurrence.

In contrast, the listening passage asserts that there is no one cause for the decline in the bee population but that the major reason is pesticides. Although cell phones, as well as global warming, contribute to the problem, they are not the major reason. The pesticides affect the bees' central nervous system and cause death. There are laws in place limiting the use of pesticides, but even low doses impact the bees' memory and the ability to return home to the hives.

Question 2 for computer-based TOEFL iBT test

Today the term talent is a word that occurs a lot in many different areas. Some people confuse talent with celebrity, which in my opinion are often very different. For me, talent can be inherited but not always developed. If people with a talent aren't trained or don't try, they can easily lose what they have or find it too late in life. Everyone has talent in different ways – music, sports, art – and it's important that parents and teachers spot this early and help children to develop. It's vital that children are encouraged and helped to succeed with a training program. To sum up, I think that everyone inherits their own talent but not everyone is given the opportunity to flourish.

Question 2 for Paper Edition

There are many talents that I wish I had that I don't have, but if I had to pick only one it would be the ability to draw. I've always had an interest in the arts, and I believe I have a good sense of design. I knit and have studied calligraphy and have dabbled in painting some abstract pieces, but I'm not able to draw realistically. I wish I were an artist.

Perhaps I'm imagining that this talent would do more for me than it could. For some reason, I believe drawing would be a stress reliever. Whenever I would be anxious or under stress of any kind, I picture myself taking out a box of colored pencils or tubes of paint and being able to block out any negative thoughts or anxieties by simply drawing. I envision myself totally immersed in creating a picture, thinking only about perspective or shading or color choice.

What else could this talent do for me? Maybe I would be so talented that I could be a professional artist and make my living from my artwork. How romantic it would be to paint in an artist's studio, surrounded by other talented artists! I close my eyes, and I'm a French Impressionist living in Paris in the 1800s. The next moment I'm sharing a studio with Picasso in Spain in the twentieth century. Or maybe it's today, and I'm living on Cape Cod and painting the seascapes. Better yet, I'm living in Soho in New York City, getting ready for my upcoming gallery show.

I do not believe that I need to be famous in order to appreciate this talent. Like any gift, the ability to draw should be appreciated for its own sake, as a means to make my current life even more fulfilling.

Practice Test 2

Speaking

Question 1

There are pros and cons to both sides of this argument, and to some extent it depends upon the companies, their products and their aims. For the first idea, getting into any market is difficult, especially if it is crowded with other products. When a company needs to get its product noticed, one of the easiest and most impactful ways is to price its product lower than the competition. This should make people at least try the product and if they like it they may try it again—even when the company raises the price of the product to match its competitors. I think this is one of the most frequently used options. On the other hand, the disadvantage of this approach is to make the product seem a bit cheap and not at all special. So another way to do this is to go in high and advertise the product as something exclusive and special.

Question 2

Dental hygiene students are conducting free dental checkups, including teeth cleaning, X-rays, and scaling on campus for students, and the two students are discussing whether they would want a student to clean their teeth. The man mentions that although the students are doing the cleaning, there is always a dentist in the clinic who walks around to make sure everything is being done correctly. The student clinicians will not be doing any procedures, such as filling cavities or pulling teeth. These dental hygiene students have had a year of coursework and have completed the state requirements in order to work on patients.

The man tells the woman that a student made an announcement about the checkups in his math class. Each dental hygiene student needs to find a certain number of volunteers. Although the man appreciates that the checkup would be free and that he would be helping a classmate who needs a patient to practice on in order to pass the clinic class, he does have a regular dentist he's been seeing for five years at home. He was planning on going to see his dentist for a regular checkup when he goes home next.

The woman agrees and adds she'd prefer to have someone licensed to do work on her teeth.

Question 3

The reading passage describes a form of taxation that governments apply to products that cause ill health, such as sugar-added drinks. Collectively these taxes are called `sin taxes' and they are becoming more common in America.

The listening passage also states that these products cause serious health issues such as heart disease but we know that if people reduce their consumption of these by 20% then it is like saving money for them. More importantly, data shows that governments can influence people's behavior by raising taxes on harmful products. For example, by increasing the price of harmful products by 20 cents, consumption fell by 16%. People in government like these taxes because they are easy to justify to the public on health grounds.

However, the listening passage also includes the counter arguments that sin taxes hurt people with less money and have the undesirable effect of creating a black market for these products. Furthermore, in some areas, sugary drinks may be the only affordable option for people. Finally, there is the general question of whether it is morally correct to interfere with people's freedom in this way.

Question 4

Excavations of Mayan weaving from the fifth century in Honduras showed that the Mayans were skilled spinners and weavers. Researchers were able to determine this fact by analyzing textiles found in a tomb there. These textiles were brought back to the United States and special equipment examined the fabrics. What was interesting was that in one woman's tomb there were 25 layers of fabric, all of which had a different structure. One of the fabrics had a thread count of over 100 yards per inch, which is high for even modern day textiles. Considering what kinds of tools these ancient spinners had at their disposal, it's truly remarkable. However, certain tools were found in the area. Tools dating from this era at this level of sophistication have not been found elsewhere. This fact speaks to the high skill level of fifth-century Mayan weavers.

Writing

Question 1

The reading passage describes the many benefits of taking a cruise. First the price is all-inclusive, so the meals, room, and entertainment are paid in advance in one amount. When everything is totaled, this vacation is typically cheaper than traveling on land. Because there are so many people on board, it is easy to meet others. Cruise ships stop at many ports, so cruising is a great way to visit numerous locations in a short amount of time. Lastly, due to the large number of onboard activities, everyone can find something enjoyable to do.

On the other hand, the listening passage enumerates the disadvantages of cruising. The all-inclusive price covers only a small interior room. Upgrades to a balcony room and other amenities are expensive. Traveling with so many people in a closed environment can be noisy, disruptive, and not to everyone's liking. If someone wants to stay longer at a site, meet locals, or sample the cuisine, it's not possible. Lastly, the weather may dampen the whole trip. Rough seas, producing seasickness, may make enjoying the many amenities impossible.

Question 2 for computer-based TOEFL iBT test

Some people claim that all university courses should be taught online. Others disagree. Experience has shown most students and professors that a combination of online lectures and in-person tutorials works well. For students who perhaps cannot travel to universities or cannot afford to, studying online affords them an opportunity previously unavailable. In addition, some people who need to work and cannot be full-time students will find online learning an appealing option. However, there are some drawbacks to learning online. It can be difficult to manage your time well and people often feel a bit isolated. In conclusion, there are circumstances where online learning is both a necessity and an opportunity. Nevertheless, if universities cease to be a place where students and faculty exchange ideas, fostering learning and development, it will be a very sad day indeed.

Question 2 for Paper Edition

Some people claim that all university courses should be taught online. Others disagree. Experience has shown most students and professors that a combination of online lectures (which can be listened to at the student's preferred time) and in-person tutorials works well. The COVID-19 pandemic showed us that many options are possible.

First, I recognize that there are those who propose online coursework only. For students in remote areas who perhaps cannot travel to universities or cannot afford to, studying online affords them an opportunity previously unavailable. In addition, some people who need to work and cannot be full-time students will find online learning an appealing option. For those who are ill or unable to travel, online learning serves a valuable purpose. I have to admit it was more comfortable to take my final exam in my pajamas lying on my bed.

I have several objections. I took an online course last semester and found it to be a positive experience overall. The professor provided insightful assignments, and we were able to communicate online with classmates. I found the course just as enjoyable and beneficial as classroom learning. I could email the professor a question, but the reply sometimes took a day or two. When the response came, I sometimes felt the professor hadn't really understood what I was asking. Fortunately, we also had remote meetings once a week so I was able to explain myself better and receive instant feedback. The interaction with classmates was in real time too. Since our classmates were all over the world, we met up in webinars and in between we posted our comments. Those interchanges were just as rich and thought-provoking as in-class discussions.

However, I felt that there were also some drawbacks to learning online. I found it was difficult to manage my time well. And I think it took longer to complete the course than it would have done if I'd been attending on-campus classes. Sometimes I felt a bit isolated.

In conclusion, I acknowledge that there are circumstances where online learning is both a necessity and an opportunity. Nevertheless, if universities cease to be what they are today, a place where students and faculty exchange ideas, fostering learning and development, it will be a very sad day indeed.

Practice Test 3

Speaking

Question 1

Some people I know really don't like surprises and before they do anything or go anywhere spend a lot of time planning what they are going to do, even down to the last detail. Some of them even try to think what they will do if their plans don't work as they thought they would, so they have plan A, plan B, and even plan C. The trouble is, if something surprising happens that's not in their plan, they can panic and not know what to do because they aren't used to thinking on their feet and reacting to situations. On the other hand, some people don't like to plan at all – they just go and do what they want without thinking about the consequences. This looks great at first because planning can take a lot of time and effort. But if things don't work out, then lack of planning can be expensive, for example, you might not be able to get cheap travel tickets because you just turned up at the train station without planning. Or resolving something can be frustrating and even take longer than the planning period would have. Still, when things do go wrong, this kind of person can react quickly and make quick decisions on the spot.

Question 2

The president of the students' university is retiring after fifteen years. It's clear they both think he's been an excellent president. He had raised money, enabled the university to start awarding doctorate degrees, and was very connected to the students. He attended sports events and college functions where the students were present.

A search committee to find a new president is looking for two students to serve on the committee. Both of them feel it would be a very special opportunity to be on this committee. Both of them also acknowledge that it will be a very big time commitment. The woman points out that some of the meetings will even be all day long. She adds that since they will both be interviewing for jobs themselves in the near future, it would be helpful. The man states that the evaluation process will also be worthwhile.

Even though they both worry about the amount of time it will take, the man states he would really like to be able to encourage the committee to find a president like Dr. Brown, especially in terms of his connection with students. He suggests maybe they both should apply.

Question 3

The reading passage explains that when papermaking reached Europe in the eleven hundreds, paper was made from plant fibers and rags. This paper with low plant fiber and more rag content has lasted really well. There's a book from the fourteen hundreds on display in Washington D.C. that is still in excellent shape. However, starting in the 1800s paper was made totally from tree fiber. Unfortunately, papermakers did not know that tree fibers stick together and form a substance that turns the pages brown. Fortunately, as the listening passage tells us, Bach, the composer, wrote his music on paper made in the eighteenth century that contained rags. As a result, his musical compositions exist almost 300 years after he wrote them. Just recently some chords he wrote in a notebook that were not part of an actual piece were discovered, and since they were legible, some musicians have made them into a new piece.

Question 4

Examples of footwear date back 9,000 years but indirect evidence from archaeology shows that we may have been wearing protective coverings on our feet for at least 50,000 years. Modern sandals first appeared 4,000 years ago in Egypt and since then have been found over most periods and in most cultures. Sandals have been made from a variety of materials including papyrus, hide, wood, and rice straw. After being introduced in America in the 1940s, flip-flops became very popular and were made with brightly colored plastic. Despite their popularity, sandals aren't great for our feet. Because they do not support our feet, people can sprain their ankles and get tendonitis by trying to hold the sandals in place. However, better quality sandals are accepted by podiatrists as adequate footwear.

Writing

Question 1

The reading passage states that there are some incorrect assumptions made about how to get a good night's sleep and what exactly that means. The first myth is that people can function on four hours of sleep a night. The passage mentions a few famous politicians who were well-known for getting very few hours of sleep a night. A doctor from Detroit claims that too little sleep can affect your health and even cause obesity and impair your judgment. In another study, female nurses who sleep five hours a night or less gained more weight than those who slept seven hours nightly. On the other hand, there are problems associated with sleeping too long. People that slept more than eight hours a night died younger than those who got between six and eight. Finally, although many believe there are benefits to napping, the value is inconclusive.

The listening passage challenges many of these points. First, the professor claims there is no magic number of hours of sleep needed. Some people even need eleven, and some can function on four. People who sleep eight hours a night may not be getting quality sleep. In contrast to the reading passage, she asserts that naps are beneficial for many reasons, including improved mood, relaxation, and having fewer accidents, and making fewer mistakes.

Question 2 for computer-based TOEFL iBT test

I totally agree with Dr Yu's statement. I believe that through traveling one begins to truly understand another culture and develop your understanding of the world and its different peoples. In my opinion it is not possible to do this by reading and watching movies. This can then lead to thoughtful reflections on one's own culture. Of course, most people love their friends and family and having a sense of place makes you feel secure. However, in my opinion, the experience and excitement of travel adds to your outlook on life and can affect how you behave and understand the wider world, that living locally just doesn't.

Question 2 for Paper Edition

What a wonderful gift it would be to travel to a foreign country, all expenses paid, for two weeks! I would choose to go to India. There are several reasons for this choice.

First of all, I have never been to that part of the world. I imagine that there are so many new experiences for my senses: the smells, the tastes, the sounds, and the sights. I've seen many Indian movies and have read several books set in India, so in my mind, I have many images that, of course, may be inaccurate. I need actually to be in India to validate my assumptions. In addition, I am sure that eating Indian food 6,000 miles away is very different from eating the same foods where they originated. As someone who loves cooking and eating, I would really look forward to that experience.

Secondly, I am fascinated by Indian crafts and textiles. I would spend a lot of time in different bazaars, looking for jewelry and clothing. I am sure the displays would be dizzying, and I would have a very difficult time making decisions. From what I've heard, many items are inexpensive in comparison to what the same products would cost at home. Since I won't have to pay for the airfare, I'll have money for gifts—for others and myself!

Finally, I believe that through traveling one begins to truly understand another culture. It is not possible to do this by reading and watching movies. This can then lead to thoughtful reflections on one's own culture.

To sum up, a two-week trip to India would stimulate my senses, enable me to purchase some of the magnificent Indian textiles and jewelry and give me valuable insights into one of the fastest-growing major economies in the world.

Practice Test 4

Speaking

Question 1

Whether or not to work on a project by myself or in a group is a really good question. I've had assignments where I had to do both, and I've come to the conclusion that I would rather work by myself.

Many teachers assign group projects because they say working in groups is what happens in the real world, and we should get used to this practice. In addition, by working in groups, each person brings a different expertise and/or experience to the project, so the entire group benefits.

Those points may be valid, but I've had too many negative group experiences to be a firm supporter of group work. One time, the other three people didn't really do what they were supposed to do. I did a really good job, but my final grade was lowered because of the others. Another time one of my group members simply vanished, and I wound up doing her part as well. So if I'm given the chance, I'll work by myself.

Question 2

For the first time, the college is going to offer summer storage to students. Students can rent a medium-sized or large-sized box and the boxes will be stored in a basement on campus that will be locked and guarded. Students can drop the boxes off after final exams and pick them up when they return.

When the man tells the woman about the announcement, she is thrilled. She didn't know what she was going to do with her stuff when she goes home this summer. It sounds as though she will definitely do it, and she and the man are going to go over to the hall to see the different box sizes.

The man, on the other hand, lives close to campus, so he'll just take his stuff home with him. She's not going to ask him if she can leave stuff at his house after he tells her about his parents being not too happy about his roommates' stuff that he took home last summer.

Question 3

The reading passage explains that the modern mystery of the Bermuda Triangle is really not a mystery at all. Since the 1940s people have been fascinated with this geographical area off the coast of the United States and attribute lost ships and aircraft, as well as mysterious occurrences, to some magical powers in the area. According to the reading passage, when researchers and scientists examine reports of the Triangle's powers, they prove to be untrue.

The listening passage supports these claims by looking at three claims. The first is that Christopher Columbus saw bright lights and a giant flame of fire there. The giant flame was probably a meteor, and the lights were probably reflections from the land. The next is the report of a famous ship from the late 1800s. The ship was found years later near Portugal. The third describes a group of American fighter planes that supposedly went missing in the Triangle. Actually, the squad leader should not have been flying, and the pilots were inexperienced and went in the wrong direction. Their plane wrecks sank so deeply in the Atlantic that they weren't immediately found.

Question 4

According to the professor, how people behave in an elevator is supported by the research of Edward T. Hall. People's personal space needs to be protected, just as animals are territorial. If you notice strangers in an elevator, they never look at or talk to one another. Everyone stands still and looks straight ahead or at the ceiling or one's cell phone as if these items have never been seen before. While in an elevator, people are very careful not to make any noise or sudden movements.

We behave irrationally in an elevator as if we are protecting our personal space. This personal space is like an imaginary bubble that surrounds us. Each culture has a different acceptable radius for this bubble, meaning that people from some cultures are more comfortable standing more closely to others than those from other cultures.

Writing

Question 1

The information in the listening passage seems to contradict many of the claims argued in the reading passage. First of all, the reading passage asserts that the fields become too hot to play on in summer days. The listening passage states that as long as practices are held in the early morning, play is possible. Next, the reading passage contends that turf fields contain chemicals that can affect the surrounding areas. The listening passage counters that tests done in the last ten years yielded only small amounts of chemicals. In contrast, grass fields need fertilizers and possibly pesticides, which are health hazards.

Although the reading passage claims that the initial cost to install the field is much greater than a grass one, the fact that it can be used more often, as explained in the listening passage, compensates for the cost. The artificial one does not need to rest, nor is it affected by rain.

The final argument in the reading passage concerns injuries. There is an unsubstantiated claim that artificial turf fields cause more injuries than grass fields do. No data were presented.

In conclusion, the listening passage challenges the reading passage's claims of grass fields having lower costs, playability, and fewer health concerns.

Question 2 for computer-based TOEFL iBT test

A controversial issue nowadays is whether animals should be used for drug testing. On one hand, new drugs have to be tested, and without animals, the only alternative is to use humans. If new drugs are not tested on animals before being given to humans, there will be no way to know if new drugs will work and the human death toll will be enormous. On the other hand, media reports of animals used in experiments show the terrible pain and suffering animals endure during tests. There is no question that without animal testing we would not have the cures for polio and smallpox that exist today. I want to believe that the animal testing done today is done as humanely as possible, minimising pain to animals but at the same time benefiting humans.

Question 2 for Paper Edition

A controversial issue nowadays is whether animals should be used for drug testing. If the question had been should animals be used for testing makeup and perfumes, of course, the answer would be no. Using animals for drug testing is a more complicated question. Many argue that the practice is inhumane, while others claim that without animal testing, many life-saving drugs could not be perfected. Although I am not totally convinced of the necessity of animal testing, I support the practice.

On the one hand, there are some animals whose DNA and organ structure is very similar to those of humans. Using animals to test new drugs enables scientists to determine the efficacy of these drugs. What is the alternative? New drugs have to be tested, and without animals, the only alternative is to use humans. Can we rationalize that practice? Of course not. I have heard the suggestion to use prisoners for drug testing. I find that idea repulsive. If new drugs are not tested on animals before being given to humans, there will be no way to know if new drugs will work and the human death toll will be enormous.

On the other hand, one need only see media reports of animals used in experiments and witness the terrible pain and suffering these animals endure to question the practice. In addition, some argue that, as animals are not humans, animal testing does not guarantee the same results in humans. I am not a scientist, but I assume that scientists are not needlessly torturing animals that are dissimilar to humans. It is important to be aware that, due to innovations in science, animal tests are being replaced in areas such as toxicity testing, neuroscience, and drug development.

There is no question that without animal testing we would not have the cures for polio and smallpox that exist today. I want to believe that the animal testing done today is done as humanely as possible with those animals most closely related to humans. In the future, we may be able to bypass animals altogether.